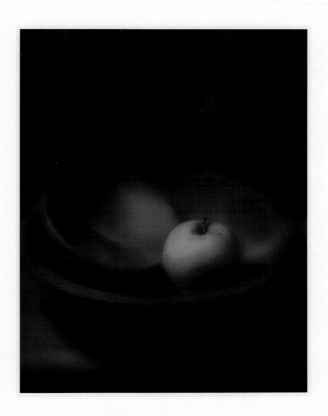

Three Rivers Renaissance
Cookbook IV

Child Health Association of Sewickley

Sewickley, Pennsylvania

First Printing 50,000
May, 2000

For information on ordering copies
of books published by
Child Health Association of Sewickley, contact:
THREE RIVERS COOKBOOKS
Child Health Association of Sewickley, Inc.
1108 Ohio River Boulevard
Sewickley, Pennsylvania 15143
(412) 741-3221 or (800) 624-8753
Fax (412) 741-3997
E-mail childhlth@juno.com
www.childhealthassociation.org
Copyright (c) 2000
ISBN 0-9607634-3-0

Printed by
Geyer Printing Company, Inc.
Pittsburgh, Pennsylvania

Child Health Association of Sewickley.

In 1923, three women recognized the need to provide fresh milk to undernourished Sewickley school children. Eight decades later, the small charitable society they formed has grown to allocate more than $2.25 million for children's programs and services throughout Western Pennsylvania. As a forerunner of volunteer action in the Pittsburgh area, the Child Health Association was named Outstanding Philanthropic Organization by the Western Pennsylvania Chapter of the National Society of Fund-Raising Executives in 1997.

The heart of Child Health today is charitable giving. Our priority is the whole child, encompassing children's emotional, physical, educational, cultural, and recreational needs. We do this with approximately 60 active volunteers and the continued support of our associate members and friends.

While many activities help us raise funds, the Three Rivers Cookbook series is our main source of revenue. The remarkable success of Volumes I, II, and III has enabled us to expand our support for child-related organizations throughout the Pittsburgh region.

Three Rivers Renaissance Cookbook IV builds on the strong legacy of the past cookbooks, while taking a fresh approach to meet today's tastes and lifestyles. With the promised success of our newest cookbook, the Child Health Association can look forward to a bright future of giving on behalf of children.

Please remember that every time you use this cookbook, you are helping to provide fresh hope to children, their families, and their community. As our children grow stronger, so does the future of the Pittsburgh region.

Susan Jones

Susan Jones
President
May, 2000

Appreciation

The support and loyalty of the people of the Pittsburgh region have made it possible to create a fourth Three Rivers Cookbook - our Renaissance edition.

Once again, we extend our sincere appreciation to all of you who so generously submitted your favorite recipes. We do not claim that all recipes included are original, only that they are favorites of the contributors, as well as the testers. We most sincerely regret that there wasn't space to include all of the outstanding recipes we received and tested. Editorial changes may have been made in order to standardize measurements and to make the directions easy to follow. We trust that any liberties taken will meet with the approval of our contributors.

We also want to extend our grateful appreciation to the following companies and organizations for their generosity in helping to underwrite the promotion and first printing of Three Rivers Renaissance Cookbook IV.

Golden Goblet Contributors
R. P. Simmons Family Foundation

Silver Spoon Contributors
Dollar Bank
The Earl Knudson Charitable Foundation
Milton Fine Revocable Trust
PNC Bank
Rudd Equipment Company

We also express our heartfelt appreciation to the following persons and companies who have donated their time and their commitment to this project.

Donna Albert
Geyer Printing Co. Inc.
Palmo, Inc.
Joanne Pompeo
Tom Samuels
Linda Topaleski
Frank Walsh

Finally, we give a special thanks to the members, associates and friends of Child Health who responded with their unique spirit and stamina during the production of this book.

Kitty Gross, *Chair*
Jane Rabe, *Co-Chair*
Bonnie Megan, *Testing Co-Chair*
Susan Nitzberg, *Testing Co-Chair*
Sara White, *Marketing Chair*
and for their tireless editing and typing
Nicki Edwards, Gaynor Grant, Nan O'Connor, Delores Samuels,
Judy Scioscia and Chris Traviss

Appetizers

Pesto and Goat Cheese Bombe

"Makes an impressive presentation"

Easy
Serves: 15–20
Preparation: 30–45 min.
Must be made ahead

Pesto:
1   **cup loosely packed fresh spinach**

1   **cup loosely packed fresh basil leaves**

1   **tsp. minced garlic**

¼   **cup olive oil**

½   **cup freshly grated Parmesan cheese**

Cheese Mixture:
1   **8-oz. pkg. cream cheese, room temperature**

1   **4-oz. pkg. soft fresh goat cheese, room temperature**

¼   **cup finely chopped walnuts**

¼   **cup oil packed sun dried tomatoes, thinly sliced**

Line a 3 cup bowl with plastic wrap, leaving a 4" overhang.

Combine spinach, basil and garlic in a food processor and chop until fine. Gradually drizzle in olive oil; add Parmesan and process until smooth.

Using an electric mixer, combine cheeses until smooth.

Spread ⅓ of cheese mixture on bottom of bowl; spread ½ of pesto over cheese; sprinkle with ½ of walnuts and arrange ½ the tomatoes on top. Spread another ⅓ of cheese mixture; repeat pesto, walnuts and tomatoes. Top with remaining cheese, smoothing the surface. Cover with plastic wrap. Refrigerate overnight. Turn out onto a plate. Let stand for 30 minutes at room temperature before serving.

Serve with crackers or sliced French bread.

Nancy H. Boland

Mediterranean Spread
"Tastes like a day in Tuscany"

Easy
Serves: 6
Preparation: 20 min.
Cooking: 15 min.

2   12-oz. jars roasted red peppers, drained and cut into strips
6   oz. goat cheese, crumbled
½   cup pine nuts, lightly toasted
1   cup fresh basil, torn into strips
4   Tbsp. olive oil
1   cup freshly grated Parmesan cheese

chopped tomatoes and chopped black olives for garnish

Preheat oven to 375°.

Coat a 9" ceramic dish with cooking spray.

Layer red peppers, goat cheese, pine nuts and basil alternately. Drizzle with olive oil and then cover with Parmesan cheese. Bake for 10–15 minutes, or until cheese is melted and slightly brown. Top with garnish.

Serve warm with French bread or crackers.

Judy Jones

Roquefort Cheese Dip

Easy
Serves: 16
Preparation: 7 min.
Must be made ahead

½   lb. Roquefort cheese, room temperature
12   oz. cream cheese
½   tsp. minced garlic
¾   tsp. Worcestershire sauce
¾   tsp. Tabasco sauce

Using an electric mixer, beat Roquefort cheese in a medium bowl until smooth. Gradually beat in cream cheese. Add remaining ingredients and beat until well combined.

Cover and refrigerate. Bring to room temperature before serving with crackers or raw vegetables.

Kristin Kingsland Brown

Caponata

"A chance to use your microwave for something other than popcorn"

Easy
Serves: 12
Preparation: 45 min.
Cooking: 1 hr. 15 min.
Must be made ahead

3 lg. onions, coarsely chopped

2 green peppers, coarsely chopped

3 stalks celery, coarsely chopped

¼ cup olive oil

2 lg. eggplants, peeled and cut into ¾" cubes

1 8-oz. can tomato sauce

1 6-oz. can tomato paste

2 cloves garlic, minced

1 6-oz. can whole pitted black olives, drained and quartered

½ cup whole pitted green olives, drained and quartered

½ cup red wine vinegar

2 Tbsp. sugar

1½ tsp. dried oregano

1 tsp. salt

1 tsp. cayenne pepper

1 tsp. black pepper

Place onions, peppers, celery and olive oil in a 4 qt. casserole. Cover with waxed paper and microwave on high for 30 minutes, stirring every 10 minutes.

Meanwhile, soak eggplant cubes in salt water for 20 minutes. Rinse and drain. Stir into the onion, pepper and celery mixture. Cover again with waxed paper and microwave for 30 minutes, stirring after 15 minutes.

Add tomato sauce and tomato paste to eggplant mixture and microwave for 10 minutes.

Stir garlic, olives, vinegar, sugar, herbs and spices together; add to the eggplant mixture. Microwave on high for 5 minutes.

Chill before serving. Serve with flatbread or plain crackers.

Amanda Dunn

Tuscan Bean Dip

Easy
Serves: 6
Preparation: 20 min.

1 14-oz. can white northern beans, drained
4 cloves garlic
¼ cup olive oil
2 Tbsp. white Worcestershire sauce
1½ Tbsp. white wine vinegar
2 tsp. red pepper flakes
2 tsp. dried thyme
2 tsp. dried rosemary
salt and pepper

Place beans and garlic in the bowl of a food processor. Add the olive oil, Worcestershire sauce, vinegar, red pepper and herbs. Process until thoroughly mixed. Season with salt and pepper. Serve with crackers or pita bread.

Mark Zappala

Southwestern Dip

"Bread bowl saves on clean up"

Easy
Serves: 8
Preparation: 10 min.
Cooking: 20 min.
Can be made ahead

1 11-oz. can of corn with red and green peppers, drained
1 bunch green onions, sliced
1 lb. Monterey Jack pepper cheese, shredded
½ cup salsa
2 Tbsp. mayonnaise
2 Tbsp. finely chopped cilantro (optional)
1 round sourdough loaf, with soft inside removed and reserved

Preheat oven to 350°.

Combine all ingredients except the bread in an ovenproof dish. Bake for 20 minutes, or until cheese is melted and dip is bubbling.

Serve in hollowed out sourdough loaf. Chop the reserved bread into bite sized pieces and serve with dip.

Lynn Bullions

Black Bean Salsa

"No last minute stress before company"

Easy
Serves: 6
Preparation: 10 min.
Must be made ahead

2 cloves garlic, minced
1 16-oz. can black beans, rinsed and drained
1 7-oz. can shoe peg corn, drained
½ cup Italian salad dressing
3 Tbsp. finely chopped fresh cilantro
½ tsp. Tabasco sauce
¾ tsp. chili powder
1 med. tomato, finely chopped
½ green pepper, finely chopped
½ red onion, finely chopped

Combine first 7 ingredients. Toss well and marinate for 4–5 hours. Just before serving, add last three ingredients. Toss well.

Serve with tortilla chips.

Tani Morrow

Chile Verde Bean Dip

"Open, layer and bake"

Easy
Serves; 6–8
Preparation: 15 min.
Cooking: 20 min.
Can be made ahead

1 8-oz. pkg. cream cheese
1 16-oz. can black beans, drained
1 4½ -oz. can chopped green chiles, drained
1 16-oz. jar picante sauce
2 cups shredded 4-blend Mexican cheese

Preheat oven to 350°.

Layer ingredients, in order, in a greased pie plate. Bake for 20 minutes.

Serve with tortilla chips.

Suzanne B. Jackson

Antipasto Salsa
"A food processor will save the day"

Easy
Yields: 5 cups
Preparation: 30 min.
Must be made ahead

1   14-oz. can artichoke
    hearts
2   4-oz. cans sliced
    mushrooms
1   4-oz. jar diced
    pimentos
1   cup pimento stuffed
    green olives
½   cup chopped green
    pepper
½   cup chopped celery
½   cup olive oil
½   cup finely chopped
    onion
1   clove garlic, minced
⅔   cup white vinegar
2½ tsp. Italian seasoning
1   tsp. seasoned salt
1   tsp. sugar
1   tsp. freshly ground
    black pepper
Belgian endive leaves,
French bread or crackers
for serving

Drain and chop artichoke hearts, mushrooms, pimentos, and stuffed olives; add green pepper and celery. Mix in a large bowl.

Over medium heat, warm olive oil in a saucepan. Add onion and garlic. Cook for 3 minutes until tender.

Add vinegar, Italian seasoning, salt, sugar and pepper. Bring to a boil. Pour over the vegetable mixture. Cover and refrigerate for 8 hours, or overnight.

Serve on fresh endive leaves or with French bread or crackers.

Nancy G. Roderick

Spinach and Chutney Dip
"Try this for a change of pace"

Easy
Serves: 8
Preparation: 15 min.
Must be made ahead

2   **10-oz. pkg. frozen chopped spinach, thawed and squeezed dry**
¾   **cup mayonnaise**
1   **Tbsp. curry powder**
1   **lg. apple, unpeeled, cored and finely chopped**
¾   **cup mango chutney**
¾   **cup coarsely chopped peanuts**

Mix all ingredients in a bowl. Refrigerate for 3–4 hours.

Serve with crackers or pita chips.

Janet Chace

Smoked Salmon Pate
"Simple yet incredibly elegant"

Easy
Serves: 4–6
Preparation: 20 min.
Can be made ahead

6   **oz. smoked salmon, cut into 1" pieces**
2   **Tbsp. fresh lemon juice**
6   **Tbsp. (¾ stick) butter, melted**
½   **cup creme fraiche, sour cream or light sour cream**
salt and pepper
fresh dill and capers for garnish

In a blender, combine salmon and lemon juice. Turn blender on high and add melted butter in a stream; blend to a puree. Transfer to a bowl and fold in ½ cup creme fraiche or sour cream. Add salt and pepper to taste.

Pour into a large ramekin or custard cup. Garnish with dill and capers. Serve with crackers.

Una Melikian

Lobster and Cucumber Mousse
"Gorgeous"

Moderately difficult
Serves: 12
Preparation: 30 min.
Must be made ahead

12 oz. cucumber, peeled and seeded

12 oz. lobster meat

2 ¼-oz. envelopes gelatin

½ cup hot water

12 oz. cream cheese

1 med. onion, finely chopped

1 green pepper, finely chopped

1 tsp. fresh lime juice

1½ tsp. vinegar

Worcestershire sauce, to taste

salt and pepper

cucumber slices and olives for garnish

Place cucumber in a food processor and pulse until finely chopped. Remove cucumber and place in a sieve to drain. Pulse lobster meat in the food processor until finely chopped. Set aside.

Combine gelatin and water in a small saucepan and allow to soften, then heat the mixture until fully dissolved. Cool to room temperature. Add the cream cheese and whip until smooth. Add onion, green pepper, lime juice, vinegar, Worcestershire sauce, and salt and pepper to taste. Fold in chopped cucumber and lobster. Adjust seasoning.

Pour into an oiled 3 cup mold. Chill for 2–3 hours, or until set. Invert onto serving platter and garnish with cucumber slices and olives.

Take the time to use a fish mold and garnish appropriately. It's worth the effort!

Carolyn S. Hammer

Caviar à la Russe

Easy
Serves: 8–10
Preparation: 25 min.
Must be made ahead

6   hard-boiled eggs
⅓   cup butter, softened
sm. amount of grated onion
1   Tbsp. mayonnaise
¼   tsp. salt
1   cup sour cream
1   4-oz. jar caviar, red or black
wheat crackers

Place the hard-boiled eggs in a food processor. Using the metal blade, process well. Add the butter, grated onion, mayonnaise and salt. Process until smooth.

Place in an 8 oz. mold and chill. When ready to serve, unmold, spread sour cream on top and decorate with caviar.

Serve with wheat crackers.

Mary Jo Johnson

Shrimp Roslyn
"A versatile dish"

Easy
Serves: 6
Preparation: 20 min.
Cooking: 3–4 min.
Must be made ahead

Sauce:
1   cup sour cream
¼   cup cider vinegar
½   cup vegetable oil
1   tsp. dill seed
1   tsp. dried dill weed or 1 Tbsp. finely chopped fresh dill
1   tsp. cayenne pepper
3   Tbsp. horseradish
½   Tbsp. pepper
2   Tbsp. grated onion
1   sm. bottle capers, drained

1½ lbs. cooked shrimp, shelled and deveined

Mix all sauce ingredients together. Add shrimp and marinate for a minimum of 5 hours, or overnight.

Makes a great appetizer or first course, or may be served over greens as a luncheon salad.

Jane Ellen Rabe

Devilled Shrimp

Easy
Serves: 8–10
Preparation: 30 min.
Cooking: 3 min.
Must be made ahead

2	lbs. med. raw shrimp
¼	cup vegetable oil
2	cloves garlic, minced
1	Tbsp. dry mustard
1	tsp. salt
½	cup lemon juice
1	Tbsp. red wine vinegar
¼	cup chopped parsley
1	lemon, thinly sliced
1	red onion, thinly sliced
1	cup pitted black olives, drained
2	Tbsp. chopped pimento

Shell and devein shrimp. Cook in boiling water for 3 minutes. Drain and rinse immediately in cold water. Shrimp can be cooked up to 24 hours in advance and refrigerated until needed.

In a bowl, combine oil, garlic, mustard, salt, lemon juice, vinegar and parsley.

In a separate bowl, combine lemon slices, onion, olives and pimento. Toss. Combine with the garlic lemon mixture and add the cooked shrimp.

Cover and chill no longer than 3 hours. Serve with toothpicks.

Dorothy W. Pusateri

Shrimp and Guacamole Tostitos

"Grab a few for yourself before they all disappear"

Moderately difficult
Serves: 8
Preparation: 30 min.
Marinate: 1 hr.

Marinade:

2 Tbsp. fresh lime juice

1 Tbsp. minced coriander

1 sm. garlic clove, minced

¼ cup vegetable oil

1 tsp. Dijon mustard

¼ tsp. ground cumin

½ tsp. salt

¼ tsp. pepper

14 lg. uncooked shrimp

6 plum tomatoes, peeled, seeded and chopped

2 fresh jalapeño peppers, seeds removed and minced, divided

1 tsp. fresh lime juice

2 ripe avocados, peeled and mashed

salt and pepper

24–28 round Tostitos

fresh coriander for garnish

Preheat oven to 350°.

Combine marinade ingredients. Mix well and set aside.

Cook shrimp in simmering water until barely pink (1–2 minutes). Drain, cool and shell. Cut in half lengthwise through back and remove vein. Combine with marinade. Refrigerate for at least 1 hour.

Heat Tostitos chips for 3–5 minutes in oven. Cool.

Combine tomatoes, half the minced peppers, lime juice, avocados, salt and pepper. Add more peppers as desired.

Drain shrimp. Put 2 teaspoons avocado mixture on each round. Place shrimp half on top, cut side down. Garnish with sprig of coriander.

Linda Castle

Salmon Tortilla Roll Ups

"Tortillas and salmon make an interesting mix"

Easy
Serves: 20
Preparation: 1 hr.
Must be made ahead

1 8-oz. pkg. cream cheese, softened
⅓ cup sour cream
2 Tbsp. fresh lemon juice
2 Tbsp. sweet pickle relish
1 tsp. Worcestershire sauce
½ lb. thinly sliced smoked salmon, divided
10 6" soft tortillas
2 lg. red peppers, cut into matchstick-sized strips
½ cup minced green onions
1 cup minced watercress
1 lg. cucumber, seeded and sliced into matchstick-sized strips

Process first 5 ingredients in a food processor. Add ½ of salmon and blend. Reserve remaining salmon.

Spread mixture over tortillas to completely cover them. Place one piece of reserved salmon over half of each tortilla. Layer remaining ingredients lightly on top of salmon. Roll up, starting on salmon side and ending with mixture. Wrap each rolled tortilla tightly in plastic wrap and refrigerate overnight. Slice into ½"–1" rounds just before serving.

Susan Vogelgesang

Beef and Tortilla Roll Ups

Easy
Serves: 4
Preparation: 15 min.
Must be made ahead

1 4-oz. pkg. Boursin cheese
½ cup mayonnaise
4 6" flour tortillas
1 Bermuda or Vidalia onion, finely chopped
¾ lb. thinly sliced roast beef

Mix cheese and mayonnaise and spread on one side of each tortilla. Sprinkle onion over cheese and place roast beef on top. Roll tightly and cut into quarters, placing a toothpick through each roll. Refrigerate for at least 2 hours before serving.

Ruth C. Hofmann

Savory English Muffins
"A savory treat for a winter gathering"

Easy
Serves: 8
Preparation: 15 min.
Cooking: 5 min.
Can be made ahead

1   6-oz. can lg. pitted black olives, drained and coarsely chopped
1   bunch green onions, green part only, chopped
2   Tbsp. mayonnaise
4   oz. grated Cheddar cheese
6   English muffins, split and toasted

Preheat broiler.

Mix olives, green onions, mayonnaise and grated cheese. Spread on top of muffins and broil until bubbling. Cut into quarters and serve.

To make ahead: Spread the topping onto the muffins and refrigerate for up to 3 hours before broiling.

Bonnie Megan

Pita Crisps
"Simple and casual"

Easy
Yields: 40 toasts
Preparation: 10 min.
Cooking: 10 min.
Must be made ahead

1   cup (2 sticks) butter, softened
2   cups parsley, chopped
2   Tbsp. finely chopped fresh chives
1   tsp. finely chopped fresh dill
3   cloves garlic, minced
2   tsp. fresh lemon juice
2   tsp. seasoned salt
2   pkgs. lg. pita bread

Preheat oven to 375°.

Mix all ingredients except pita. Let stand at room temperature for 1 hour. Split pita bread horizontally; cut each thin sheet in half. Spread butter mixture on each half. Cut each half into triangles.

Arrange on a baking sheet. Bake for 10 minutes or until lightly browned.

Debra Gibbs

Brie Quesadilla
"So good it's worth the calories"

Easy
Serves: 4
Preparation: 20 min.
Cooking: 10 min.

1   **pkg. 7" flour
    tortillas**
1   **5-oz. container of
    spreadable Brie**
8   **oz. Monterey Jack
    cheese, shredded**
12 **oz. bacon, cooked**
1   **bunch green onions
    (white and light green
    part only) chopped**
garlic powder

cooking spray

**sour cream and salsa for
garnish**

Spread 1 tablespoon of Brie on half of a tortilla. Sprinkle 1 oz. of Monterey Jack cheese on top of Brie. Sprinkle 2 strips of crumbled bacon and some green onions on top of cheese and dust with garlic powder. Fold over to close.

Repeat with remaining tortillas.

Coat a non-stick pan or electric skillet with cooking spray. Heat over low to medium heat.

Place tortillas in pan and allow to heat until cheese begins to melt. Turn several times to brown evenly.

Serve with sour cream and salsa.

For a little more "zing," use Gouda or Cheddar cheese.

P.J. Forbes

Tangy Cheese Tips

Easy
Serves: 10
Preparation: 15 min.
Cooking: 5 min.

12 **oz. sharp Cheddar
    cheese**
1   **sm. onion, finely
    chopped**
6–8 slices cooked bacon

8–10 green olives, chopped

1½ **tsp. Worcestershire
    sauce**
pinch of garlic powder

¾   **cup mayonnaise**

8–10 pieces of toast

Preheat broiler.

Grate cheese into a large bowl and let soften at room temperature. Mix in onion, bacon and olives. Add Worcestershire sauce, garlic powder and mayonnaise and mix thoroughly.

Spread on toast and place under broiler until bubbly. Cut into triangles and serve.

Wende Woodworth

Tomato and Feta Bruschetta

"Delicious when your homegrowns ripen"

Easy
Serves: 8
Preparation: 20 min.
Cooking: 10 min.

2   lg. shallots, finely chopped
1   Tbsp. extra virgin olive oil
2   cups vine ripened tomatoes, seeded and chopped
salt and pepper
⅓   cup feta cheese, finely diced
2   Tbsp. finely chopped cilantro
2   tsp. balsamic vinegar

In a small skillet, cook shallots in oil over moderate heat, stirring until softened. Stir in tomato and add salt and pepper to taste. Cook, stirring continuously, until just heated through.

In a bowl, toss tomato mixture with feta, cilantro, vinegar and salt and pepper to taste.

Spread tomato and feta mixture onto bruschetta toasts and serve.

Susan Clay Russell

Bruschetta Toasts

Easy
Yields: 45 toasts
Preparation: 10 min.

1   French or crusty Italian loaf
1   clove garlic
¼   cup extra virgin olive oil

Preheat grill or broiler.

Using a serrated knife, cut bread crosswise into ½" slices. Grill or broil slices until golden brown on both sides, but still soft inside. Rub toasts with garlic on one side, then lightly brush the same side with oil.

Susan Clay Russell

Red Pepper Bruschetta

"Purchased pesto makes this a snap"

Easy
Serves: 4
Preparation: 10 min.

1   French Baguette, cut
     into 8 diagonal slices
     ¾" thick
½   cup soft goat cheese
¼   cup homemade or
     purchased basil pesto,
     excess oil drained off
1   7-oz. jar roasted red
     peppers, drained and
     cut into ½" wide strips
snipped fresh herbs such
as basil, oregano or thyme

Preheat grill or broiler.

Toast or grill bread slices.

Spread each slice with goat cheese. Top with basil pesto and pepper strips. Garnish with snipped herbs and serve immediately.

Linda D. Orsini

Beef and Roasted Pepper Crostini

Easy
Serves: 8
Preparation: 10 min.
Cooking: 8–12 min.

2   8-oz. baguettes, cut
     into ½" slices
3   Tbsp. garlic flavored
     olive oil
¾   lb. thinly sliced deli
     roast beef
1   12-oz. jar roasted red
     peppers, rinsed,
     drained and chopped
2   cups shredded Italian
     cheese blend

Preheat oven to 450°.

Lightly brush top side of each bread slice with olive oil. Arrange on 2 baking sheets. Bake 6–8 minutes, or until light golden brown.

Layer equal amounts of beef, red pepper and cheese over toasted bread. Return to oven and bake an additional 2–4 minutes, or until cheese is melted.

Serve immediately.

Paula A. Doebler

Pecan Brie Tarts

Easy
Yields: 36 tarts
Preparation: 30 min.
Cooking: 15 min.
Can be made ahead

1   11-oz. pkg. pie crust
    mix
¼   lb. Brie cheese
¼   cup ground pecans

Preheat oven to 375°.

Prepare pie crust mix following package directions. Divide into 36 balls and press into 2" tart pans. Press up sides and prick sides and bottom with a fork. Bake 8–10 minutes, or until crisp and lightly browned. Midway through baking, press down to retain shape.

Cut Brie into 36 ½" squares. Place one square in each shell. Sprinkle with ground pecans.

Bake until Brie melts and starts to bubble, about 5 minutes. Serve hot.

Allison M. Miller

Sugar Nut Brie
"A delicious combination of flavors"

Easy
Serves: 16–20
Preparation: 10 min.
Cooking: 5 min.
Must be made ahead

¼   cup brown sugar
¼   cup broken walnuts,
    pecans, macadamias or
    almonds
1   Tbsp. whiskey or
    brandy
1   14-oz. round Brie
apple wedges and crackers
for serving

In a small mixing bowl or a wide mouthed jar, combine sugar, nuts of your choice and whisky or brandy. Cover and chill up to 1 week.

Place sugar mixture in a 2 cup glass measuring cup. Cook in microwave at 100% power for 1 minute. Split Brie in half horizontally. Place sugar mixture between cheese halves.

Place cheese in a 9" glass pie plate. Microwave uncovered at 50% power for 1½–2 minutes until cheese is heated through, but not melted.

Serve with fruit and crackers.

Alice F. Gault

Baked Brie En Croute

"Your guests will think you spent hours on this"

Easy
Serves: 8–10
Preparation: 15 min.
Cooking: 30–35 min.
Can be made ahead

1 **10"x 9" sheet of frozen puff pastry, thawed**

1 **14-oz. round Brie**

2 **4-oz. pkg. Boursin cheese**

2 **Tbsp. finely chopped fresh basil or parsley**

1 **egg, beaten**

1 **Tbsp. water**

crackers for serving

Preheat oven to 375°.

Roll puff pastry on lightly floured baking sheet to remove folds. Place whole Brie on pastry and spread top with 1 package of Boursin.

Sprinkle with 1 tablespoon of basil or parsley, pressing into cheese with spoon.

Turn cheese over, and repeat with other package of Boursin and remaining basil or parsley.

Bring pastry up and over sides of cheese, wrapping completely and trimming the excess. Seal tightly.

Turn over and place seam side down. Roll out pastry scraps and cut into decorative shapes.

Place decorations on pastry, sealing with a little water. Combine the egg with 1–2 tablespoons water and mix well. Brush this egg wash over the entire pastry.

Pastry may be refrigerated at this point. Bring to room temperature before continuing.

Bake for 30–35 minutes, or until pastry is golden brown. Let stand 10 minutes. Serve warm with crackers.

Jane Ellen Rabe

Roquefort Cheesecake
"Wow your guests with this one"

Moderately difficult
Serves: 12
Preparation: 20 min.
Cooking: 1 hr. 40 min.
Must be made ahead

⅓ **cup fine bread crumbs**

¼ **cup freshly grated Parmesan cheese**

4 **8-oz. pkg. cream cheese, room temperature**

3 **eggs**

½ **cup heavy cream**

8 **slices bacon**

1 **med. onion, minced**

½ **lb. blue cheese, crumbled (Roquefort, Stilton or Gorgonzola)**

2–3 **drops Tabasco sauce**

salt and freshly ground pepper

Preheat oven to 300°.

Sprinkle bread crumbs and Parmesan cheese in a buttered, watertight 8" round springform pan. Wrap outside of pan with foil for better seal. Set aside.

Using an electric mixer, combine cream cheese, eggs and cream.

Sauté bacon until crisp. Drain and finely chop. Reserve 1 tablespoon of bacon drippings.

Sauté onion in reserved bacon drippings until soft.

Add onion, bacon, blue cheese, and Tabasco to cream cheese mixture. Add salt and pepper to taste. Pour into prepared pan.

Set pan inside a larger one. Pour boiling water 2" deep into larger pan.

Bake for 1 hour and 40 minutes. Turn off oven and let cake remain in oven for 1 hour.

Remove from water and cool in refrigerator for 2 hours. Release from pan and serve cold with crackers.

Debra Gibbs

Chile Cheesecake

Easy
Serves: 12
Preparation: 30 min.
Cooking: 45 min.
Must be made ahead

1 cup tortilla chips, crushed

3 Tbsp. butter, melted

2 8-oz. pkg. cream cheese

2 eggs

1 4-oz. can green chiles, drained and diced

1 fresh jalapeño pepper, cored, seeded and diced

8 oz. shredded Colby and Monterey Jack Cheese

¼ cup sour cream

½ cup chopped tomatoes

¼ cup chopped green onions

¼ cup chopped black olives

Preheat oven to 350°.

In a medium bowl, combine tortilla chips and butter. Press into bottom of 9" springform pan. Bake for 15 minutes and remove from oven.

In a large bowl, combine cream cheese and eggs until well blended. Add diced green chiles, jalapeño and cheeses. Pour over crust and bake for 30 minutes. Do not overcook.

Remove from oven and cool in pan for 5–10 minutes. Run knife around inside edge and remove sides from pan.

Spread sour cream on top. Top with chopped tomatoes, onions and olives.

Serve at room temperature with tortilla chips.

Lynn M. Smith

Renaissance Tart

Easy
Serves 6–8
Preparation: 20–30 min.
Cooking: 50 min.

2   med. red onions, each
    cut into 12 wedges

3   Tbsp. olive oil

salt and pepper

1   sheet frozen puff
    pastry, thawed for 30
    minutes

1   egg, slightly beaten

8   oz. softened goat
    cheese

¼   cup pesto

¼   cup whipping cream

3   Tbsp. finely chopped
    fresh basil, divided

Preheat oven to 400°.

Lightly oil a 13"x9" pan. Toss onions with olive oil and put in pan. Season with salt and pepper. Roast in oven for 20–30 minutes, stirring once after 15 minutes.

Roll out pastry into 14"x11" rectangle. Cut ½" strip from all four sides, and reserve. Transfer pastry to baking sheet. Glaze a ½" border of the pastry with beaten egg, taking care not to allow the egg to drip down the sides of the dough. Reserve remaining egg. Place the reserved strips on top, pressing gently to adhere. Pierce bottom of pastry with fork several times. Bake 14 minutes, or until lightly browned. Remove from oven. Cool slightly. Reduce oven temperature to 350°.

Stir cheese, pesto, cream and 2 tablespoons basil together until smooth. Season with salt and pepper. Mix in remaining beaten egg. Spread over pastry. Puffed pastry will flatten in center. Top with roasted onions.

Bake until browned, about 20 minutes. Cool to room temperature. Cut into squares, top with remaining basil and serve.

Melissa C. Delaney

Charleston Artichoke Turnovers

"Capers add zest"

Moderately difficult
Yields: 48
Preparation: 30 min.
Cooking: 12–15 min.
Can be made ahead

1   **8-oz. jar marinated artichoke hearts, undrained**

1   **14-oz. can artichoke hearts, drained**

¼   **tsp. garlic powder**

1   **cup freshly grated Parmesan cheese**

2   **Tbsp. capers, drained**

2   **Tbsp. finely chopped parsley**

salt and pepper to taste

1   **17¼-oz. box frozen puff pastry, thawed**

1   **egg yolk mixed with 1 tsp. water**

Preheat oven to 400°.

Finely chop undrained marinated artichoke hearts in a bowl, then add finely chopped canned artichokes. Add remaining ingredients except pastry and egg wash. Mix well with a wooden spoon.

Take one pastry sheet and divide into thirds. Roll each piece into a 12"x6" rectangle on a lightly floured surface. Cut into 3" squares. Repeat with other pastry sheet.

Put 1 tablespoon of the artichoke filling into the center of each square. Moisten edges of the pastry with water and fold in half to form a triangle. Press edges with a fork to seal and place on greased baking sheets. Brush with egg wash. At this point the turnovers can be tightly covered with plastic wrap and stored in the refrigerator for one day.

Bake for 12–15 minutes, or until golden brown. Serve immediately.

Mary Lee Parrington

Potato Griddle Cakes with Smoked Salmon

"Great with champagne"

Moderately difficult
Serves: 8
Preparation time: 30 min.
Cooking: 15 min.

6   lg. russet potatoes, peeled

2   sm. red onions, peeled

1   cup flour

2   eggs

2   tsp. salt

1   tsp. ground pepper

1   tsp. finely chopped chives

vegetable oil for frying

½   cup sour cream

8   thin slices of smoked salmon, cut into 1" strips

fresh chives or dill for garnish

Shred potatoes and onions with processor or grater. Blot excess liquid with a paper towel. Sprinkle flour over mixture, then stir and toss to combine.

In a separate bowl, whisk the eggs, salt, pepper and chives. Add to the potato mixture and combine.

Heat a lightly greased griddle. Spoon 2 tablespoons of mixture onto griddle and form into cakes. Cook until golden, about 3 minutes on each side. Transfer to a paper lined plate or baking sheet and keep warm while cooking remaining batter.

To serve, top cakes with a teaspoon of sour cream and a thin strip of salmon. Garnish with fresh chives or dill. Serve warm.

Carolyn S. Hammer

Savory Basil and Tomato Phyllo Pizza
"The delicate crust makes this pizza unique"

Moderately difficult
Serves: 10
Preparation: 30 min.
Cooking: 30 min.

6   Tbsp. unsalted clarified butter, melted

8   sheets phyllo pastry, defrosted and refrigerated

8   Tbsp. freshly ground Parmesan cheese

1   cup coarsely shredded whole milk mozzarella cheese

1   cup thinly sliced red onion

2   lbs. plum tomatoes, thinly sliced, drained on paper towels

½   tsp. dried oregano

½   Tbsp. finely chopped fresh thyme or ½ tsp. dried

2   tsp. finely chopped fresh basil

feta cheese or Kalamata olives, optional

Preheat oven to 375°.

Using a 2" wide pastry brush, lightly coat a heavy jelly-roll pan with butter. Set aside.

Lay 1 sheet of phyllo pastry on the pan. Brush lightly with butter. Sprinkle with 1 tablespoon Parmesan cheese. Repeat, using 7 more sheets of phyllo and cheese. Press down gently to compact phyllo.

Sprinkle the mozzarella cheese over the entire surface and scatter with red onion.

Place the well-blotted tomato slices evenly over the phyllo. Sprinkle with oregano and thyme.

Bake pizza in middle of oven for 30 minutes, or until the edges are golden brown. Rotate the pan halfway through baking. Remove from oven and place on cooling rack for 5 minutes.

Cut into small squares, sprinkle with basil and serve.

May also sprinkle with a small amount of feta cheese or Kalamata olives.

Penny Lawrence

Spinach Tartlets
"You will love these rich, bite-sized morsels"

Easy
Yields: 30 tartlets
Preparation: 15 min.
Cooking: 5–7 min.
Can be made ahead

2 **pkg. frozen phyllo tartlet shells (15 shells per package)**

2 **Tbsp. butter**

4 **shallots, finely chopped**

4 **mushrooms, chopped (optional)**

1 **10-oz. pkg. frozen chopped spinach, thawed and well drained**

1 **tsp. Dijon mustard**

⅛ **tsp. nutmeg**

6 **oz. cream cheese**

Preheat oven to 425°.

Put tartlet shells on cookie sheet to thaw while preparing filling.

Melt butter and sauté shallots (and mushrooms, if desired) for 3 minutes. Add other ingredients. Cook over low heat, stirring until cheese is thoroughly incorporated and mixture is well blended.

Fill shells with spinach mixture and bake for 5–7 minutes. Serve hot.

Carolyn S. Hammer.

Hot Stuffed Banana Peppers
"Spice up your party with these"

Easy
Serves: 6–8
Preparation: 15 min.
Cooking: 30 min.

2 **lbs. loose sausage, hot or sweet**

2 **eggs, lightly beaten**

½ **tsp. garlic salt**

½ **cup Romano cheese, grated**

8 **slices of bread, with crust on, roughly chopped**

12 **hot or mild banana peppers, cut in half lengthwise, seeded and cored**

Preheat oven to 350°.

Place a baking sheet on the middle shelf of the oven. (This will prevent the bottom of the peppers from burning).

In a bowl, combine sausage, eggs, garlic salt and Romano cheese until well blended. Add chopped bread to the stuffing mixture, incorporating until all the bread is used.

Place peppers on a clean baking sheet and fill the cavities with the stuffing mixture. Place on top of the heated baking sheet. Cook for 30 minutes, or until golden brown. Serve immediately.

Donna Adipietro

Soups

Red Bell Pepper Soup

Easy
Serves: 4–6
Preparation: 30 min.
Cooking: 45 min.

3   Tbsp. butter, room
    temperature, divided

4   med. red peppers,
    cored and chopped

2   leeks, white part only,
    chopped

1   med. carrot, peeled and
    chopped

1   med. onion, chopped

2   cups chicken broth

2   cups whipping cream
    or 2 potatoes, peeled
    and chopped

salt and white pepper

Melt 1 tablespoon butter in a large saucepan and sauté the vegetables on low heat for about 10 minutes.

Add the broth and cream or potatoes. Simmer for 30 minutes, or until the vegetables are soft. Puree in batches in a blender or food mill. Simmer again and reduce to desired texture. Season with salt and pepper to taste.

Add the remaining 2 tablespoons of butter and serve.

Mary C. Hall

Hot Fennel Soup
"An elegant choice for fennel lovers"

Easy
Serves: 8
Preparation: 10 min.
Cooking: 1 hr. 5 min.

2   Tbsp. butter

1   med. red onion, finely
    chopped

1   med. potato, peeled
    and finely chopped

2   lg. or 3 sm. fennel
    bulbs, peeled and
    chopped (reserved)

4   cups chicken broth

2   cups whipping cream

salt and pepper

Melt butter in a heavy saucepan. Add onion and potato and cook about 15 minutes. Add fennel. Cook for 20 minutes, or until tender. Stir in broth and cream and simmer for another 30 minutes.

Puree in batches in a blender or food mill. Reheat and season with salt and pepper. Sprinkle with reserved fennel leaves before serving.

Una Melikian

Spicy Split Pea Soup

Easy
Serves: 6
Preparation: 2 hrs.
Cooking: 30 min.

5 cups chicken broth
5 cups water
1 lb. dried split peas
2 Tbsp. butter
½ cup chopped onion
1 clove garlic, minced
1 Tbsp. curry powder
1 tsp. crushed coriander seeds
¼ tsp. crushed red pepper
1 tsp. salt
½ cup light cream or milk

Combine chicken broth, water and split peas in a large saucepan; heat to boiling. Turn off the heat, cover and let stand for 1 hour. Reheat and simmer over low heat for 45 minutes.

Melt butter in a skillet over medium heat; sauté the onion, garlic and spices for about 7 minutes. Stir spice mixture into split peas. Cover and cook over low heat for 20 minutes. Cool slightly. Puree 2 cups of the soup in a blender. Repeat until all has been pureed.

Stir in cream, heat and serve.

Ann Steytler

Indian Pea Soup
"An exotic blend of flavors"

Easy
Serves: 4
Preparation: 15 min.
Cooking: 10 min.

¼ cup flour
⅓ cup water
1 16-oz. can peas, drained, liquid reserved
3 cups chicken broth
2 tsp. curry powder
1 tsp. sugar
¼ cup slivered almonds
¼ cup raisins
½ cup light cream
salt and white pepper

Place flour in a small bowl and gradually incorporate the water, using a whisk, to prevent lumps.

Place peas in a food processor and process with the metal blade until smooth. In a large saucepan, put peas, reserved liquid, broth, curry, sugar and flour mixture. Bring to a boil, stirring constantly. Add the almonds and raisins. Simmer for 5 minutes. Soup may be made ahead to this point. Remove from heat and add cream.

Season to taste with salt and pepper. Serve at once.

If making ahead, heat just before serving, then add the cream.

Irene Gates

Portobello Soup

Easy
Serves: 4
Preparation: 20 min.
Cooking: 25 min.

2   Tbsp. olive oil
2   Tbsp. finely chopped shallots
2   cloves garlic, minced
1   leek, white part only, thinly sliced
2   carrots, peeled and chopped
2   stalks celery, chopped
1   lb. portobello mushrooms, diced
4   cups chicken broth

1   Tbsp. soy sauce
salt and pepper
2   Tbsp. finely chopped herbs for garnish

Heat oil in a large saucepan. Add shallots and garlic. Cook over medium heat until softened, about 2 minutes, stirring frequently. Add the leek, carrots, celery and mushrooms and cook. Stir frequently, until the vegetables begin to soften, about 5 minutes. Add chicken broth and soy sauce. Simmer for 15 minutes. Season with salt and pepper to taste. Garnish with herbs before serving.

Sally M. Wood

Italian Tomato Soup
"A simple solution to a busy day"

Easy
Serves: 4
Preparation: 10 min.
Cooking: 20 min.

2   cloves garlic, minced
3   Tbsp. extra virgin olive oil, divided
1   28-oz. can whole plum tomatoes in puree, coarsely chopped
1   14½-oz. can chicken broth
¼   cup finely chopped basil, plus extra for serving
salt and pepper
4   slices Italian bread, 2"–3" across
1½ cups shaved Parmesan cheese

Preheat oven to 400°.

In a large saucepan, cook garlic in 2 tablespoons olive oil over medium heat for 30 seconds. Add tomatoes, broth, basil, and salt and pepper to taste. Cover and simmer for 20 minutes.

Drizzle bread with remaining 1 tablespoon olive oil. Bake on baking sheet for about 10 minutes, until crisp and golden, turning once.

Place toasted bread in individual soup bowls. Sprinkle cheese on bread, ladle soup on top and garnish with reserved basil.

Grace Clark Benjamin

Soup of Chanterelles
"Perfect for a dinner party"

Easy
Serves: 4
Preparation: 30 min.
Cooking: 30 min.

½ cup chopped bacon
½ cup chopped shallots
2 cups sliced, cleaned chanterelles or other wild mushrooms
½ cup white wine
3 Tbsp. flour
3 cups hot chicken broth
pinch of ground caraway seeds
ground lemon zest
½ cup heavy cream
salt and pepper
1 tsp. finely chopped Italian parsley

Brown bacon lightly in a large saucepan. Add shallots and stir on low heat until translucent. Add chanterelles and sauté until softened. Place flour in a small bowl and gradually incorporate the wine. Add to saucepan and allow the liquid to reduce a little. Let vegetables sweat, but do not brown.

Add chicken stock gradually, while stirring to avoid lumps. Let mixture come to a boil. Simmer for 30 minutes. Season with ground caraway seeds and lemon zest. Let simmer for 5 minutes more. Add heavy cream and bring to simmer. Add salt and pepper to taste. Stir in chopped parsley just before serving.

Willi Daffinger, Executive Chef
Rolling Rock Club

35

Fresh Mushroom Soup
"You'll feel like you're dining in the Governor's Mansion"

Easy
Serves: 6
Preparation: 10 min.
Cooking: 55 min.

6 Tbsp. butter
2 cups minced yellow onions
2 tsp. sugar
1 lb. fresh mushrooms
¼ cup flour
1 cup water
1¾ cups chicken broth
1 cup dry Vermouth
1 tsp. salt
¼ tsp. pepper

Melt butter in a large saucepan and cook onions and sugar slowly until golden, about 30 to 45 minutes.

Meanwhile, slice ⅓ of the mushrooms and finely chop the rest. Add all the mushrooms to the saucepan and sauté for 5 minutes. Gradually incorporate the flour, stirring to a smooth consistency. Cook 2 minutes, stirring constantly. Pour in water and stir again until smooth. Add the remaining ingredients and heat to boiling, stirring constantly. Reduce heat and simmer uncovered for 10 minutes.

Tom Ridge
Governor of Pennsylvania

Cashel Cheese and Celery Soup
"Swirl in your cheese, and smile"

Easy
Serves: 6–8
Preparation: 20 min.
Cooking: 40 min.

4 Tbsp. butter

3 lg. onions, quartered and thinly sliced

4 cups chopped celery

6 cups chicken broth

1 Tbsp. fresh thyme

black pepper

¼ lb. blue cheese

½ cup heavy cream

½ cup parsley, finely chopped

½ cup chopped celery leaves

1 cup seasoned croutons

Melt butter and sauté onions and celery. Add the chicken broth and simmer 30 minutes. Add fresh thyme and pepper to taste. Simmer 5 minutes more. Soup may be refrigerated at this point if desired. In a microwave safe dish, crumble the blue cheese and add the cream. Warm in the microwave for 1 minute on high, or place on the stove top to warm, but do not boil. Whisk mixture until smooth. Set aside.

Add the parsley and celery leaves to the hot stock just before serving. Ladle into individual bowls, and pass the blue cheese and cream mixture separately so that guests may swirl in the amount they wish. Garnish with seasoned croutons.

Susan Vogelgesang

White Bean, Garlic, and Gorgonzola Soup
"A rich, creamy indulgence"

Easy
Serves: 12–14
Preparation: 10 min.
Cooking: 40 min.

4 Tbsp. butter

¾ cup minced garlic

8 cups chicken broth

8 cups cream or half-and-half

1 cup grated Pecorino Romano cheese

2 cups crumbled Gorgonzola cheese

6 cups canned Northern white beans, drained

pepper to taste

In a large stockpot or Dutch oven, melt the butter and brown the garlic.

Add chicken broth and remaining ingredients, and cook over low heat until the cheeses are melted. Serve.

Cut recipe in half for a smaller crowd.

Café Georgio

Annie's Soup
"For the hearty appetite"

Easy
Serves: 6–8
Preparation: 15 min.
Cooking: 1 hr. 15 min.

1½ lbs. lean ground beef
2   cups coarsely chopped cabbage
1   lg. onion, chopped
2–3 stalks celery, coarsely chopped
4–5 carrots, sliced
3   med. potatoes, peeled and cubed
1   16-oz. can tomatoes
1   6-oz. can tomato paste
1   10½-oz. can beef broth
1   10½-oz. can condensed French onion soup
3   soup cans water
1   16-oz. can kidney beans
salt and pepper
fresh herbs, finely chopped

In a medium stockpot, brown beef over medium heat. Add cabbage, onion, celery and carrots. Sauté for 15 minutes, stirring frequently.

Add remaining ingredients and let simmer for 1 hour. Additional water may be added as needed.

This recipe is flexible. Any fresh or leftover vegetables you have on hand can be added.

Beth Rom

Black Bean and Pumpkin Soup

Easy
Serves: 8
Preparation: 10 min.
Cooking: 40 min.

3   15½-oz. cans black beans, rinsed and drained
1   10-oz can whole tomatoes, chopped and drained
4   Tbsp. butter
2   med. onions, chopped
3   cloves garlic, minced
1   tsp. salt
1   tsp. fresh ground pepper
1½ Tbsp. ground cumin
4   cups chicken or beef broth
1   16-oz. can pumpkin
½   cup dry sherry
sour cream and chopped green onions for garnish

In a blender, puree beans and tomatoes. In a large saucepan, melt butter and sauté onion, garlic, salt, pepper and cumin until onion is soft and lightly browned.

Stir in the bean and tomato puree. Add the broth, pumpkin and sherry.

Simmer for 30 minutes. Garnish with sour cream and chopped green onions just before serving.

Bonnie Casper

Poblano Soup Gratinee
"Spice up a winter day"

Easy
Serves: 6–8
Preparation: 20 min.
Cooking: 35 min.

1–2 poblano chiles

3 Tbsp. butter

1 Tbsp. vegetable oil

3 cups thinly sliced onions

3 Tbsp. flour

8 cups chicken broth

1 cup fresh corn kernels

1 cup diced, poached chicken

½ tsp. ground cumin

½ tsp. salt

toast rounds

Monterey Jack cheese, grated

Roast the poblano chiles over a gas flame or under a broiler, turning often, until charred all over. Place in a paper bag, seal and let steam for 10 minutes. Peel the poblanos, discarding the stems, ribs and seeds. Cut into ⅛" strips.

In a large saucepan, melt butter and oil over medium heat. Cook the onions for 15 minutes. Stir in flour and cook 2 minutes. Add chicken broth and continue cooking. Add the peppers and simmer for 30 minutes. Stir in the corn and chicken and cook for an additional 5 minutes before seasoning with cumin and salt.

Pour the soup into individual flame-proof bowls; float toast rounds on top and sprinkle with grated cheese. Heat under broiler until bubbly and golden.

Kit Muire

Tortilla Rice Soup
"For a south of the border supper"

Easy
Serves: 4
Preparation: 10 min.
Cooking: 30 min.

cooking spray

⅓ cup green onions, sliced

4 cups chicken broth

1 14½-oz. can diced tomatoes with green chiles, undrained

1 cup cooked chicken breast, cubed

2 4-oz. cans chopped green chiles

salt and pepper

1 Tbsp. fresh lime juice

2 cups cooked rice

tortilla chips

½ cup chopped tomato

½ cup cubed avocado

4 lime slices and chopped cilantro, for garnish

Coat a Dutch oven or large saucepan with cooking spray. Sauté onions over medium high heat until tender. Add broth, tomatoes, chicken and chiles. Reduce heat. Cover and simmer for 20 minutes. Stir in salt, pepper and lime juice. Just before serving, add rice.

Pour into soup bowls and top with tortilla chips, chopped tomatoes and avocado. Garnish with lime slices and cilantro.

Leslie S. Kelly

Chilled Carrot Soup
"A cool delight on a hot summer's day"

Easy
Serves: 8
Preparation: 10 min.
Cooking: 35 min.
Must be made ahead

¼ cup olive oil

2 cups chopped onions

2 cloves garlic, minced

2 tsp. curry powder

2 Tbsp. peeled, minced fresh ginger

2 lbs. carrots, chopped

½ tsp. freshly ground pepper

salt to taste

10 cups chicken broth

chopped chives, for garnish

In a large pan, sauté the onion and garlic in oil for a few minutes. Add curry powder and cook 2 minutes. Stir in the remaining ingredients, except the chives, and simmer, covered, for about 30 minutes. Vegetables should be covered with broth. Cool and then puree in batches in a blender. Thin with additional broth, if needed. Chill at least 6 hours before serving. Garnish with chopped chives.

Mary C. Hall

Hot "Be Be" Soup

"Good served with corn bread or crusty Italian bread"

Easy
Serves: 6
Preparation: 10 min.
Cooking: 45 min.

1   Tbsp. olive oil
1   lg. onion, chopped
2   cloves garlic, minced
½   cup chopped green, yellow or red pepper
3   14½-oz. cans beef broth
1   14½-oz. can stewed tomatoes
¾   cup picante sauce
1   Tbsp. finely chopped basil
½   tsp. Italian seasonings
1   12-oz. pkg. frozen sausage tortellini
¾   cup grated Parmesan cheese

Heat olive oil in a 4 qt. soup pot. Sauté onions, garlic and peppers. Add broth, tomatoes, picante sauce, basil and seasonings. Let simmer for 30 minutes.

Bring to a boil and add the tortellini. Simmer for 10 minutes, or until the tortellini float on the surface.

Place in soup bowls and sprinkle with Parmesan cheese before serving.

Christine Sunderman

Roma Ravioli Soup
"Your whole family will adore this"

Easy
Serves: 6
Preparation: 10 min.
Cooking: 35 min.

1 Tbsp. olive oil
1 green pepper, chopped
1 sm. onion, finely chopped
3 lg. cloves garlic, minced
1 Tbsp. dried basil
2 tsp. fennel seeds
¼ tsp. crushed red pepper
6 cups chicken broth
2 med. zucchini, chopped
1 carrot, chopped
1 9-oz. pkg. fresh cheese ravioli

1½ cups diced cooked chicken

salt and pepper

In a large saucepan, heat oil over medium heat. Add green pepper, onion, garlic, basil, fennel seeds and crushed red pepper. Sauté until the vegetables are just tender, about 10 minutes. Add the broth. Cover and simmer for 10 minutes. Add the zucchini and carrot. Cover and simmer until the carrot is almost tender, about 5 minutes. Increase the heat to high and bring the soup to a boil. Add the ravioli and cook for about 5 minutes, or until the ravioli are tender. Add the chicken and cook until heated through, about 1 minute. Season with salt and pepper to taste.

Ruth C. Hofmann

Tortellini Soup
"Simplicity itself"

Easy
Serves: 6
Preparation: 10 min.
Cooking: 15 min.

2 Tbsp. butter
1 tsp. minced garlic
4 14½-oz. cans chicken broth
1 9-oz. pkg. fresh cheese tortellini
1 14½-oz. can chopped tomatoes
1 Tbsp. Italian seasonings
½ 10-oz. pkg. frozen chopped spinach, thawed

Romano or Parmesan cheese

Melt butter in a large saucepan. Add garlic and sauté over low heat until softened. Add chicken broth and bring to a boil. Add the tortellini, reduce the heat and cook for 7 minutes. Add tomatoes and Italian seasoning. Continue to cook until hot. Add the spinach and heat through. Do not overcook. Just before serving, sprinkle with grated cheese.

Debra Gibbs

Sausage and Bean Chowder
"A welcome sight for hungry eyes"

Easy
Serves 8–10
Preparation: 15 min.
Cooking: 1 hr. 45 min.

1 lb. bulk hot pork sausage
2 16-oz. cans kidney beans, drained
2 14-oz. cans stewed tomatoes, undrained
2 cups tomato juice
1 lg. onion, chopped
1 bay leaf
1 tsp. salt
½ tsp. garlic salt
½ tsp. chili powder
1 tsp. thyme
½ tsp. pepper
1 cup whole kernel corn
1 stalk celery, chopped
1 green pepper, chopped

In a large skillet, brown sausage and drain off excess fat.

Combine sausage with all remaining ingredients in a large kettle. Simmer covered for 1½ hours. Remove bay leaf before serving.

Susan O. McEwen

Peanut Soup

Easy
Serves: 6
Preparation: 10 min.
Cooking: 20 min.

4 Tbsp. butter
1 lg. onion, diced
4 ribs celery, diced
1 sm. green pepper, diced
½ cup flour
1 bay leaf
4 cups chicken broth
2 cups heavy cream
24 oz. peanut butter
2 tsp. Tabasco
salt and pepper
2 bunches green onions, diced, and ½ cup chopped peanuts, for garnish

Melt butter in a heavy stockpot. Sauté onion, celery and green pepper until onion is translucent. Stir in flour and cook for 3–4 minutes. Add bay leaf and chicken broth. Stir frequently and bring to a boil. Reduce heat and simmer, uncovered, for 10–15 minutes.

Stir in heavy cream and peanut butter until smooth. Add Tabasco and adjust seasoning to taste. Serve garnished with green onions and peanuts.

Chef Jack Hahn
The Inn at Turkey Hill,
Bloomsburg, PA

Shrimp Soup with Crisp Tortilla Strips

"This lively soup will give you a glow"

Moderately Difficult
Serves: 4
Preparation: 45 min.
Cooking: 1 hr.

2   med. poblano chiles

4   6" corn tortillas, halved and cut into ¼" strips

¾   lb. med. shrimp, shelled and deveined, shells reserved and shrimp cut in half

2   cups water

½   cup white wine

3   green onions, cut into 1" pieces

1   cilantro sprig plus 3 Tbsp. coarsely chopped cilantro, for garnish

1   tsp. oregano

1   bay leaf

1   tsp. salt

2   tsp. olive oil

1   med. onion, thinly sliced

4   lg. cloves of garlic, minced

2   lg. tomatoes, peeled, seeded, finely chopped

1   Tbsp. hot paprika

2   cups chicken broth

1   cup fresh or frozen corn kernels

lime wedges for serving

Preheat the oven to 350°.

Roast chiles over a gas flame or under a broiler, turning often, until charred all over. Transfer to a paper bag, seal and let steam 10 minutes. Peel the chiles, discarding stems, ribs and seeds. Cut chiles into thin strips and set aside.

Toast tortilla strips on a baking sheet until crisp, about 10 minutes, or fry the strips. Set aside.

In a medium nonreactive saucepan, combine the shrimp shells, water, wine, green onions, cilantro sprig, oregano, bay leaf and salt. Bring to a boil over high heat. Lower temperature, cover and simmer for 15 minutes. Strain the broth into a bowl, discarding the solids. Heat oil in a large nonreactive saucepan. Add onion and garlic. Cook over moderate heat, stirring, until softened, about 3–4 minutes. Add the tomatoes. Raise the heat to high, and cook, stirring frequently, until the liquid is almost completely evaporated, about 4–5 minutes. Stir in paprika and cook for 30 seconds. Stir in shrimp broth and chicken broth.

Bring soup to a boil over moderately high heat. Add the shrimp, chiles and corn. Lower the heat and simmer until the shrimp turn pink, about 2–3 minutes. Ladle soup into bowls. Sprinkle with the chopped cilantro. Pile tortilla strips on top and serve with lime wedges.

Susan Foradas

Oyster Stew Rafalko

"A wonderful taste of coastal cuisine"

Easy
Serves: 10
Preparation: 15 min.
Cooking: 20 min.

1 onion, cut into pieces

1 celery stalk including leaves, cut into pieces

1 carrot, cut into pieces

1 Tbsp. finely chopped fresh parsley

2 Tbsp. bacon fat

½ cup (1 stick) unsalted butter

2 cups chicken broth

3 lg. boiling potatoes, peeled and cut into ¾" cubes

2 tsp. salt

½ tsp. white pepper

2 tsp. Old Bay Seasoning

1 pt. shucked oysters with liquid

3 Tbsp. cornstarch dissolved in 3 Tbsp. cold water

4 cups half-and-half

In a food processor, finely chop the onion, celery, carrot and parsley. Over a moderate heat, melt bacon fat and butter in a kettle. Add the onion mixture and cook, stirring occasionally, until softened. Add the broth, potatoes, salt, pepper and Old Bay Seasoning. Continue cooking, covered, over a very low heat for 15 minutes, or until the potatoes are almost tender. Add the oysters and their liquid and simmer an additional 5 minutes.

In a separate saucepan, scald the half-and-half. Stir the cornstarch mixture into the soup. Add the scalded half-and-half and simmer, stirring, for 15 seconds or until thickened. Serve immediately.

David M. Rafalko, M.D.

Fish Chowder
"An American tradition"

Easy
Serves: 4
Preparation: 10 min.
Cooking: 25 min.

1   **12-oz. can clam broth**

3   **cups chopped red potatoes**

2   **celery stalks, chopped**

1   **onion, chopped**

1   **lb. white fish fillets, chopped (preferably cod)**

1   **Tbsp. dried tarragon**

½   **tsp nutmeg**

salt and white pepper

¼   **cup butter**

¼   **cup flour**

2   **cups heavy cream**

salt and pepper

lemon wedges for garnish

In a heavy soup kettle, simmer clam broth, potatoes, celery, onion and fish fillets. When vegetables are tender, season with tarragon, nutmeg, and salt and pepper to taste.

In another saucepan, melt butter. Add flour and cook over low heat for 5 minutes, stirring constantly. Stir the butter and flour mixture into vegetables and simmer until thickened. Gradually stir in cream. Simmer for another 10 minutes. Season to taste.

Ladle into soup bowls and garnish with lemon wedges.

Tom and Robin Adams
Patrick Henry's Restaurant
Hanover, NH

Cream Of Chicken and Wild Rice Soup

"A family favorite that company will love too"

Easy
Serves: 6
Preparation: 15 min.
Cooking: 20 min.

1   Tbsp. vegetable oil

1   8-oz. chicken breast,
    boned and skinned, cut
    into bite-sized pieces

2   cups sliced fresh
    mushrooms

1¼ cups chopped onion

2   cloves garlic, minced

1   6-oz. box long-grain
    and wild rice mix,
    prepared according to
    directions

2   14½-oz. cans chicken
    broth

2   Tbsp. dry white wine

¼   tsp. dried tarragon

¼   tsp. dried thyme

1   Tbsp. cornstarch

1   12-oz. can evaporated
    lowfat milk, divided

sliced green onions and
green peppers for garnish

Heat oil in a large saucepan over medium high heat. Add chicken, mushrooms, onion and garlic. Cook for 5–8 minutes, or until vegetables are tender and chicken is no longer pink.

Add prepared rice, broth, wine, tarragon and thyme. Bring to a boil. Combine a small amount of evaporated milk and cornstarch in a small bowl. Stir until smooth. Stir into soup mixture with remaining evaporated milk.

Reduce heat to low. Cook, stirring occasionally, for 8–10 minutes, or until soup is thickened. Garnish with green onions and pepper slices.

Nancy B. Williams

Breads

Basic Bread Dough

Moderately difficult
Yields: 4 loaves
Preparation: 45 min.
Rising time: 3 hrs.
Cooking: 25–30 min.
Can be frozen

2 **pkg. active dry yeast**
1 **Tbsp. sugar**
½ **cup lukewarm water (105°–115°)**
1 **cup milk**
½ **cup (1 stick) unsalted butter**
3 **eggs**
2 **egg yolks**
1½ **tsp. salt**
6½ **cups (or more) flour**
parchment paper
1 **egg beaten with 1 Tbsp. milk, for glaze**
sesame seeds

Preheat oven to 375°.

To proof, dissolve yeast with sugar in warm water; set aside for 10 minutes, until it foams. In a small saucepan, heat milk to just below boiling point. Remove milk from heat. Add butter, stirring until butter just begins to melt.

Combine milk/butter mixture, yeast mixture, eggs, yolks, salt and 2 cups of flour in a food processor. (If using processor with small capacity, mix dough in 2 batches). Process until well blended. Add 4 ½ cups flour and process until ball forms. Knead on floured surface until no longer sticky, adding more flour if necessary. Put dough in large greased bowl and let rise in a warm, draft-free area until doubled in volume, about 1–1½ hours. Punch dough down.

Prepare glaze. Divide dough into 4 equal parts. Divide each part into 3 long ropes. Braid the ropes, forming a long braid of bread. Repeat with remaining dough. Place braids on parchment lined baking sheets.Brush with egg wash and sprinkle with sesame seeds. Allow to rise again until doubled in size.

Bake bread in oven until golden brown, about 25–30 minutes. When tapped on bottom, bread should sound hollow. Cool before slicing.

Rania Harris

Layered Olive Bread
"A savory loaf with cocktails"

Moderately difficult
Serves: 12
Preparation: 30 min.
Rising time: 1 hr.
Cooking: 35–40 min.
Can be frozen

½ **cup (1 stick) unsalted butter**

1 **med. onion, finely chopped**

¾ **cup coarsely chopped pimento-stuffed green olives**

1 **cup coarsely chopped pitted Greek black olives**

freshly ground black pepper

parchment paper

½ **batch basic bread dough (see Basic Bread Dough recipe)**

1 **egg beaten with 1 tsp. water, for glaze**

sesame seeds

Preheat oven to 375°.

Melt butter in heavy medium skillet over medium low heat. Add onion and cook until just golden. Mix in olives and pepper. Cool completely.

Line a baking sheet with parchment paper. Using ½ batch basic bread dough after first rising, roll out on a lightly floured surface to a 18"x12" rectangle. Spread with olive mixture, leaving ½" border. Starting at one long side, roll up tightly, jelly-roll style. Pinch ends and seam to seal. Arrange loaf, seam side down, on prepared sheet. Cut several diagonal slashes across the top. Prepare egg wash and brush. Sprinkle with sesame seeds. Cover with greased plastic wrap. Let bread rise in a warm draft-free area until almost double in volume, about 1 hour.

Bake for 35–40 minutes, until golden brown. Loaf should sound hollow when tapped on bottom. Cool on rack. Serve at room temperature.

Rania Harris

49

Feather Yeast Rolls
"So good, they inspired a marriage proposal"

Easy
Makes: 32
Preparation: 20 min.
Rising time: 5 hrs.
Cooking: 12 min.

1   pkg. active dry yeast, dissolved in 1 Tbsp. warm water (105°–115°)

1½ cups scalded milk, cooled

½   cup sugar

1   tsp. salt

½   cup (1 stick) melted butter

2   well-beaten eggs

5   cups flour

additional ½ cup melted butter for brushing dough

Preheat oven to 350°.

Mix all ingredients, except flour, with an electric mixer. Stir in flour all at once. Cover and refrigerate 3–4 hours, or overnight.

Cut dough into quarters. Working with one quarter of dough, roll into a circle. Brush with melted butter. Cut circle into 8 pie-shaped wedges.

Roll each wedge up from wide to narrow end, tucking under tip; shape into crescent. Place on nonstick or buttered baking sheet. Brush crescents generously with butter. Repeat with rest of dough. Let rise 2 hours, or until double in size. Bake for 12 minutes.

Suzanne Martinson
Food Editor, Pittsburgh-Post Gazette

Focaccia Bread with Cambazola
"The mellow topping perfects this loaf"

Easy
Serves: 8–10
Preparation: 30 min.
Cooking: 10 min.

6   cloves garlic

¼   cup plus 1 Tbsp. olive oil, divided

2   yellow peppers, cored, seeded, cut into strips

2   green peppers, cored, seeded, cut into strips

2   red peppers, cored, seeded, cut into strips

2   loaves focaccia bread

½   lb. Cambazola cheese

Preheat oven to 350°.

Coat unpeeled garlic cloves with 1 tablespoon oil. Place on baking sheet and roast 15–20 minutes, until softened. Cool slightly and squeeze out pulp. Set aside. Adjust oven to 325°.

In a large skillet, cook pepper strips in remaining oil until tender, but still firm, about 10 minutes. Remove from heat.

Spread roasted garlic on bread and place in oven for about 10 minutes. Spread with cheese and top with peppers. Cut bread into serving size wedges. Serve warm.

Debra Gibbs

Cheese Bread
"Fills the house with mouth-watering aroma"

Easy
Yields: 2 loaves
Preparation: 30 min.
Rising time: 2 hrs.
Cooking: 45 min.
Can be frozen

2   pkgs. active dry yeast

1½ cups warm water
    (105°–115°)

2   Tbsp. sugar

2¼ tsp. salt

4½–5 cups flour

2   eggs, beaten

1   lb. sharp Cheddar
    cheese, grated

Preheat oven to 325°.

Grease 2 9"x5" loaf pans.

To proof, dissolve yeast in warm water. Set aside for 10 minutes, until it foams.

In the large bowl of an electric mixer fitted with a dough hook, mix sugar, salt and 2 cups flour. Add eggs and cheese. Add yeast and water mixture. Beat well. Add remaining flour and continue to beat until dough is very smooth, using hands if necessary to blend. Knead lightly in the bowl. Divide into loaf pans. Let rise in a warm place until double in size, about 2 hours.

Bake bread for 45 minutes. Leave in pan for 10 minutes after baking.

Anne G. Phipps

51

The Best Garlic Bread In The Universe
"Out of this world"

Easy
Serves: 8–10
Preparation: 10 min.
Cooking: 15 min.

1   cup (2 sticks) butter,
    softened

1   cup freshly grated
    Parmesan cheese

½   cup mayonnaise

5   cloves garlic, minced

3   Tbsp. finely chopped
    parsley

½   tsp. dried oregano

1   lg. loaf Italian or
    French bread, cut in
    half lengthwise

Preheat oven to 375°.

Mix the first six ingredients in a bowl and spread on bread. Place bread halves on cookie sheet. Bake for 15 minutes, until melted and bubbly.

Cool slightly before slicing.

Barbara W. Gordon

Jalapeño Jack Cheese Spoon Bread
"Great for a southwest buffet"

Easy
Serves: 6–8
Preparation: 40 min.
Cooking: 30 min.

52

2   jalapeño chiles, seeded
    and finely chopped
2   cloves garlic, minced
2   shallots, peeled and
    finely chopped
2   cups milk
1   cup cornmeal
1   cup grated Jalapeño
    Jack cheese
1   cup (2 sticks) unsalted
    butter, softened
1   Tbsp. maple syrup
salt
4   eggs, separated
1   Tbsp. Tequila

Preheat oven to 350°.

Butter a 2 qt. casserole.

Combine jalapeño chiles, garlic, shallots and milk in a medium saucepan, over medium high heat. Bring just to boil; immediately stir in cornmeal, beating thoroughly. Lower heat and cook 5 minutes, or until thick. Remove from heat and beat in cheese, butter, syrup and salt to taste, until combined well. Set aside to cool.

Beat egg yolks in a small bowl and stir into cooled cornmeal. Beat egg whites until stiff and fold into cornmeal. Add Tequila, stirring just enough to mix. Pour into a prepared casserole. Cover and bake for about 30 minutes, or until the tip of a knife inserted in the center comes out clean. Serve hot.

Susan Vogelgesang

Onion Bread
"Great with soup or sauce dishes"

Easy
Yield: 1 loaf
Preparation: 30 min.
Rising time: 1 hr.
Cooking: 30 min.
Can be frozen

2   frozen loaves of bread dough

3   Tbsp. butter

1   cup chopped onion

1   tsp. garlic salt, optional

Preheat oven to 350°.

Defrost loaves until almost completely thawed. Using your hands, roll dough into a long cylinder, approximately 14" long. Make a slit lengthwise, being careful not to cut through the bottom.

Sauté onions in butter; sprinkle with garlic salt if desired. Fill slits with onions, seal shut. Lay loaves side by side on greased baking sheet and wrap them around each other to form a twist. Let rise until doubled in size, about 1 hour. Bake for 30 minutes, or until browned.

Mrs. Joanne Vargo

53

Caraway Bread
"Substitute dill for a different taste"

Easy
Yield: 1 loaf
Preparation: 15 min.
Rising time: 1 hr. 40 min.
Cooking: 40–50 min.

1   pkg. active dry yeast

¼   cup luke warm water (105°–115°)

1   cup cottage cheese, heated (105°–115°)

2   tsp. sugar

1   Tbsp. melted butter

1   Tbsp. minced onions

2   tsp. caraway seeds

1   tsp. salt

¼   tsp. baking soda

2½ cups flour

additional butter and salt for glaze

Preheat oven to 350°.

Grease an 8" casserole.

To proof, dissolve yeast in warm water and set aside for 10 minutes until it foams.

Combine all ingredients, except flour. Mix well. Add flour slowly to form stiff dough. Cover and let stand in warm place until double in size, about 50–60 minutes. Punch down dough and put into prepared casserole. Let rise 30–40 minutes.

Bake for 40–50 minutes until golden brown. Brush with butter and sprinkle with salt.

Sally W. Bruce

Café Georgio's Flat Bread
"Your guests can choose their own toppings"

Difficult
Serves: 10–12
Preparation: 1 hr.
Rising time: 1½ hrs.
Cooking: 10–15 min.

Fresh Herb-infused Oil:
2   cups olive oil
2   Tbsp. chopped fresh basil
1   Tbsp. chopped fresh parsley
1   Tbsp. chopped fresh oregano
2   cloves garlic, minced
salt and pepper
2   whole red chile peppers

Dough:
1   cup warm water (105°–115°)
2   Tbsp. active dry yeast
2½–3 cups flour
¼   cup fresh herb-infused oil (see above)
½   Tbsp. crushed red pepper
pinch salt and sugar
fresh basil, finely chopped
fresh parsley, finely chopped
flour and cornmeal

Toppings:
fresh tomatoes
sun dried tomatoes
Asiago cheese
feta cheese
hot pepper cheese
sautéed peppers, onions, spinach and garlic
sliced onions
capers
fresh herbs, finely chopped

Preheat oven to 450°.

Fresh Herb-infused Oil:
Mix all ingredients in a jar. The flavor becomes more intense with age. Store in the refrigerator.

Dough:
To proof, dissolve yeast in warm water; set aside for 10 minutes until it foams. Add to large bowl and fold in flour. Add oil, salt, sugar, pepper flakes, basil, and parsley. Knead, either by hand or in an electric mixer fitted with a dough hook, until dough is very smooth to the touch. Cover bowl and let stand in a warm place until doubled in size. Divide into three pieces.

Assembly of Flat Bread:
Lightly dust each piece of dough with flour. Roll each bread out on cornmeal covered board; don't worry about the symmetry. Transfer to a baking sheet. Bake at 450° until just beginning to brown, about 5 minutes. Remove from oven, and paint baked flatbread surface with herb-infused oil.

Toppings:
Layer with any combination of toppings, and return to oven until cheese melts, about 5 minutes. Finish with capers and fresh herbs if desired.

Café Georgio

Martha's California Pizza
"Everyone loves it"

Easy
Serves: 2–3
Preparation: 45 min.
Rising time: 1½ hrs.
Cooking: 15–20 min.

Crust:
1 pkg. active dry yeast

1 tsp. sugar

⅔ cup warm water
   (105°–115°)

1⅔ cup flour

¾ tsp. salt

2 tsp. olive oil

Topping:
1 14-oz. can artichoke
   hearts, drained

⅓ cup roasted red
   peppers from jar,
   drained

1 2¼- oz. can sliced black
   olives

4 oz. grated mozzarella
   cheese

⅓ cup freshly grated
   Parmesan cheese

Preheat oven to 450°.

To proof, dissolve yeast with sugar in warm water; set aside for 10 minutes until it foams. Put flour and salt in food processor. With machine on, pour yeast mixture through feed tube. Process about 15 seconds, until dough pulls away from sides of bowl. Add oil and process for 20 seconds. If dough sticks to sides of bowl, add 1 tablespoon of flour at a time, processing for 10 seconds after each addition. Dough should leave sides of bowl but remain soft. Remove from food processor and knead dough a few times. Place dough in lightly oiled bowl, turning to coat completely. Let dough rise slightly before using, or leave all day. Roll into 1 large pizza. Prepare topping.

Topping:
Combine artichoke hearts, peppers and olives in food processor. Pulse until finely chopped and blended, but not pureed. Spread onto crust. Top with cheeses. Bake pizza for approximately 15–20 minutes.

Susan N. Dobbins

Roasted Onion and Garlic Pizza
"This is a winner"

Easy
Serves: 6
Preparation: 30 min.
Cooking: 10 min.

4   Tbsp. olive oil

2   lg. sweet onions, cut into thin wedges

1   red onion, cut into thin wedges

1   lg. leek, thinly sliced

6   cloves garlic, thinly sliced

2   sprigs fresh thyme

1   bay leaf

1   Tbsp. balsamic vinegar

salt and pepper to taste

1   prepared pizza crust

½   cup shaved Romano cheese

Preheat oven to 425°.

In a large skillet, heat oil over medium heat. Add onions, leek, garlic, thyme and bay leaf. Cook, stirring, until moisture begins to release and onions soften. Lower heat to medium low and, stirring occasionally, caramelize ingredients over heat for at least 30 minutes. Add vinegar and cook until moisture has evaporated. Remove thyme and bay leaf. Season with salt and pepper. The sauce can be refrigerated at this point.

Brush pizza crust with oil. Spread with sauce. Bake for 10 minutes, or until sauce is bubbly and crust is golden. Remove from oven and top with shaved Romano cheese. Serve immediately.

Ann Hunt

Date Nut Bread

Easy
Yield: 2 loaves
Preparation: 25 min.
Cooking: 1 hr.
Can be made ahead

8   oz. dates, chopped

2   tsp. baking soda

2   cups boiling water

½   cup (1 stick) margarine

2   cups sugar

2   eggs

1   tsp. salt

½   tsp. vanilla

1   cup chopped nuts

4   cups flour

Preheat oven to 325°.

Grease two 9"x5" loaf pans.

Mix dates, baking soda and boiling water. Set aside to cool.

Put margarine, sugar, eggs, salt, vanilla and chopped nuts in a bowl and mix well. Add flour and date mixture alternately. Pour into loaf pans. Bake for 1 hour. Cool before serving.

Eloise F. Montgomery

Orange Poppy Tea Bread
"Pour a cup of coffee and relax"

Easy
Yield: 1 loaf
Preparation: 20 min.
Cooking: 50–55 min.
Must be done a day ahead
Can be frozen

¾ cup sugar

½ cup (1 stick) butter
softened

1 cup sour cream

2 eggs

1 Tbsp. poppy seeds

2 Tbsp. grated orange
rind

2 Tbsp. orange juice

2 cups flour

1 tsp. baking powder

1 tsp. baking soda

½ tsp. salt

Preheat oven to 325°.
Grease a 9"x5" loaf pan.

Place sugar, butter and sour cream in the bowl of an electric mixer and beat until light and fluffy. Add the eggs, poppy seeds, orange rind and orange juice. Continue to beat until well mixed. Add flour, baking powder, baking soda and salt. Beat at low speed. Pour into the loaf pan and bake for 50–55 minutes, until center springs back when lightly pressed with finger.

Let bread cool in pan for 5 minutes before removing. Cool bread completely. Wrap in plastic wrap and let sit overnight before serving.

Lynn B. Popovich

57

Lemon Blueberry Bread

Easy
Yield: 1 loaf
Preparation: 15 min.
Cooking: 55–60 min.
Can be frozen

2 cups flour

2½ tsp. baking powder

1 tsp. salt

¼ cup (½ stick) butter

¾ cup sugar

2 eggs

¾ cup milk

grated zest of 1 lemon

2 Tbsp. fresh lemon juice

1 tsp. vanilla extract

1½ cups blueberries

½ cup powdered sugar

1½ Tbsp. milk

Preheat oven to 350°.
Grease 9"x5" loaf pan.

Combine flour, baking powder and salt in a small bowl. Using an electric mixer, cream butter and sugar in a large bowl. Beat in eggs, milk, lemon zest, lemon juice and vanilla. Add flour mixture. Fold in blueberries. Pour into prepared pan. Bake for 55–60 minutes.

Remove from pan. Mix powdered sugar and milk. Drizzle over bread while warm.

Jane Ellen Rabe

Banana Zucchini Bread

Easy
Yield: 2 loaves
Preparation: 25 min.
Cooking: 45–55 min.
Can be frozen

3   eggs, beaten
1   cup oil
½   cup mayonnaise
2   cups sugar
2¾ cups flour
1   Tbsp. vanilla
1   tsp. baking soda
1   tsp. cinnamon
¼   tsp. baking powder
2   cups shredded zucchini
2   ripe bananas, mashed

Preheat oven to 350°.
Grease two 9"x5" loaf pans.

Combine eggs, oil and mayonnaise. Add remaining ingredients except zucchini and bananas. Mix batter well. Fold in zucchini and bananas. Pour into loaf pans.

Bake for 45–55 minutes, or until tester comes out clean.

In memory of Jordan Riazzi

Lemon Zucchini Bread

"This bread is loved by all who receive it"

Easy
Yield: 2 loaves
Preparation: 20–25 min.
Cooking: 1 hr.

3   eggs
1   cup oil
1½ cups sugar
2   tsp. lemon flavoring
juice and rind of 1 lemon
2   cups grated zucchini
3¼ cups flour
1   tsp. salt
1   tsp. baking soda
1   tsp. baking powder
½   cup coconut
1   box lemon instant pudding
1   cup chopped walnuts (optional)
powdered sugar

Preheat oven to 350°.
Grease and flour two 9"x5" loaf pans.

In a large bowl, beat eggs and oil until mixed. Add sugar, lemon flavoring, lemon juice and rind. Mix well. Stir in zucchini.

Sift together flour, salt, soda and baking powder. Blend this with the creamed lemon mixture. Fold in coconut, pudding and nuts, if desired. Pour into prepared loaf pans. Bake for 1 hour.

When cool, remove from pans and sprinkle with powdered sugar.

Dorothy P. Schettler

Maine Blueberry Muffins

"Think of these when blueberries are abundant"

Easy
Yields: 18 muffins
Preparation: 20 min.
Cooking: 30 min.

½ cup (1 stick) butter
1 cup sugar
2 eggs
2 cups flour
½ tsp. salt
2 tsp. baking powder
¾ cup milk
1 tsp. vanilla
2 cups blueberries

Preheat oven to 375°.

In a large bowl, cream butter and sugar. Beat in eggs, one at a time.

Sift together dry ingredients. Mix well. Add dry ingredients to creamed mixture alternately with milk and vanilla. Gently fold in berries. Fill paper-lined muffin tins. Bake for 30 minutes.

Store uncovered.

Bernice A. Born

Double Chocolate Banana Muffins

"Combine, mix, fold and fill"

Easy
Yields: 12–16 muffins
Preparation: 15 min.
Cooking: 20–25 min.

1½ cups flour
1 cup sugar
¼ cup cocoa
1 tsp. baking soda
½ tsp. baking powder
½ tsp. salt
1⅓ cups mashed ripe
    bananas
⅓ cup vegetable oil
1 egg
1 cup chocolate chips

Preheat oven to 350°.

Combine first 6 ingredients. Mix bananas, oil and egg and add to dry ingredients. Fold in chocolate chips. Fill greased or paper-lined muffin cups.

Bake for 20–25 minutes

Jean Whitehill Schnatterly

French Toast with Orange Butter
"So delicious you won't miss the syrup"

Easy
Serves: 8
Preparation: 15 min.
Cooking: 15 min.

4   eggs

¼   cup flour

¼   cup sugar

3   cups milk

2   tsp. vanilla

½   tsp. cinnamon

8   ¾" thick sliced, firm white bread

vegetable oil for frying

Orange Butter:
¼   cup (½ stick) butter

1   cup light brown sugar

1½ tsp. grated orange rind

In a large bowl, beat eggs and blend in flour. Add sugar, milk, vanilla and cinnamon. Beat until completely smooth.

Soak both sides of bread in batter, until thoroughly saturated.

In a large skillet, heat oil. Fry bread for about 3 minutes on each side, or until brown and puffed.

Orange Butter:
Combine all ingredients and mix well. Serve with French toast.

Linda D. Orsini

Pecan Pie Mini Muffins
"Sweet enough for dessert"

Easy
Yields: 28 mini muffins
Preparation: 15 min.
Cooking: 20–25 min.

1   cup packed brown sugar

½   cup flour

1   cup chopped pecans

⅔   cup melted butter

2   eggs, beaten

Preheat oven to 350°.

In a bowl, combine brown sugar, flour, and pecans. Set aside.

Combine butter and eggs; mix well. Stir into flour mixture until just moistened. Pour into greased mini-muffin pans, filling ⅔ full. Bake for 20–25 minutes. Remove and cool.

Betty Miller

Entrees

Filet Roast
"A surefire success"

Easy
Serves: 10
Preparation: 25 min.
Cooking: 45 min.

1   lb. fresh mushrooms,
    coarsely chopped

2   green or red peppers,
    coarsely chopped

4   med. onions, chopped

5   Tbsp. butter

1   4–5 lb. beef tenderloin,
    trimmed

salt and pepper

1   Tbsp. Herbs de
    Provence

Preheat oven to 350°.

Sauté vegetables in butter. Season roast with salt, pepper and Herbs de Provence. Place roast in large roasting pan. Surround with cooked vegetables.

Bake for 30 minutes. Stir vegetables around in the pan. Bake for another 15 minutes to serve rare.

Susan L. Nitzberg

Standing Rib Roast with Sauce

"An outstanding sauce for a standing rib roast"

Moderately difficult
Serves: 10
Preparation: 30 min.
Cooking: 2–3 hrs.

½　cup (1 stick) butter, softened

1　Tbsp. minced garlic

2　tsp. finely chopped fresh thyme

½　tsp. freshly ground pepper

1　tsp. sea salt

¼　cup finely chopped parsley

1　4 lb. standing rib roast

2　carrots

1　onion

2　stalks celery

2　cloves garlic

3　Tbsp. butter

3　Tbsp. flour

1　cup beef stock

1　Tbsp. tomato paste

½ –1 cup dry red wine

Preheat oven to 325°.

Mix butter, garlic, thyme, pepper, salt and parsley to make a paste. Score fat side of meat in a cross pattern. Fill holes with the butter paste. Spread any remaining paste on the sides of the beef.

Finely chop carrots, onion, celery and garlic in a food processor. Press mixture onto the exterior of the beef. Place the beef roast, vegetable side up, on a rack in a large roasting pan. Sprinkle with salt and pepper. Roast for 2–2½ hours for rare, or 2½–3 hours for medium. Remove the roast from the oven.

To make sauce, melt 3 tablespoons butter over medium heat. Add flour and cook 2 minutes. Add the beef stock a little at a time, whisking thoroughly to prevent lumps. Add tomato paste and wine. Simmer 1–2 minutes. Scrape vegetables off the roast and add to the simmering sauce. Boil for 5 minutes and strain through a sieve. Reduce over medium heat until the sauce is the consistency of heavy cream. Slice the roast and serve the sauce on the side.

Susan Vogelgesang

Stuffed Tenderloin
"Take the time for this splendid dish"

Moderately difficult
Serves: 8
Preparation: 30–45 min.
Cooking: 45–50 min.

1   5 lb. beef tenderloin, trimmed

1   cup (2 sticks) butter, softened

2–3 cloves garlic, minced

3   eggs, beaten

8   oz. fresh spinach, finely chopped (about 6 cups)

¾   cup soft bread crumbs

seasoned salt, optional

1   10½-oz. can condensed beef broth

1   lb. tiny new potatoes

8   oz. lg. whole mushrooms

1   Tbsp. butter

3   med. onions, cut into wedges

½   cup dry sherry

Preheat oven to 400°.

Prepare a double butterfly cut in the beef by first making a single, lengthwise cut down the center of the roast (cutting to within ½" of the bottom). Then make 2 more cuts, one on each side of the first cut, being careful not to cut through the beef, only to ½". Pound meat with a mallet to an 10"x8" rectangle. Mix butter and garlic and spread over beef.

In a medium bowl, mix eggs, spinach and bread crumbs. Spoon on top of butter mixture. Roll meat, jelly-roll style, beginning with the long side. Place meat, seam side down, on a rack in a shallow roasting pan. Sprinkle with seasoned salt, if desired. Roast uncovered for 45 minutes, or until a meat thermometer registers 140°, for rare.

Meanwhile, in a small saucepan, bring beef broth to a boil; then reduce heat. Simmer, uncovered, for 15 minutes, until reduced to ⅔ cup. In a separate pan, cook potatoes in boiling salted water for 10 minutes. Drain and keep warm. In another pan, cook mushrooms in butter for 6 minutes. Drain and keep warm.

Remove beef from pan, reserving drippings. Keep warm. Cook onions in reserved drippings until tender, but not brown. Stir in reduced beef broth and sherry and heat through. Remove onions with a slotted spoon. Slice meat crosswise into 1" thick slices. Arrange on serving platter, with slices overlapping. Place potatoes, mushrooms and onions on either side of platter. Drizzle broth/sherry mixture over meat.

Aileen Magnotto

Jane's Beef Brisket
"Rave reviews"

Easy
Serves: 8
Preparation: 30 min.
Cooking: 4 hrs. 30 min.
Can be frozen

1   3 lb. beef brisket
vinegar
¼   cup Liquid Smoke
Sauce:
1   Tbsp. dry mustard
4   Tbsp. cider vinegar
4   Tbsp. Worcestershire
    sauce
2   14-oz. bottles ketchup
1   cup water
1   cup brown sugar

2   tsp. paprika
2   tsp. chili powder
2   tsp. celery seed
½   tsp. Tabasco sauce

Preheat oven to 300°.

Wash brisket in vinegar and coat with liquid smoke. Wrap brisket in foil. Bake for 4 hours. Cool. Remove fat from brisket and slice against the grain.

Sauce:
Mix all ingredients well. Simmer, stirring occasionally, for 10 minutes. Put meat into the sauce and heat thoroughly.

Jebby Potter

Sweet and Sour Brisket
"Heavenly the first day. Divine the second"

Easy
Serves: 8
Preparation: 15–20 min.
Cooking: 3 hrs.
Can be made ahead

1   Tbsp. oil
1   3 lb. beef brisket
2   onions, sliced
½   cup brown sugar
¼   cup cider vinegar
1   cup ketchup
1   cup water

Heat oil in a large deep skillet. Brown brisket on both sides. Remove from pan. Add sliced onions and sauté till golden.

Mix brown sugar, vinegar, ketchup and water in a bowl.

Place brisket in skillet with onions. Pour sauce over meat and cover. Simmer over low heat for 3 hours.

Slice against grain and serve.

Esther M. Neft

Carbonade Flammade
"Warm and satisfying"

Easy
Serves: 6
Preparation: 20 min.
Cooking: 2 hrs.
Can be made ahead

½   cup flour

1   tsp. salt

1   tsp. black pepper

3   lbs. chuck steak, cut
     into 1" cubes

¼   lb. bacon, cut into
     small pieces

3   lg. onions, thinly sliced

3   garlic cloves, minced

safflower oil

2½ cups dark brown beer

2   Tbsp. dark brown sugar

1   bay leaf

4   slices whole wheat
     bread, crusts removed,
     cut into wedges

Dijon mustard

Combine flour, salt and pepper in a medium bowl. Toss meat in flour mixture, a few pieces at a time.

Fry bacon pieces in a sauté pan over high heat, until bacon is browned and fat is rendered. Remove with a slotted spoon and reserve. Add onion and garlic to the pan and cook for about 5 minutes over medium heat, or until translucent. Remove with a slotted spoon and set aside.

Increase heat to high and brown meat pieces in the pan, a few at a time. Sear meat on all sides, adding a little oil if the pan becomes dry. Add beer to the pan and, using a wooden spoon, scrape up browned pieces from the bottom.

Place meat, onions, garlic and bacon in a large casserole and add beer mixture along with brown sugar and bay leaf. Cover and cook over a low heat for 1½ hours, or until meat is tender.

Spread both sides of bread with Dijon mustard and place on top of meat. Spoon some of the stew juices over bread and meat. Cover and cook another 30 minutes. Remove the bay leaf before serving.

Gaynor Grant

Boozy Stew

"Settle in for this simmering stew"

Easy
Serves: 8
Preparation: 20 min.
Marinate: 3 hrs.
Cooking: 3 hrs.
Can be made ahead

1   cup apple brandy
¼   cup vegetable oil
6   shallots, chopped
4   cloves garlic, minced
¼   tsp. dried thyme
1   bay leaf
juice of 1 lemon
freshly ground pepper
3   lbs. beef chuck, cubed
2   cups beef broth
3   carrots, peeled and
    chopped
3   turnips, peeled and
    chopped

4   parsnips, peeled and
    chopped
2   Tbsp. cornstarch
¼   cup water
salt and pepper

In a large bowl, combine apple brandy, oil, shallots, garlic, thyme, bay leaf, lemon juice and pepper. Mix well and add meat. Cover bowl and marinate 3–24 hours. Put meat and marinade in a pot with the beef broth. Bring to a boil, cover and simmer for 2 hours. Add carrots, turnips and parsnips. Simmer, covered, until vegetables are fork tender, about 45 minutes.

Mix cornstarch with ¼ cup water and add to the stew to thicken the gravy. Season to taste with salt and pepper.

Emilie Szakach

Mexican Lasagna

Serves: 6–8
Easy
Preparation: 15 min.
Cooking: 40–45 min.
Can be frozen

1½ lbs. ground beef
1   med. onion, chopped
1   pkg. taco seasoning
1   pkg. 10" tortillas
2   cups sour cream
6   oz. Cheddar cheese,
    shredded
6   oz. mozzarella cheese,
    shredded
shredded lettuce

2   tomatoes, chopped
1   24-oz. jar of salsa

Preheat oven to 325°.

In a large skillet, brown beef, onion and taco seasoning. Drain. Spread ½–1 cup salsa in a 13"x9" pan. Layer tortillas first, then ½ the meat, sour cream, cheese and salsa. Repeat layers. Cover with foil and bake for 40–45 minutes. Let stand for 10 minutes, uncovered, before serving. Top with shredded lettuce, chopped tomatoes and salsa.

Good served with Italian bread.

June E. Resetarits

Pop's Chow Mein

"Chicken or pork work equally well"

Easy
Serves: 4
Preparation: 40 min.
Cooking: 20 min.
Can be made ahead

2½ tsp. cornstarch

⅓ cup water

1 Tbsp. oil

2 lbs. steak, cut into bite-sized pieces

2 lg. onions, chopped

3 cups diced celery

¼ cup water

1 8-oz. can sliced water chestnuts, drained

½ green pepper, diced

4 oz. jar sliced mushrooms, drained

½ cup soy sauce, divided

pinch black pepper

1 14-oz. can bean sprouts

1 lg. can crispy chow mein noodles or cooked rice

sliced almonds, optional

Combine corn starch and ⅓ cup cold water. Set aside to thicken.

Heat oil in a large skillet; add beef and brown. Add onion, celery and ¼ cup water. Cover and steam for 2 minutes. Add water chestnuts, green pepper and mushrooms. Cook until tender, about 5 minutes.

Stir ¼ cup soy sauce into cornstarch mixture; add to skillet with black pepper. Add remaining ¼ cup soy sauce and the bean sprouts.

Heat slowly and serve over rice or noodles. Sprinkle with almonds if desired.

Barbara A. Veazey
Daughter of Larry Hatch, Founder of Eat'n Park Restaurants, Inc.

Taos Green Chili
"Most authentic chili east of the Mississippi"

Easy
Serves: 10
Preparation: 30 min.
Cooking: 2 hrs.
Can be made ahead

1   lb. ground beef
1   lb. ground pork
1   lb. boneless sirloin, cut
    into ½" cubes
½   cup (1 stick) unsalted
    butter
1   lg. onion, chopped
3   cloves garlic, minced
1   cup fresh cilantro,
    finely chopped
1½ Tbsp. Tabasco sauce
2   tsp. dried oregano
1   tsp. ground cumin
½   cup parsley,
    finely chopped
2   tsp. black pepper
6   Tbsp. flour
1½ tsp. salt
6   cups chicken broth
1   cup Mexican beer, not
    dark
4   mild banana peppers,
    roasted, finely chopped
2–6 jalapeño peppers,
    roasted, finely chopped
2   green peppers, roasted,
    chopped
2   tomatoes, chopped
½   lb. Monterey Jack
    cheese, grated
1   cup sour cream
fresh cilantro, finely
chopped

In a skillet, brown the ground beef over moderately high heat and, using a slotted spoon, transfer to a kettle. In the same skillet, brown the pork and sirloin separately, again transferring them to the kettle. Discard any remaining fat in the skillet.

Add the butter and cook the onion, garlic and cilantro over moderately high heat, until the onion is softened. Add the Tabasco, oregano, cumin, parsley, black pepper, flour and salt and cook for 2 minutes. Add this to the kettle with the broth, beer, roasted peppers and tomatoes. Bring to a boil, lower heat and simmer for 2 hours. Top with Monterey Jack cheese, sour cream and cilantro.

Debra Gibbs

69

Hearty Beef and Bean Casserole
"Turn your basic beans into tonight's dinner"

Easy
Serves: 8–10
Preparation: 10 min.
Cooking: 45 min.
Can be made ahead

1 **lb. ground beef**

1 **env. onion soup mix**

2 **15-oz. cans pork and beans in tomato sauce**

1 **15-oz. can kidney beans, drained**

1 **cup ketchup**

1 **cup brown sugar**

½ **cup cold water**

2 **Tbsp. prepared mustard**

2 **tsp. vinegar**

Preheat oven to 350°.

Grease a 2½ qt. casserole.

In a large skillet, brown the meat. Drain excess fat. Stir in the remaining ingredients and mix. Pour into the prepared casserole and bake for 35 to 40 minutes, until hot and bubbly.

Fay S. Wright

Crock Pot Pizza
"The dinner answer for your busiest day"

Easy
Serves: 4–6
Preparation: 15 min.
Cooking: 5 hrs.
Can be made ahead

1 **lb. browned ground beef, drained**

¾ **box rigatoni, cooked**

2 **12-oz. pkg. shredded mozzarella cheese**

1 **7-oz. can mushrooms**

onion powder, to taste

1 **2 lb. 13-oz. can pasta sauce**

1 **6-oz. pkg. pepperoni slices**

Preheat crock pot to 300°.

Alternate layers of all ingredients in a crockpot. Make three layers of each. Bake for 5 hours.

This makes a great, quick family dinner that children will like.

Peter Skudra
Pittsburgh Penguins

Jagr's Czech Beef Rolls
"Jaromir's favorite dish"

Easy
Serves: 4
Preparation: 30 min.
Cooking: 20 min.

4 thin slices of sirloin steak
salt and pepper
4 tsp. mustard
2 med. onions, finely chopped, divided
1 hard-boiled egg, sliced
8 oz. kielbasa, cut into ¼" slices
4 pickles, sliced
4 cups beef broth
1 tsp. oil
4 Tbsp. flour
1 cup water, or more as needed
salt and pepper
Worcestershire sauce and mustard, optional
cooked rice

Season both sides of beef slices with salt and pepper. Spread one teaspoon mustard on one side. Divide one onion, sliced egg, kielbasa and pickle into four, and layer on each of the beef slices. Roll each piece of beef and secure with 1 or 2 toothpicks.

Sauté the second onion in a little oil, until golden. Add beef rolls and brown on all sides. Add broth to the pan contents. Cook 5 minutes more. Remove beef rolls.

In a small bowl, slowly mix 4 tablespoons flour with 1 cup water and stir into pan juices. Cook 10 minutes, adding water if necessary, to yield 3–4 cups. Season sauce by adding salt, pepper, Worcestershire sauce and extra mustard. Remove toothpicks from the beef rolls and return to the pan. Heat through and serve with rice.

Anna Jagr
Pittsburgh Penguins

Snappy Glazed Meatballs
"Also makes a terrific appetizer"

Easy
Serves: 4
Preparation: 30 min.
Cooking: 15 min.
Can be frozen

1   lb. ground chuck
¼   cup dry bread crumbs
1   egg, slightly beaten
1   sm. onion, chopped
1   tsp. salt
1   cup chili sauce
¾   cup grape jelly

Combine meat, bread crumbs, egg, onion and salt. Mix well. Shape into 1" balls. Brown meatballs in skillet, turning occasionally. Drain.

Combine chili sauce and jelly. Pour over meatballs and simmer for 15 minutes.

Bobby H. Dollas
Pittsburgh Penguins

Mary Bottcher's Flank Steak
"Your entire family will thank you"

Easy
Serves: 6
Preparation: 15 min.
Marinate: 6 hrs.
Cooking: 12 min.
Must be made ahead

½   cup olive oil
½   cup soy sauce
½   cup bourbon
1   tsp. pepper
1   tsp. dry mustard
1   Tbsp. peeled, freshly grated ginger
2   sm. onions, chopped
2   cloves garlic, minced
splash of wine vinegar
1   2 lb. flank steak, scored

Combine all marinade ingredients and soak scored flank steak in marinade 6–24 hours. Broil or grill to desired doneness.

Anne B. Tomson

Sewickley Café Flank Steak

"Turn an ordinary meal into an extraordinary experience"

Moderately difficult
Serves: 4
Preparation: 20 min.
Cooking: 30 min.

1   lb. mushrooms
1   2 lb. flank steak
¼   cup finely chopped
    shallots
1   cup (2 sticks) butter
1   10-oz. bag spinach,
    washed, trimmed,
    blanched
3   cloves garlic, minced
½–1 cup freshly grated
    Parmesan cheese
kosher salt

Finely chop the mushrooms. Place a small handful in a clean dish towel and squeeze well to extract liquid. Continue with remaining mushrooms. Melt butter and sauté the shallots until golden. Add mushrooms and continue to cook until all additional mushroom liquid has evaporated. Set aside to cool.

Pound flank steak as thinly as possible without breaking through. Cover the steak with spinach. Layer on the cooled mushroom mixture and sprinkle with garlic and Parmesan cheese. Roll the steak lengthwise, jelly-roll style, and tie shut. Sprinkle with kosher salt. Grill, turning every 5 minutes, for 20 to 25 minutes. Allow to cool for 10 minutes, then slice into 1" slices.

73

Jon S. Olson and Don L. Reinhardt, Jr.
The Sewickley Café
Sewickley, PA

Stuffed Flank Steak
"Tantalizing"

Moderately difficult
Serves: 4–6
Preparation: 30 min.
Cooking: 40 min.
Can be prepared up to 1 day ahead

1 **cup coarsely chopped fresh spinach**
1 **cup coarsely chopped fresh basil**
1 **large clove garlic**
¼ **cup olive oil**
½ **cup freshly grated Parmesan cheese**
1½ **lb. flank steak, butterflied**
4 **oz. prosciutto, thinly sliced**
3 **red peppers, roasted**
1 **hot cherry pepper, cored, seeded and minced**

salt and pepper

Preheat oven to 350°.

Combine spinach, basil and garlic in food processor and chop finely. With the machine running, drizzle in olive oil; add Parmesan cheese and process until smooth. Set aside.

Season steak with salt and pepper. Place prosciutto in one layer on steak and top with layer of roasted peppers. Spread spinach/basil mixture over top. Sprinkle with minced cherry pepper.

Starting with long side, roll the steak and tie with string about every 2".

Roast for 40 minutes for medium rare. Slice and serve.

Nancy H. Boland

Chilean Malaya
(Rolled Stuffed Flank Steak)

Serves: 6
Moderately difficult
Preparation: 30 min.
Marinate: Overnight
Cooking: 2 hrs.
Must be made ahead

Steak and Marinade:

1   2 lb. flank steak

½   tsp. salt

⅛   tsp. freshly ground black pepper

2   tsp. finely chopped fresh thyme or ½ tsp. dried

1   med. onion, chopped

3   Tbsp. finely chopped fresh parsley

3   Tbsp. red wine vinegar

Stuffing:

½   cup fresh bread crumbs

½   cup chopped cooked spinach (10-oz. pkg. fresh)

½   cup cooked frozen peas

¼   cup finely grated carrot

1   Tbsp. grated Cheddar cheese

1   hard-boiled egg, chopped

3   cooked bacon slices, crumbled

2   Tbsp. olive oil

1   14.5-oz. can beef broth

Steak and Marinade:
The day before serving, score one side of the flank steak in a diamond pattern. Sprinkle both sides with salt, pepper and thyme. Place in a large bowl or a resealable bag. Add the onion, parsley and vinegar. Refrigerate overnight.

Stuffing:
About 2 hours before serving, combine bread crumbs, spinach, peas, carrot, cheese, chopped egg and bacon. Remove steak from the marinade, reserving the liquid. Spoon stuffing onto the scored side of the flank steak, then pat it neatly to the steak's edges. Roll jelly-roll style and tie securely with string at 1" intervals.

In a heavy pot, brown flank steak in olive oil on all sides. Add beef broth and marinade liquid. Simmer, covered, about 2 hours, or until the steak is fork tender. Place the meat on a heated platter. Skim fat from the cooking juices. Remove the strings, slice and serve with the pan juices.

Good served with barley or risotto and a tomato salad.

Amanda Dunn

Veal Scallopini with Mushrooms
"Always a winner"

Easy
Serves: 4
Preparation: 20 min.
Cooking: 15 min.

1   cup seasoned bread
    crumbs
1   cup freshly grated
    Romano cheese
1   egg, lightly beaten
¼   cup milk
1   lb. veal scallopini
¾   cup (1½ sticks)
    unsalted butter,
    divided
1¾ cups dry white wine,
    divided
1½ lbs. mushrooms, sliced
⅓   cup finely chopped
    parsley

In a bowl, mix bread crumbs and Romano cheese. Set aside.

Mix egg and milk and place in shallow dish. Set aside.

Reserve 3 tablespoons of butter and ½ cup wine, for the sauce.

Melt 3 tablespoons of butter in a large non-stick pan, over medium high heat; add ⅓ cup of wine. Dip the veal in the egg mixture, roll in the bread crumbs and save remaining bread crumbs for later. Sauté the veal approximately 3 minutes on each side. Add additional butter and wine as needed. Remove veal to a large plate and keep warm in the oven at low temperature.

Meanwhile, add 3 tablespoons butter and ½ cup wine to the skillet. Stir in mushrooms and sprinkle ⅓ cup of the remaining bread crumb mixture over them. Cook until mushrooms are tender. Remove skillet from heat and stir in the parsley.

Remove the veal from the oven, cover with the mushroom mixture and serve immediately.

Nancy H. Boland

Veal Tarragon
"Serve with nutty brown rice"

Easy
Serves: 6
Preparation: 15 min.
Cooking: 20 min.

1½ lbs. veal scallopini

¼ cup flour

1 tsp. salt

½ tsp. pepper

¼ cup olive oil

1 14-oz. can chicken broth

1 tsp. dried tarragon

1 Tbsp. fresh lemon juice

Pound the veal to approximately ⅛" thickness. Mix flour with salt and pepper. Lightly coat the veal with the flour. Heat oil over medium high heat in a 12" skillet and cook the veal, a few pieces at a time, until browned on both sides. Set veal aside. Add chicken broth and tarragon to the skillet and bring to a boil over high heat, making sure skillet is deglazed.

Return the veal to the pan and heat to boiling. Reduce heat and simmer, covered, for 20 minutes. Stir in lemon juice and serve.

Ellen Hagerty

Tuscan Veal Cutlets

Easy
Serves: 2
Preparation: 50 min.
Cooking: 30 min.

2 Tbsp. butter

salt and pepper

2 6-oz. veal cutlets

1 hard-boiled egg, finely chopped

1 Tbsp. capers

1 8-oz. can tomato sauce containing oregano and garlic

Pound the veal cutlets, cutting out any bone to save for soup, or to put in the skillet for added flavor.

Heat butter, salt and pepper in a skillet. Sauté the cutlets about 3 minutes on each side. Put the capers, along with their juice, on top of each cutlet. Sprinkle with the chopped egg and pour half of the tomato sauce over each piece of meat. Cover and cook for 30 minutes on low heat.

Bonnie Moorhead

Grilled Veal Chops with Herbed Butter
"Simply delicious"

Easy
Serves: 4
Preparation: 5 mins.
Cooking: 15 mins.

4   veal chops, approx.
    1½" thick

3   Tbsp. butter, softened

2   Tbsp. Dijon mustard

fresh tarragon, chopped

Preheat grill.

Cream together butter, mustard, and tarragon.

Spread half the butter mixture over chops. Grill, turning once and coating other side of chops with butter mixture. Grill until meat thermometer registers 160°.

Cindy Dyer

Barbecue Veal With Rice
"Tender, tangy tidbits"

Easy
Serves: 8
Preparation: 25 min.
Cooking: 2 hrs.
Can be frozen

3   lbs. boneless breast of
    veal, cut into 2" cubes

2   Tbsp. oil

salt and pepper

1   8-oz. can tomato sauce

½   cup ketchup

½   cup water

1   med. onion, sliced

½   cup chopped celery

2   Tbsp. brown sugar

2   Tbsp. Dijon mustard

1   Tbsp. Worcestershire
    sauce

Preheat oven to 350°.

In a large pot, heat oil. Add veal in batches and brown on all sides. Transfer to a covered casserole. Season with salt and pepper. Combine remaining ingredients, pour over meat and bake, covered, until tender, about 2 hours. Remove the cover for the last 20 minutes. Spoon off excess fat. Serve over rice or noodles.

Jean Whitehill Schnatterly

Italian Veal Shanks (Osso Buco)

"Melts in your mouth"

Easy
Serves: 8
Preparation: 20 min.
Cooking: 2 hrs. 30 min.
Can be frozen

1   4¾ qt. clay cooker

6   lbs. veal shanks cut into 2" thick slices

salt and white pepper

ground nutmeg

flour

1   med. carrot, peeled and shredded

1   lg. onion, sliced

4   cloves of garlic, minced, divided

1   14½-oz. can tomatoes, chopped, with liquid

½   cup dry white wine

1   tsp. salt

1   tsp. sugar

½   tsp. dried thyme

¼   tsp. dried sage

⅓   cup finely chopped parsley

1   Tbsp. grated lemon rind

Soak the top and bottom of the clay cooker in water about 15 minutes, then drain.

Sprinkle veal with salt, pepper and nutmeg. Coat lightly with flour.

Place veal, carrot, onion and half the garlic in the cooker. In a bowl, combine the tomatoes, including liquid, with wine, salt, sugar, thyme and sage; add to the cooker. Place the cooker in a cold oven, and set the temperature to 425°. Bake, stirring occasionally, until the veal is very tender, about 2½ hours.

Combine remaining 2 cloves of garlic, parsley and lemon rind. Place cooked veal on a platter.

Ladle the liquid from the cooker into a large skillet, and bring to the boil. Cook until thick. Stir in half the parsley mixture. Pour the sauce over the veal shanks and sprinkle with the remaining parsley mixture.

Carole A. Frisch

Rack of Lamb with Port and Currant Sauce

"Glorious for entertaining"

Easy
Serves: 8
Preparation: 30 min.
Cooking: 30 min.

3   1½ lb. racks of lamb,
     boned (reserve bones
     and trimmings)
2   Tbsp. finely chopped
     fresh oregano
1   Tbsp. finely chopped
     fresh thyme

salt and freshly ground
black pepper

1   cup plus 2 Tbsp. fresh
     lemon juice
3   lg. garlic cloves, minced

Port and Currant Sauce:
1   cup plus 2 Tbsp. ruby
     port
⅔   cup orange juice
¾   cup red currant jelly
6   Tbsp. fresh lemon juice
3   Tbsp. matchstick-sized
     strips orange zest
3   Tbsp. matchstick-sized
     strips lemon zest

fresh rosemary sprigs for
garnish

Preheat oven to 500°.

Season lamb with oregano, thyme, salt and pepper. Sprinkle with lemon juice; rub with garlic. Arrange on rack in roasting pan. Add bones to pan. Cook until thermometer inserted in thickest part of meat registers 130° for medium rare, 15 to 20 minutes. Tent lamb with foil and allow to stand for 15 minutes.

Port and Currant Sauce:
Combine port, orange juice, jelly, lemon juice and citrus zest in a heavy medium saucepan. Bring to a boil. Reduce heat; simmer until sauce thickens slightly, about 5 minutes. This sauce can be made up to 3 days ahead. Cover and keep refrigerated.

Slice lamb against grain and arrange slices on a large dinner plate. Cover with sauce and garnish with rosemary sprigs. Serve remaining sauce on the side.

Rania Harris

Rack of Lamb with Mustard Thyme Crust

"A savory classic"

Easy
Serves: 2
Preparation: 10 min.
Cooking: 30 min.

⅓ cup Dijon mustard

1 Tbsp. minced garlic

1 Tbsp. finely chopped fresh thyme, or 1 tsp. dried

1½ lb. rack of lamb, well trimmed

salt and pepper

1 cup fresh bread crumbs

2 Tbsp. olive oil

fresh thyme sprigs for garnish

Preheat oven to 425°.

Whisk mustard, garlic and chopped thyme in a small bowl. Sprinkle lamb with salt and pepper. Place lamb on baking sheet, rounded side up. Spread mustard mixture evenly over lamb. (Lamb can be prepared up to 6 hours ahead.) Refrigerate uncovered.

Stir bread crumbs and oil in a heavy medium skillet, over medium heat, until crumbs begin to crisp. Cool slightly. Press crumbs into mustard coating on lamb. Roast lamb until thermometer inserted into center registers 130° for medium rare, about 30 minutes. Garnish with thyme sprigs and serve.

Mary Lee Parrington

Marlene's Leg of Lamb

Easy
Serves: 8
Preparation: 20 min.
Cooking: 2½ hrs.

1 lg. clove garlic, minced

½ tsp. marjoram

½ tsp. salt

2 Tbsp. fresh lime juice

¼ tsp. Tabasco sauce

1 5 lb. boned and rolled leg of lamb

4 strips raw bacon, cut into ½" pieces

30 sm. pimento-stuffed green olives

Preheat oven to 350°.

Mix garlic, marjoram and salt. Add lime juice and Tabasco. Cut 1½" deep holes in meat in 15 places. Widen the holes with the handle of a wooden spoon, or use your finger. In each hole push a stuffed olive, piece of bacon, ½ teaspoon garlic/lime mixture, another piece of bacon and another olive. Spread the remaining garlic mixture over the top of the meat.

Roast the lamb, fat side up, on a rack in an open roasting pan, allowing 25–30 minutes per pound for medium.

Sharon Schaefer

Casbah Lamb Shanks
"Kevin McClatchy's favorite"

Moderately difficult
Serves: 4
Preparation: 30 min.
Marinate: Overnight
Cooking: 3 hrs.

Tabil Spice Blend:

¼ **cup coriander seeds**

¼ **cup caraway seeds**

¼ **cup cumin seeds**

¼ **cup red pepper flakes**

¼ **cup kosher salt**

4 **lamb shanks**

1 **lg. onion, chopped**

3 **carrots, peeled and chopped**

2 **stalks celery, chopped**

¾ **cup honey**

1 **whole head of garlic, sliced across the middle**

5 **Tbsp. Tabil Spice Blend (see above)**

garlic mashed potatoes

Preheat oven to 400°.

Tabil Spice Blend:
Lightly toast the seeds in a hot skillet. Do not burn. Grind cooled seeds in a spice mill and place in a bowl. Add pepper flakes and salt. Mix well. Store in an airtight container.

The day before cooking, coat shanks with 4 tablespoons of the Tabil Spice Blend. Cover and refrigerate overnight.

Heat skillet over high flame. Brown the shanks on all sides. Meanwhile, roast carrots, onions and celery in oven until browned. Remove and lower oven temperature to 300°.

Place the shanks in the bottom of a large casserole. Cover with roasted vegetables. Add enough water to completely cover the shanks. Add the honey, garlic and the remaining Tabil Spice Blend.

Cover the casserole and bake for 3 hours.

Serve the shanks in individual large bowls over garlic mashed potatoes. Strain the vegetables from the lamb cooking liquid and serve as a sauce.

Lou Durbin
Casbah Restaurant

Moroccan Lamb Stew

Moderately Difficult
Serves: 6
Preparation Time 45 min.
Cooking Time: 2 hrs.

3   Tbsp. olive oil
2   Tbsp. butter
1   3½ lb. boned leg of lamb, cut into 1" cubes
4   cups finely chopped onions
6   cloves garlic, minced
2   Tbsp. flour
3   cups peeled and chopped fresh tomatoes or a 28-oz. can plum tomatoes, drained and chopped
1   cup chicken broth
1   tsp. ground cumin
½   Tbsp. finely chopped fresh cilantro

1   3" stick cinnamon
½   tsp. ground cardamom
½   tsp. cayenne pepper
1   cup golden raisins

Preheat oven to 350°.

Heat oil and butter in a large sauté pan, over medium high heat. Add lamb pieces, a few at a time, and brown on all sides. Transfer to a casserole.

Place onion and garlic in the same pan and sauté until they turn light brown. Add the flour, stir well, then add the tomatoes and chicken broth. Bring the mixture to a boil, deglazing the bottom of the pan with a wooden spoon. Remove the pan from the heat and add the remaining ingredients. Stir well. Pour sauce over the lamb, cover and bake for 2 hours.

Gaynor Grant

83

Lamb Marinade

Easy
Serves: 8
Preparation: 10 min.
Marinate: Overnight

1   16½-oz. can whole plums, roughly chopped
2   Tbsp. butter
1   med. onion, chopped
⅓   cup sugar
¼   cup chili sauce
2   Tbsp. soy sauce
1   tsp. ground ginger
2   tsp. fresh lemon juice
4   lbs. lamb, butterflied

Mix first 8 ingredients in a saucepan and let simmer 30 minutes. Cool. Pour over lamb. Cover and refrigerate overnight.

Roast or grill lamb, allowing 15–20 minutes per pound for medium rare.

Jane M. Reilly

Pork Tenderloin

Easy
Serves: 6
Preparation: 10 min.
Marinate: 4 hrs.
Cooking: 20–40 mins.

Marinade:

¾ cup fresh lemon juice

½ cup light soy sauce

½ cup honey

2 shallots, finely chopped

2 cloves garlic, minced

2 tsp. dry mustard

1 tsp. peeled, freshly grated ginger

2 1 lb. pork tenderloins

Combine marinade ingredients and place in a large resealable plastic bag. Add pork and marinate for at least 4 hours.

Remove tenderloin, reserving marinade. Grill or broil tenderloin to desired doneness. Heat the remaining marinade until boiling and serve as a sauce.

Missy Zimmerman

Pork Tenderloin with Savory Cream
"Great with wild rice casserole"

Easy
Serve: 2
Preparation: 10 min.
Marinate: 8 hrs.
Cooking: 1 hour

Marinade:

¼ cup soy sauce

¼ cup bourbon

2 Tbsp. brown sugar

1 pork tenderloin

Sauce:

⅓ cup sour cream

⅓ cup mayonnaise

1 tsp. dry mustard

1 tsp. finely chopped shallots

1½ tsp. white wine vinegar

Preheat oven to 325°.

Mix marinade ingredients and place in a resealable plastic bag with pork tenderloin. Marinate for 8 hours or overnight.

Mix sauce ingredients and refrigerate for 8 hours.

Remove pork tenderloin from bag and discard marinade. Place tenderloin in a roasting pan and cook for 1 hour. Serve with sauce.

Greer C. Lerchen

Southwestern Grilled Pork

"Fun for a casual dinner"

Easy
Serves: 6
Preparation: 25 min.
Marinate 2 hrs.
Cooking: 30 min.

Marinade:
½ cup dry red or white wine
2 Tbsp. balsamic vinegar
2 Tbsp. olive oil
½ tsp. salt
2 tsp. chopped fresh thyme, or ½ tsp. dried
freshly ground pepper
2 1 lb. pork tenderloins
Guacamole:
3 ripe avocados
1 lg. tomato, peeled and finely chopped
1 clove garlic, minced
2 Tbsp. finely chopped fresh cilantro
2 Tbsp. fresh lime juice
¼ tsp. red pepper sauce
1 tsp. finely chopped jalapeño
salt and pepper

6 warm tortillas

Mix marinade ingredients. Put tenderloin in a resealable plastic bag and cover with marinade. Refrigerate for at least 2 hours, turning occasionally.

Guacamole:
Peel, pit and chop avocados coarsely, leaving small lumps. Add tomato, garlic, cilantro, lime juice, red pepper sauce and jalapeño. Add salt and pepper to taste. Refrigerate.

Remove tenderloin from marinade and reserve. Pat meat dry; grill for about 20 minutes, or until center reaches 150°. Brush often with reserved marinade. Remove from grill and allow to rest about 5 minutes. Cut into thin slices. Place inside warm tortillas and spread with guacamole.

Good served with corn salsa and black beans.

Mary Jo Hottenstein

85

Pork Tenderloin with Dried Cherries and Caramelized Onions
"An incredible marriage of flavors"

Moderately difficult
Serves: 8
Preparation: 1 hr.
Marinate: 8 hrs.
Cooking: 1 hr.

Marinade:
1 cup thinly sliced onions
⅓ cup water
3 Tbsp. dry red wine
2 Tbsp. olive oil
2 cloves garlic, minced
salt and pepper
2 1 lb. pork tenderloins

Dried Cherry Chutney:
4 cups dried cherries
3 cups sugar
2 cups water
1½ cups red wine vinegar
1 cup diced Vidalia or other sweet onion
2 Tbsp. peeled, minced fresh ginger
1 Tbsp. jalapeño pepper, minced
2 tsp. ground coriander
1 tsp. ground cardamom
1 tsp. cumin
1 tsp. grated orange rind
3 whole cloves
1 3" cinnamon stick

Caramelized Onion Sauce:
1 Tbsp. butter
3 cups thinly sliced onions
1 cup dry red wine
3 cups chicken broth
salt and pepper

Mix marinade ingredients and pour into a resealable plastic bag. Add pork and marinate in refrigerator for at least 8 hours.

Dried Cherry Chutney:
Combine all ingredients in a large saucepan and bring to a boil. Reduce heat to medium and simmer uncovered until thick, about 1 hour. Stir occasionally. Discard cloves and cinnamon stick. Serve warm or at room temperature. The chutney may be made up to 2 weeks in advance.

Caramelized Onions:
Melt butter over medium high heat and add onions. Cook 5 minutes, stirring frequently. Cook 15 minutes longer until deep golden brown, stirring constantly. Add wine and cook 5 minutes, or until liquid evaporates. Remove onions from pan and chop finely. Return to pan and add broth, salt and pepper. Bring to a boil. Cook until reduced to 2 cups, about 10 minutes.

Remove and discard marinade. Sprinkle pork with salt and pepper and grill until meat thermometer register 160°.

Serve slice of pork, ¼" thick, in a pool of onion sauce, topped with chutney.

Cindy Dyer

Grilled Pork with Sweet Mustard Sauce
"Sweet and Tangy"

Easy
Serves: 4
Preparation: 10–15 min.
Marinate: 5–6 hrs.
Cooking: 18–20 min.

Marinade:

6 Tbsp. frozen orange juice concentrate, thawed

4 Tbsp. grainy style Dijon mustard

4 Tbsp. vegetable oil

4 Tbsp. honey

3 Tbsp. soy sauce

2 tsp. minced garlic

2 tsp. peeled, minced fresh ginger

freshly ground pepper

2 1 lb. pork tenderloins

Sauce:

6 Tbsp. frozen orange juice concentrate, thawed

4 Tbsp. apricot, peach or orange preserves

4 Tbsp. grainy style Dijon mustard

2 Tbsp. fresh lemon juice

2 tsp. grated lemon zest

2 tsp. dry mustard

Preheat grill or broiler.

Mix marinade ingredients. Pour over pork. Refrigerate 5–6 hours or overnight. Return meat to room temperature before grilling.

Grill pork about 18–20 minutes, until barely pink at the center. Remove from grill or broiler and cover with foil for about 10 minutes.

In a small saucepan, combine sauce ingredients. Bring to a boil and cook until smooth and heated through.

Slice the tenderloin and serve topped with sauce.

Patty Wynn

Onion Marmalade Stuffed Pork Tenderloin

Moderately difficult
Serves: 6–8
Preparation: 40 min.
Marinate: 1-8 hrs.
Cooking: 1 hr 40 min.

3   **1 lb. pork tenderloins, trimmed**

1   **Tbsp. olive oil**

3   **cloves garlic, minced**

¼   **tsp. ground cumin**

¼   **tsp. cayenne pepper**

¼   **tsp. ground cloves**

salt and freshly ground black pepper

Onion Marmalade:
2   **Tbsp. olive oil**

2   **yellow onions, thinly sliced**

1   **tsp. grated orange zest**

¾   **cup fresh orange juice**

⅓   **cup golden raisins**

¼   **cup sherry vinegar or white wine vinegar**

2   **tsp. sugar**

1   **cup water**

salt and freshly ground pepper

½   **cup dry white wine**

1   **cup chicken broth**

parsley for garnish

Butterfly the pork tenderloins by making a long slit down the length of each tenderloin, cutting just deep enough so the tenderloin opens up to lay flat. Do not cut all the way through. Flatten tenderloins and pound gently with a meat mallet. Set aside.

In a small bowl, combine olive oil, garlic, cumin, cayenne, cloves, and salt and black pepper to taste. Rub the pork with the mixture and cover. Refrigerate for at least 1 hour, or up to 8 hours.

Onion Marmalade:
Heat oil in a skillet over medium heat. Add onions and sauté, stirring occasionally, until lightly golden, about 15 minutes. Add the orange zest, juice, raisins, vinegar, sugar, water, salt and pepper to taste. Cover and cook over low heat until the onions are very soft, about 30 minutes. Uncover, raise the heat to medium high and cook until the onions are dry, about 10 minutes.

Lay the pork tenderloins, cut side up, on a work surface. Spread the onion mixture over the pork, distributing evenly. Close up the tenderloins and tie them with string at 1" intervals.

Place the pork in a heavy bottomed pan and add the wine and chicken broth. Cover and bring to a boil. Reduce the heat to very low and simmer until pork is firm to the touch and pink when cut in the thickest portion, about 30 minutes. Transfer the pork to a cutting board and keep warm. Raise the heat to high. Reduce the broth by half, stirring occasionally, about 10 minutes. Strain the broth and keep warm.

Snip the strings on the tenderloins. Cut crosswise into ½" slices. Arrange on a warmed platter and spoon the broth over the top. Garnish with parsley and serve.

Daniel J. Dooley
Executive Chef
Penn Brewery

Pork Roast with Cinnamon Apple Glaze
"Pork and apples, a classic duo"

Easy
Serves: 6
Preparation: 20 min.
Cooking: 40–45 min.

1   3 lb. pork loin
salt and pepper
Glaze:
1   Tbsp. butter
1   Tbsp. cinnamon
½   cup brown sugar
½   cup white wine vinegar
1   cup apple juice or cider
Apples:
1   Tbsp. butter
4   Granny Smith or Rome apples, peeled, cored and sliced into rings
½   cup apple juice or cider

Preheat oven to 375°.

Season pork with salt and pepper. Place in a roasting pan, uncovered. Roast for 45–55 minutes, or until meat thermometer reads 150°–155°. Remove and cover with foil to keep warm.

Glaze:
In a medium saucepan, melt butter; add cinnamon and sugar. Mix well, then add vinegar and cider. Bring to a boil and stir until sugar is fully dissolved. Lower heat and cook for 8–10 minutes, until mixture thickens slightly. Set aside.

Apples:
In a large skillet, melt butter; add apples and cider. Cook, turning apples often until they are brown and soft, about 5 minutes. Pour glaze over apples.

To serve, place slices of pork on plate and spoon apples over top.

Lynn B. Popovich

Herbed Roast Pork Loin with Mustard Sauce
"A little extra work for a lot of extra taste"

Moderately difficult
Serves: 16
Preparation: 15 min.
Marinate: 4 hrs.
Cooking: 1½ hrs.

2 **6 lb. pork loins, bone in, but cracked by butcher for easy carving**

Seasoned Salt Mixture:
2 **Tbsp. kosher salt**
1 **Tbsp. plus 1 tsp. finely chopped fresh rosemary, or 2 tsp. dried**
1 **Tbsp. plus 1 tsp. black peppercorns**
2 **tsp. finely chopped fresh thyme, or 1 tsp. dried**
6–8 cloves garlic, minced
¼ **cup fresh lemon juice**
¼ **cup extra virgin olive oil**

Mustard Sauce:
pan drippings from pork loin
1 **cup dry white wine**
⅓ **cup champagne vinegar or white wine vinegar**
1½ **cups water**
1 **cup heavy cream**
1 **Tbsp. plus 1 tsp. Dijon mustard**
1 **Tbsp. cornstarch, dissolved in ¼ cup water**
salt and freshly ground pepper
4 **Tbsp. unsalted butter, cut into tablespoons**

Preheat oven to 425°.

Trim fat around pork loins to a thin layer, and score in a diamond pattern. Wipe roasts dry. Place bone down on a rack, in 1 or 2 roasting pans.

In a spice grinder or food processor, combine the salt, rosemary, peppercorns and thyme. Process until peppercorns are coarsely ground and transfer mixture to a small bowl. Add garlic, lemon juice and olive oil to form a paste. Smear all over the pork loins. Set aside at room temperature for 3–4 hours.

Roast the pork for 15 minutes. Reduce the oven temperature to 325°; roast for 1½ hours, or until the pork registers 150°–155°. Cover with foil, and let stand about 10 minutes.

Mustard Sauce:
Pour fat out of roasting pan; put roasting pan over moderately high heat. Add the white wine and vinegar. Bring to a boil, scraping up the brown bits from the bottom of the pan. Boil until the liquid is reduced by half. Add 1½ cups water and boil for 2 minutes. Whisk the cream and mustard until blended. Gradually whisk into liquid in the pan. Boil for 2 minutes. Stir in the dissolved cornstarch and boil, stirring until thickened. Season with salt and pepper. Remove from heat, whisk in the butter and serve with roast.

Toni Fammartino

Pork Loin with Port and Leek Sauce
"Tender, with great flavor"

Moderately difficult
Serves: 4
Preparation: 40 min.
Cooking: 30 min.

2 cups chicken broth
1 cup beef broth
1 Tbsp. olive oil
1 lb. boneless pork loin
salt and pepper
1 lg. leek, white and pale green part only, chopped
2 shallots, finely chopped
1 cup port

Preheat oven to 425°.

Boil both broths in a medium sauce-pan until reduced to ⅔ cup, about 25 minutes. Set aside.

In a heavy ovenproof skillet, heat oil. Season pork with salt and pepper. Add to skillet and brown on all sides, about 5 minutes. Transfer skillet to oven. Roast pork until meat thermometer reads 150°–155°, about 20 minutes. Transfer pork to a serving plate and cover with foil to keep warm. Do not clean skillet.

Add leek and shallots to same skillet. Cook over medium heat until tender, about 8–9 minutes. Add reduced stock and port. Boil until reduced by half. Slice pork and serve with sauce.

Dorothy M. Price

91

Garlic Spareribs
"Start these ahead and you're ten minutes from dinner"

Easy
Serves: 6
Preparation: 30 min.
Marinate: 12 hrs.
Cooking: 20 min.

6 lbs. boneless country style ribs
4 lg. cloves garlic
1 Tbsp. salt
1 cup chicken broth
1 cup orange marmalade
¼ cup red wine vinegar
¼ cup ketchup

Microwave ribs in a covered dish for 20 minutes, turning once after 10 minutes. Cool.

Crush garlic with salt. Add chicken broth, marmalade, vinegar and ketchup. Pour mixture into a shallow glass dish. Add the cooled ribs, turning to coat with marinade. Cover and refrigerate for at least 12 hours, turning ribs several times.

Barbecue over low heat for about 10 minutes on each side, basting with marinade throughout cooking.

Jean Kestner

Boneless Pork Roast with Stuffing

Easy
Serves: 8
Preparation: 20 min.
Cooking: 1½–2 hrs.

1 10-oz. pkg. frozen spinach, cooked and drained
¾ lb. bulk sweet sausage
½ cup Italian bread crumbs
½ cup sliced almonds
2 eggs
1 Tbsp. onion powder
1 Tbsp. beef bouillon paste or soup base
1 tsp. minced garlic
2 tsp. dried thyme

1 4 lb. boneless pork loin
2 Tbsp. oil, mixed with 1 clove garlic, minced

Preheat oven to 350°.

In a large bowl, combine all ingredients except pork loin and oil. Set aside.

Slice pork horizontally through the meat, stopping 1" from the back. Lay pork out flat. Cover with spinach mixture. Roll up pork and tie with string to secure while roasting. Rub with oil and garlic mixture. Roast for 1½–2 hours, or until meat thermometer reads 150°–160°.

Jeanne Vanich

Rio Grande Pork Roast
"Pork with a saucy personality"

Easy
Serves: 6
Preparation: 20 min.
Cooking: 3 hrs.

1 4 lb. boneless rolled pork loin roast
½ tsp. salt
½ tsp. minced garlic
1 tsp. chili powder, divided
½ cup apple jelly
½ cup ketchup
1 Tbsp. white wine vinegar
1 cup crushed corn chips

Preheat oven to 325°.

Place pork, fat side up, in a shallow roasting pan. Combine salt, garlic and ½ tsp chili powder. Rub into roast. Roast for 2–2½ hours, or until meat thermometer registers 145°.

Meanwhile, boil jelly, ketchup, vinegar and remaining ½ teaspoon chili powder, in a small saucepan. Reduce heat and simmer for 2 minutes.

Brush roast with glaze and sprinkle with corn chips.

Roast 10–15 minutes more, until thermometer registers 155°–160°. Remove from oven. Let stand, covered with foil, for 10 minutes. Cut into slices.

Add water to pan juices to yield 1 cup. Reheat and serve.

Marge Brodbeck

Risotto, Sausage, Sun Dried Tomatoes and Escarole

"Enticing entree or a super side dish"

Easy
Serves: 4
Preparation: 20 min.
Cooking: 40 min.

3 Tbsp. olive oil, divided

1 lb. hot Italian sausage, cut into ¾" slices

6 sun dried tomatoes, oil packed, drained and finely diced

1 sm. yellow onion, finely diced

1½ cups Arborio rice

5 cups chicken broth, hot

1 cup escarole, coarsely chopped

½ tsp. salt

½ tsp. pepper

1 cup grated Parmesan cheese, divided

¼ tsp. freshly grated nutmeg

freshly chopped basil and Parmesan cheese for garnish

Preheat oven to 400°.

Grease a 2 qt. baking dish.

Heat 1 tablespoon of oil in a large skillet and cook the sausage pieces until browned. Remove with slotted spoon. Add sun dried tomatoes to the sausage. Set aside.

In a heavy saucepan, heat remaining 2 tablespoons of oil. Cook onion over medium heat until softened, about 3–5 minutes. Add rice and cook 2 minutes, stirring constantly. Add chicken broth and cook over high heat until the mixture begins to boil, 3–4 minutes. Remove from heat. Add sausage mixture, escarole, salt and pepper and ½ cup Parmesan cheese. Pour into the prepared baking dish and sprinkle with remaining Parmesan cheese and nutmeg. Cover tightly with foil and bake until rice is cooked through and most of the liquid is absorbed, about 30–40 minutes. Risotto should be creamy.

Serve in heated soup plates, with cheese and chopped basil sprinkled on top.

Bill Cardone

93

Crispy Oven Baked Pork Chops
"Terrific with chicken too"

Easy
Serves: 4–6
Preparation: 15 min.
Cooking: 30 min.

1 cup Italian style bread crumbs

3 Tbsp. grated Parmesan or Romano cheese

1 tsp. dried basil, thyme or Italian seasoning

¼ tsp. ground black pepper

2 Tbsp. butter, melted

2 eggs, beaten

4–6 center cut pork chops, ¾"–1" thick

Preheat oven to 375°.

Coat baking pan with cooking spray.

Combine bread crumbs, Parmesan cheese, dried seasoning, pepper and butter in a bowl. Place beaten eggs in another bowl. Dip each chop in egg, then crumb mixture. Bake for 30 minutes or until tender.

Judy B. Scioscia

Barbecued Ribs or Pork Chops
"Effortless"

Easy
Serves: 8
Preparation: 15 min.
Cooking: 2 hrs.

1 8-oz. can tomato sauce

1½ tsp. dry mustard

1 med. onion, chopped

½ cup molasses

2 Tbsp. vinegar

1 Tbsp. Worcestershire sauce

¼ tsp. garlic powder

4 lbs. spareribs or pork chops

Preheat oven to 350°.

Mix all ingredients except pork.

Place pork in a casserole, pour sauce over it and cover. Bake for 1½ hours. Remove cover and continue to bake for 30 minutes.

Mrs. Robert Becker

Chicken Breasts in Phyllo Pastry

"A grand gift for your guests"

Moderately difficult
Serves: 8
Preparation: 45 min.
Cooking: 40 min.

1 cup mayonnaise

⅔ cup chopped green onion

3½ Tbsp. fresh lemon juice

1 sm. clove garlic, minced

¾ tsp. dried tarragon

8 chicken breasts, boned and skinned

¼ tsp. salt

⅛ tsp. pepper

16 sheets phyllo pastry, thawed

cooking spray or melted margarine

3½ Tbsp. grated Parmesan cheese

Preheat oven to 350°.

In a small bowl, combine the first 5 ingredients. Set aside. Sprinkle chicken with salt and pepper.

Place one sheet of phyllo pastry on a sheet of plastic wrap. Spray evenly with cooking spray, or brush with margarine. Place another sheet of phyllo on top. Spray or brush with margarine.

Spread 3 tablespoons of mayonnaise mixture over breast. Place chicken breast diagonally in one corner of pastry. Fold pastry sides over breast and carefully roll up. Place seam side down on ungreased 15"x10"pan. Repeat procedure with remaining chicken breasts. Spray tops of bundles with cooking spray, or brush with margarine. Sprinkle with Parmesan cheese.

Bake for 40–45 minutes, or until done. Serve immediately.

Jacki Ronning

Chicken and Crab Richele

"Impress that special someone"

Moderately difficult
Serves: 2
Preparation: 30 min.
Cooking: 20 min.

10 oz. jumbo lump crabmeat, cleaned

½ Tbsp. diced red pepper

½ Tbsp. diced green pepper

2 Tbsp. mayonnaise

salt and pepper to taste

⅛ Tbsp. chopped fresh tarragon

2 10-oz. chicken breasts, boned and skinned

2 med. tomatoes

2 Tbsp. olive oil

⅛ Tbsp. minced garlic

½ Tbsp. chopped fresh basil

⅛ Tbsp. oregano

1 Tbsp. olive oil

1 med. zucchini, sliced

Preheat oven to 350°.

Mix crabmeat, red pepper, green pepper, mayonnaise, salt, pepper and tarragon.

Place raw chicken breasts on a cutting board and flatten with a kitchen mallet. Put 5 ounces of crabmeat mixture in the center of each chicken breast and fold over. Place in greased baking pan. Bake for 20 minutes.

Slice tomatoes in half; place under broiler until cooked. Put cooked tomatoes in a food processor with olive oil, garlic, basil and oregano. Blend until smooth. Transfer sauce to a saucepan and heat. Sauté zucchini in olive oil.

Place sauce over entire plate. Add zucchini around the border of the plate and place chicken breast in the center. Serve.

William K. Ward, CWC
Butler Country Club

Sue's Chicken

Easy
Serves: 3–4
Preparation: 45 min.
Cooking: 30 min.

3   chicken breasts, boned
    and skinned
3   eggs, beaten
½   tsp. salt
1   cup fine bread crumbs
½   cup (1 stick) butter
½   lb. mushrooms, sliced
1   tsp. dried thyme
4   oz. Gruyere or Swiss
    cheese, shredded
½   cup chicken broth
juice of 1 lemon

Preheat oven to 350°.

Cut chicken into strips. Mix beaten eggs and salt. Dip each strip in egg; then roll in bread crumbs.

In a large heavy skillet, melt butter. Lightly brown chicken, turning occasionally. Do not cook through. Transfer to 1½ qt. casserole. Add mushrooms and thyme. Sprinkle with cheese. Pour over chicken broth and bake for 30 minutes. Squeeze fresh lemon juice over casserole right before serving.

Tom and Megan Barrasso
Pittsburgh Penguins

97

Chicken Giraldi
"No consumer complaints"

Easy
Serves: 4
Preparation: 40 min
Cooking: 1 hour

6   chicken breasts, boned
    and skinned
¼   cup flour
2   Tbsp. vegetable oil
2   Tbsp. butter
1   tsp. salt
dash white pepper
1½ cups hot water
2   chicken bouillon cubes
3   Tbsp. brandy
2   tsp. fresh lemon juice
1   cup sour cream
2   9-oz. pkgs. frozen
    artichoke hearts or 2
    cans artichoke hearts,
    drained

Preheat oven to 350°.

Coat chicken breasts with flour. Heat oil in a large skillet. Add chicken and brown on both sides. Place chicken in a 13"x9" baking dish. Set aside.

In a 2 qt. saucepan, melt butter. Add 2 tablespoons flour, salt and pepper and stir until smooth. Gradually stir in 1½ cups water with dissolved bouillon, brandy and lemon juice. Cook, stirring constantly, until thick and smooth. Using a wire whisk, blend in sour cream. Pour over chicken. Cover baking dish tightly with foil, and bake for 45 minutes. Add artichoke hearts and bake for 15 minutes longer, or until chicken and artichokes are fork tender.

Serve over cooked rice.

Wendy Bell,
WTAE TV

Chicken Antonio

"The smell is as heavenly as the taste"

Easy
Serves: 4
Preparation: 15 min.
Cooking: 25 min.

⅓ cup flour

salt and white pepper

2 eggs, beaten

1 Tbsp. Parmesan cheese

pinch garlic powder

pinch white pepper

3 sprigs parsley, chopped

4 8-oz. chicken breasts, boned and skinned

1 Tbsp. olive oil

2 cloves garlic, minced

1 sm. shallot, finely chopped

3 Tbsp. white wine

3 Tbsp. butter

1 tsp. fresh lemon juice

1 4-oz. jar sliced mushrooms

8 slices prosciutto ham

4 slices provolone cheese

⅓ cup chicken broth

Preheat oven to 325°.

Season flour with salt and white pepper. Mix beaten eggs, Parmesan cheese, garlic, white pepper and chopped parsley. Cover chicken breasts with flour, then dip into egg wash.

In a large Dutch oven, heat olive oil. Add chicken and brown on both sides, about 2 minutes. Remove chicken. Add garlic and finely chopped shallots; brown lightly. Return chicken to pan. Add wine, butter, lemon juice and sliced mushrooms. Top each chicken breast with 2 thin slices of prosciutto ham, 1 slice provolone cheese and pour broth over chicken. Bake for 20 minutes.

Nicholas Longobardi

Poulet Parisienne
"Deliriously delicious"

Moderately difficult
Serves: 6
Preparation: 30 min.
Cooking: 35 min.

1   stick plus 2 Tbsp. butter, divided
⅔   cup minced onion
1   cup chicken broth, divided
2½ Tbsp. flour
2   lbs. chicken breasts, boned and skinned
4   Tbsp. oil
1   cup chopped onions
4   cups sliced mushrooms
⅔   cup brandy
1   Tbsp. dried tarragon
4   Tbsp. ketchup
2   cups heavy cream
1   tsp. tarragon vinegar
salt and white pepper
cooked white rice or rice pilaf
finely chopped fresh parsley for garnish

In a small pan, melt 4 tablespoons butter. Add ⅔ cup onion and saute over low heat, until soft. Add ⅔ cup chicken broth. Bring to a simmer and whisk in flour. Stir and simmer until mixture is very thick, 5–7 minutes. Remove from heat and set aside.

Trim chicken breasts of all fat and flatten, with a kitchen mallet, between 2 pieces of plastic wrap. In a large skillet, melt 2 tablespoons butter. Brown chicken breasts lightly on each side, then remove to a platter. Repeat with more butter and remaining chicken breasts. Remove from pan and set aside (or refrigerate). In the same pan, heat remaining butter and oil. Add 1 cup onions and cook gently for several minutes. Raise heat to medium high. Add mushrooms and cook 2 minutes. Lower heat and pour in brandy carefully, so it does not flame. Add remaining ⅓ of chicken broth. Bring to a boil and cook until liquid in pan is reduced by one half.

Stir in chicken broth, onion and flour mixture. Mix thoroughly; add tarragon and ketchup. Add cream, bring to a simmer and cook until sauce is thickened, 20–30 minutes. Stir in vinegar and season with salt and white pepper.

Return chicken to pan. Simmer gently until chicken is just tender and cooked through, 5 minutes.

Place chicken breasts on rice or rice pilaf and ladle sauce over chicken. Sprinkle with chopped parsley.

Wayne Murphy

Caper Chicken
"Lively"

Easy
Serves: 4–6
Preparation: 5 min.
Cooking: 25 min.

4–6 **chicken breasts, boned and skinned**
½ **cup flour, seasoned with salt and pepper to taste**
2 **Tbsp. margarine**
1 **cup chicken broth**
1 **cup artichoke hearts, quartered**
¼ **cup pitted black olives, halved**
4 **Tbsp. capers**
¼ **cup white wine**

Dredge chicken breasts in seasoned flour.

In a large skillet, melt margarine. Add chicken breasts and brown on both sides. Add chicken broth and simmer for 10 minutes, or until chicken is cooked through. Add artichoke hearts, olives, capers and wine. Cook until heated through. Serve.

Marilyn A. Walters

Greek Chicken
"Makes dinner a breeze"

Easy
Serves: 4
Preparation: 5 min.
Cooking: 25 min.

¼ **cup flour**
½ **tsp. salt**
1 **Tbsp. dried oregano**
4 **chicken breasts, boned, skinned and slightly pounded**
3 **Tbsp. olive oil**
1 **14-oz. can diced tomatoes**
½ **cup dry white wine**
1 **2¼-oz. can sliced black olives**
2 **Tbsp. capers, rinsed**
4 **oz. crumbled feta cheese**
salt and pepper

Combine flour, salt and oregano. Dredge chicken in flour mixture.

In a large skillet, heat olive oil. Sauté chicken until golden brown on both sides. Add remaining ingredients and simmer until chicken is tender and sauce thickens, about 15 minutes. Season with salt and fresh pepper to taste.

Diane Verdish

Herb Chicken with Vegetable Couscous

"A meal to remember"

Easy
Serves: 4
Preparation: 45 min.
Marinate: 2–3 hrs.
Cooking: 20 min.

Chicken:

1   cup olive oil

1   tsp. salt

1   tsp. black pepper

2   cloves garlic, minced

1   cup fresh herbs, finely minced (tarragon, parsley, chives, basil)

4   chicken breasts, boned and skinned

Couscous:

1   yellow squash, cut into ½" slices

1   sm. zucchini, cut into ½" slices

1   head endive, cut into quarters

2   baby eggplants, cut in half

1   portobello mushroom

5   asparagus spears

olive oil

salt and pepper

3   cups cooked couscous

Coulis:

1   red pepper, roasted and peeled

1   yellow pepper, roasted and peeled

1   cup olive oil

½   cup rice wine vinegar

salt and pepper

Preheat grill.

Chicken:
Combine all ingredients, except chicken, in a shallow glass dish. Add chicken breasts and marinate for 2–3 hours. Remove from marinade and grill until done. Chill until ready to serve.

Couscous:
Rub all vegetables with olive oil and season with salt and pepper. Grill vegetables in a basket until tender. Remove and cool. Once they are cold, reserve 4 pieces of zucchini, 4 slices yellow squash and eggplant. Finely dice the remaining vegetables. Combine the diced vegetables and cooked couscous and adjust seasonings.

Coulis:
Cut red pepper into pieces and place in a blender. Add ¼ cup vinegar and blend until smooth. With the motor running, slowly add ½ cup olive oil. Season to taste. Repeat process using the yellow pepper.

Place ¾ cup of couscous onto each plate. Lay one piece each of the remaining grilled vegetables on top. Slice the chicken and fan out across the front of the couscous. Garnish with a small portion of dressed salad greens and a tablespoon of red and yellow pepper coulis.

Jacky Fracnois
The Westin William Penn

Brandywine Chicken with Goat Cheese

Easy
Serves: 3–4
Preparation: 20 min.
Cooking: 10 min.

4 chicken breasts, boned, skinned, and pounded flat
1 Tbsp. olive oil
¼ cup (½ stick) butter, divided
4 oz. goat cheese, sliced
3 tomatoes, thinly sliced
1 Tbsp. finely chopped fresh rosemary
½ cup dry white wine

In a large skillet, heat oil and 2 tablespoons butter. Sauté chicken breasts until golden on both sides. Alternate slices of tomato and cheese on each breast. Sprinkle with rosemary. Pour wine around chicken and cover. Cook until tomato and cheese are heated through. (Cheese will not melt completely.) Remove chicken to a warm platter and cover with foil to keep warm.

Reduce remaining liquid over high heat until it thickens and coats the back of a spoon. Gradually add remaining 2 tablespoons butter. To serve, pour sauce over chicken.

Sara L. White

Lime and Yogurt Marinated Chicken Breasts

Easy
Serves: 4
Preparation: 15 min.
Marinate: overnight
Cooking: 10 min.

1 lg. green onion, minced
3 med. garlic cloves, minced
¾ tsp. ground cumin
1 tsp. ground coriander
1 tsp. grated lime zest
1½ Tbsp. fresh lime juice
½ cup plain yogurt
⅓ tsp. salt
⅓ tsp. ground black pepper
4 chicken breasts, boned and skinned

Preheat grill or broiler.

In a large nonreactive baking dish or plastic container, mix all marinade ingredients, including salt and pepper. Add chicken breasts in a single layer and turn to coat. Marinate overnight in the refrigerator.

Grill or broil chicken, turning once, until cooked through, about 5 minutes on each side.

Slice each chicken breast across the grain into ¼" thick slices and serve. Chicken pieces may also be served whole.

Susan Clay Russell

Country Captain
"A symphony of spices"

Easy
Serves: 4
Preparation: 15 min.
Cooking: 25–30 min.

1   med. chicken, cut up
    (or 4 whole legs, or 4
    chicken breasts)
¼   cup flour
1   tsp. salt
½   tsp. paprika
½   tsp. pepper
½   tsp. cayenne pepper
¼   cup olive oil, divided
1   med. onion, diced
1   sm. green pepper, diced
1   clove garlic, minced
1½ tsp. curry powder
½   tsp. dried thyme
1   14-oz. can stewed or
    diced tomatoes
⅓   cup currants, soaked in
    Marsala wine

Condiments:
toasted almonds, chutney,
chopped parsley

Cut excess fat from chicken, leaving the skin on. Place flour in a plastic bag; add salt, paprika and cayenne pepper. Shake bag to mix.

Heat 2 tablespoons olive oil in a skillet. Toss chicken pieces one at a time in the flour, shake off the excess and add them, skin side down, a few at a time to the skillet. If spattering, lower the heat a bit. Cook, turning once, until the skin is golden brown, then transfer pieces to a plate. Repeat until all chicken is browned.

103

Add 1 tablespoon of olive oil to skillet. Add onions, green pepper and garlic. Cook until soft. Add curry powder and thyme and mix well. Add tomatoes with their juice and mix again. Place chicken on top of vegetables. Bring to a boil, lower the heat, cover and simmer for 25–30 minutes. When the chicken is cooked, toss the soaked currants over the top.

Serve with condiments.

Patricia Prattis Jennings
Pianist, Pittsburgh Symphony

Artichoke Chicken

Easy
Serves: 4
Preparation: 30 min.
Cooking: 45 min.

4 chicken breasts, boned and skinned

salt and pepper to taste

2 cloves garlic, minced, divided

1 sm. onion, chopped

8 oz. fresh mushrooms, chopped

3 Tbsp. olive oil

1 14-oz. can stewed tomatoes

2 6-oz. jars marinated artichoke hearts

1 8-oz. can tomato sauce

½ cup dry white wine

oregano to taste

Preheat broiler.

Place chicken breasts on a broiler pan. Season with salt, pepper and half the garlic. Broil and set aside. Cut into cubes when cool.

Heat oil in a 12" skillet. Sauté onion, mushrooms and remaining garlic. Add stewed tomatoes and marinated artichoke hearts. Stir, then add tomato sauce, wine and oregano. Heat to boiling. Reduce heat and simmer, covered, for 25 minutes. Remove cover and continue to simmer for 10 minutes.

Serve with rice or noodles.

Lisa Elchik

Curry Chicken
"An exotic blend"

Easy
Serves: 4
Preparation: 20 min.
Cooking: 30 min.

4 chicken breasts, boned and skinned

¼ cup flour

2 Tbsp. oil

1 16-oz. can stewed tomatoes

1 cup water

1 envelope dry onion soup

1 Tbsp. chopped fresh parsley

1½ tsp. curry powder

¼ tsp. garlic powder

½ tsp. thyme

⅛ tsp. pepper

¼ cup raisins

¼ cup sliced almonds

Place chicken breasts between 2 pieces of plastic wrap; and pound using a kitchen mallet. Dredge chicken in flour. In a large skillet, heat oil; add chicken and cook for 5 minutes on each side.

Mix remaining ingredients, except almonds. Add to chicken and cook for 25–30 minutes. Serve over rice or pasta. Sprinkle with almonds.

This recipe can be easily doubled or tripled for larger groups.

Judy F. Loughren

Chicken Capri

"Lovely for a luncheon"

Easy
Serves: 8
Preparation: 15 min.
Cooking: 40–50 min.

8   chicken breasts, boned, skinned and cut into 2"–3" pieces

salt and pepper

1   13¾-oz. can artichokes, drained

8   oz. mushrooms, sliced

1   12-oz. jar roasted red peppers, sliced into strips

1½ cups shredded Cheddar cheese

1½ cups bread crumbs

3   Tbsp. butter

Preheat oven to 350°.

Coat 11"x9" dish with cooking spray.

Line dish with chicken pieces in a single layer. Do not crowd dish. Season with salt and pepper.

Layer artichokes, mushrooms, and peppers on top. Sprinkle with cheddar cheese.

Mix bread crumbs with melted butter and sprinkle over the top of the cheese.

Bake for 40–50 minutes.

Beth Rom

105

Chicken Delicious

"Rave reviews from the ravenous"

Easy
Serves: 4–6
Preparation: 10 min.
Cooking: 1 hour 30 min.

4   med. potatoes, peeled and quartered

1   tsp. oregano

1   tsp. paprika

1   tsp. garlic powder

1½ tsp. salt

½   tsp. pepper

1   frying chicken, cut up

1   lb. Italian sausage links (hot, sweet or a combination)

⅓   cup vegetable oil

Coat a roasting pan or large casserole with cooking spray. Mix seasonings. Put potatoes in pan, drizzle with half the oil and sprinkle with half of the seasonings.

Arrange chicken and sausage on top. Pour the remaining oil over the meats and sprinkle with remaining seasoning.

Cover and bake for 1 hour. Uncover, turn sausage and bake for 30 minutes more, or until everything is well browned.

Serve with Italian bread.

Jean Lopilato

Chili Marinated Chicken with Pineapple Salsa
"Delightful on a warm summer night"

Easy
Serves: 4–6
Preparation: 30 min.
Marinate: 8–24 hrs.
Cooking: 16 min.

Marinade:
1   Tbsp. chili powder
1   Tbsp. minced red onion
2   tsp. minced garlic
¼   cup fresh chopped cilantro
2   Tbsp. chopped fresh oregano, or 2 tsp. dried
1   tsp. ground cumin
¼   cup fresh lime or lemon juice
¼   cup olive oil
salt, pepper and cayenne pepper
6   chicken breasts, boned and skinned

Salsa:
1   lg. pineapple, peeled, cored and roughly chopped
¾   cup minced red onion
1   cup fresh cilantro, finely chopped
1   Tbsp. rice or white wine vinegar
½   tsp. cayenne pepper
salt and pepper

Marinade:
Place all ingredients in a nonreactive container with a tight fitting lid. Mix well. Add chicken and cover. Shake occasionally to coat chicken. Marinate in refrigerator for 8–24 hours.

Salsa:
Place chopped pineapple in a strainer and drain for about 5 minutes. Transfer pineapple to a bowl and add remaining ingredients. Stir to combine, cover and refrigerate for at least 2 hours.

Remove chicken from marinade. Grill for 7–8 minutes on each side. Serve with salsa.

Elise Keely Smith

Thai Chicken
"A lively, creamy curry"

Easy
Serves: 2
Preparation: 10 min.
Cooking: 15 min.

Béchamel Sauce:
2　Tbsp. butter

2　Tbsp. flour

¼　tsp. salt

dash of pepper

1　cup half-and-half

Curry:
1½ cups broccoli florets

2　Tbsp. corn oil

1　tsp. green Thai curry paste

12 oz. chicken, boned, skinned and cut into strips

¼　tsp. salt

2　Tbsp. sugar

½　tsp. minced garlic

2　Tbsp. soy sauce

¼　cup roasted peanuts

hot cooked rice

Béchamel Sauce:
Melt butter in a small saucepan. Stir in flour and salt and pepper. Cook and stir over low heat for a few minutes. Gradually add half-and-half and stir until thickened. Set aside.

Curry:
Blanch broccoli for 1 minute in boiling water. Drain and set aside.

In a large skillet, heat corn oil. Stir in curry paste and cook for 1 minute over low heat. Increase heat to medium. Add chicken, salt, sugar and garlic. Stir fry until sugar begins to caramelize. Add soy sauce and continue to stir fry until liquid has almost evaporated and chicken is cooked. Blend in béchamel sauce. Thin with additional milk, if needed. When sauce is smooth, add broccoli and peanuts and quickly heat through. Serve at once over rice.

Connie Stumbras

Poultry

Chicken Enchiladas
"A taste of Texas"

Easy
Serves: 6–8
Preparation: 20 min.
Cooking: 20 min.

Sauce:
1   14-oz. can green
     enchilada sauce
1   4-oz. can chopped
     green chiles
8   oz. sour cream
1   cup grated Cheddar
     cheese
1   cup shredded Monterey
     Jack cheese

Filling:
1   Tbsp. butter
¼   cup chopped onion
1½–2   cups cooked, diced
        chicken
¼   cup pitted black olives,
     chopped
12 flour tortillas

Topping:
¼   cup shredded Monterey
     Jack or Cheddar cheese

Preheat oven to 350°.

Sauce:
Mix all ingredients in a saucepan and
cook on low heat until melted.

Filling:
Sauté onions in butter. Combine with
the remaining filling ingredients. Set
aside.

Coat a baking dish with cooking spray.
Cover each tortilla with some sauce,
spoon in filling, roll up and place in
dish. Cover with remaining sauce and
top with cheese. Bake for 20 minutes.

Terry Hilton

White Chicken Chili
"This won't pale by comparison"

Easy
Serves: 8
Preparation: 1 hr.
Cooking: 1 hr. 30 min.
Must be made ahead

½ **lb. dried navy beans, picked over**

½ **cup (1 stick) unsalted butter, divided**

1 **lg. onion, chopped**

¼ **cup flour**

1 **cup chicken broth**

2 **cups half-and-half**

2 **tsp. Tabasco sauce**

1½ **tsp. chili powder**

1 **tsp. ground cumin**

½ **tsp. salt**

½ **tsp. white pepper**

2 **4-oz. cans whole mild green chiles, drained and chopped**

1 **4-oz. can of jalapeño peppers, drained and chopped**

5 **chicken breasts, boned, skinned, cooked, and cut into ½" pieces**

1½ **cups grated Monterey Jack cheese**

½ **cup sour cream**

1 **jar salsa**

fresh cilantro for garnish

In a large kettle, soak beans in cold water overnight. Drain beans and return to kettle. Cover with water by 2". Simmer beans until tender, about 1 hour. Drain.

In a skillet, melt 2 tablespoons butter. Sauté onion over medium heat until softened. In a 6–8 quart heavy pot, melt remaining 6 tablespoons butter over low heat and whisk in flour. Cook roux, whisking constantly, 3 minutes. Stir in onion. Gradually add broth and half-and-half, whisking constantly. Bring mixture to a boil and simmer, stirring occasionally, 5 minutes, or until thickened.

Stir in Tabasco, chili powder, cumin, salt and white pepper. Add beans, chiles, peppers, chicken and cheese. Cook for 20 minutes over medium low heat, stirring frequently.

Stir sour cream into chili. Ladle chili into individual bowls, garnish with a spoonful of salsa and cilantro sprigs. Serve with warm tortillas.

This can be easily doubled or tripled for a crowd.

Hilary Rose

109

Salmon Provencal
"Zesty and tantalizing"

Easy
Serves: 8 to 10
Preparation: 30 min.
Cooking: 25 min.

1½–2 lbs. fresh salmon
  fillet

¼ cup fresh lemon juice

2 Tbsp. olive oil, divided

¼ cup packed fresh basil
  leaves, finely sliced

2 tsp. lemon peel, grated
  and divided

1 tsp. salt, divided

½ tsp. ground black
  pepper, divided

8–10 plum tomatoes,
  sliced

1 med. garlic clove,
  minced

½ cup sliced pitted black
  olives

2½ Tbsp. capers

fresh basil for
garnish

Preheat broiler.

Coat broiler pan with cooking spray. Place salmon, skin side down, in the pan. Set aside.

Stir together lemon juice, 1 tablespoon oil, 2 tablespoons basil, 1 teaspoon lemon peel, ½ teaspoon salt and ¼ teaspoon pepper. Pour over the salmon and broil for 10–15 minutes.

Meanwhile, in a skillet over medium high heat, cook the tomatoes and garlic in the remaining oil for 2 minutes, or until tender. Stir in all remaining ingredients and serve over the salmon. Garnish with fresh basil.

Joyce A. Scalerico

Barbecued Salmon

"This versatile marinade enhances swordfish and chicken too"

Easy
Serves: 4
Preparation: 20 min.
Marinate: 1 hr.
Cooking: 8 min.

2   lemons, zest and juice
2   limes, zest and juice
⅓   cup brown sugar
2   Tbsp. olive oil
2   Tbsp. lite soy sauce
2   Tbsp. peeled, freshly grated ginger
4   6-oz. salmon fillets at least 1" thick

Preheat grill.

Mix the lemon and lime zests and juices with sugar, oil, soy sauce and grated ginger. Pour over salmon fillets and marinate, at room temperature, for 1 hour in a nonreactive bowl.

Drain the marinade into a small saucepan and boil for 1 to 2 minutes. Strain.

Grill the salmon for 6 minutes, skin side down. Baste with the marinade; turn and grill for 3 minutes more depending on the thickness of the fillets. Do not overcook.

Serve marinade on the side, or spoon over the salmon just before serving.

Lorraine P. Trice

Salmon Zucherro

"Savory and sumptuous"

Moderately difficult
Serves: 1
Preparation: 15 min.
Cooking: 20 min.

¼   tsp. cayenne pepper
½   cup sugar
½   tsp. dried basil, crushed
¼   tsp. dried oregano, crushed
1   8-oz. salmon fillet
2   Tbsp. olive oil
5   oz. white Zinfandel wine
8   oz. heavy cream

Preheat oven to 375°.

Mix cayenne, sugar, basil and oregano. Toss salmon in the mixture until well coated.

Heat oil in a sauté pan and brown salmon on both sides. Remove salmon to a separate pan and cook in the oven until done. Meanwhile, deglaze the sauté pan with the wine.

Transfer cooked salmon back to the original pan on the stovetop and add the whipping cream. Reduce cream until sauce thickens. Serve immediately.

Michael Geiger

Salmon with Lime Yogurt Sauce
"Creamy, yet light and refreshing"

Moderately difficult
Serves: 4
Preparation: 30 min.
Cooking: 15 min.

Sauce:
½ cup plain nonfat yogurt
1½ tsp. finely chopped fresh chives
½ tsp. finely chopped fresh parsley
½ tsp. minced lime zest
½ tsp. fresh lime juice
salt and pepper

Salmon:
2 Tbsp. finely chopped fresh parsley
2 Tbsp. finely chopped fresh basil
2 Tbsp. finely chopped fresh chives
1 tsp finely chopped fresh thyme
cooking spray
1 cup chopped onion
1 bunch fresh spinach, stemmed, chopped or 1 10-oz. pkg. frozen, chopped
1 med. tomato, chopped
1 clove garlic, minced
4 4-oz. salmon fillets

Preheat grill or broiler.

Sauce:
Combine all ingredients in a bowl and season with salt and pepper.

Salmon:
Combine the herbs in a shallow dish and set aside.

Coat a large nonstick skillet with cooking spray and heat over medium heat. Add the onion; sauté until tender, about 4 minutes. Add the spinach, tomato and garlic. Add the herb mixture and sauté until the spinach wilts, about 3 minutes. Set aside.

Grill or broil the salmon until cooked through, about 3 minutes per side. Reheat the spinach mixture.

Serve the salmon over a bed of the spinach and spoon sauce over each portion.

Dorothy M. Price

Sugared Salmon with Spicy Mango Sauce
"A provocative blend of fruit and spice"

Moderately difficult
Serves: 4
Preparation: 20 min.
Cooking: 14 min.

Salsa:
½ cup diced fresh mango
1 tsp. seeded, minced
    fresh jalapeño chile
2 Tbsp. diced red onion
2 Tbsp. finely chopped
    fresh cilantro
3 Tbsp. fresh lime juice
salt and pepper

Salmon:
½ cup yellow corn meal
½ cup sugar
½ tsp. cinnamon
1 Tbsp. paprika
1 Tbsp. cocoa powder
½ cup chili powder
2 Tbsp. ground cumin
2 tsp. ground black
    pepper
2 Tbsp. salt
3 Tbsp. olive oil, divided
4 8-oz. salmon fillets

Preheat oven to 350°.

Salsa:
Prepare salsa by combining mango, jalapeño, onion, cilantro and lime juice in a nonreactive bowl. Season with salt and pepper. Refrigerate. Can be made up to 12 hours ahead.

Salmon:
Combine the corn meal, sugar and spices in a shallow bowl. Rub the salmon on both sides with 1 tablespoon of the olive oil. Dredge the salmon in the spice mixture, making sure to coat generously.

Heat a cast iron or heavy sauté pan over medium high heat; add 1 table-spoon of oil and heat. Gently add the spiced salmon and cook about 3 to 5 minutes, or until a crisp crust forms. Carefully turn salmon over, adding 1 tablespoon of oil if needed, and continue cooking until the same results occur on the bottom of the fillet. Transfer the fish to an ovenproof dish. Cook in oven for about 5 to 7 minutes, or until the fish is cooked through. Serve at once with a generous portion of mango salsa.

Martin Thomas
Westmoreland Country Club

113

Salmon and Rice En Croute
"Elegance in presentation and taste"

Moderately difficult
Serves: 4
Preparation: 1 hr.
Cooking: 30 min.

2   Tbsp. butter
½   cup minced leek, white and pale green parts only
6   oz. fresh shitake mushrooms, stemmed, chopped
½   cup long grain rice, cooked
salt and pepper
2   sheets frozen puff pastry (17¾-oz. pkg. thawed)
4   6-oz. skinless salmon fillets
1   egg beaten with 1 Tbsp. water

Dill Sauce:
⅔   cup bottled clam juice
½   cup dry white wine
1¼ cup crème fraiche
3   Tbsp. minced fresh dill
salt and pepper

Preheat oven to 400°.

Melt butter in a heavy skillet and sauté the leek until just softened. Add mushrooms and cook until the liquid is released. Increase the heat and sauté until all liquid has evaporated. Transfer to a bowl; add the rice and season with salt and pepper. Set aside and cool.

Butter a large baking sheet. Roll out one sheet of pastry to a 12-inch square. Cut into four equal squares. Divide the rice mixture and mound in the center of each square. Shape the filling into an oval shape, with the ends towards the two corners of the pastry and place a fillet on top. Sprinkle with salt and pepper. Bring pastry corners up around the salmon; pastry will not enclose salmon completely. Roll out remaining pastry into a 13-inch square. Cut into four equal squares and lay one square on top of each salmon fillet, tucking corners under the bottom to enclose completely. Pinch edges to seal. Brush with some of the egg mixture. Arrange salmon packages on baking sheet, seam side down. Cover and chill 30 minutes, or up to 8 hours ahead.

Brush the top of the pastry with the remaining egg mixture. Bake until golden, about 30 minutes.

Dill Sauce:
Combine clam juice and wine in a heavy non-aluminum saucepan. Boil until reduced to ⅓ cup, about 9 minutes. Reduce heat to medium and whisk in the crème fraiche. Bring back to a boil and continue to cook until reduced to 1 cup, about 5 minutes. Remove from heat, stir in the dill and season with salt and pepper. Serve salmon with the sauce.

Dorothy M. Price

Sole Duxelle
"A delicious classic dish."

Easy
Serves: 4
Preparation: 20 min.
Cooking: 25 min.

1 lb. fillet of sole
3 Tbsp. white wine
2 Tbsp. fresh lemon juice
salt and pepper
3 Tbsp. butter
3 Tbsp. flour
1 cup half-and-half
¼ lb. mushrooms, chopped, sautéed
2 Tbsp. buttered bread crumbs
2 Tbsp. grated Parmesan cheese

Preheat oven to 375°.

Place sole in a buttered baking dish. Sprinkle with wine, lemon juice, salt and pepper. Cover with aluminum foil and bake for 15 minutes.

In a small saucepan, melt the butter. Add flour and cook, stirring for 1 to 2 minutes. Add half-and-half and cook, whisking continuously, until the sauce thickens. Do not season.

When the sole is ready, remove the dish from the oven and pour the liquid from the dish into the sauce. Stir in the mushrooms, season to taste and pour the sauce over the fish. Top with the bread crumbs and cheese and return to the oven for 10 minutes, or until the surface is nicely browned.

Susan L. Tedesko

Orange Roughy with Parmesan Cheese
"A tasty time saver"

Easy
Serves: 4
Preparation: 10 min.
Cooking: 8 min.

2 lbs. orange roughy
2 Tbsp. fresh lemon juice
½ cup freshly grated Parmesan cheese
4 Tbsp. butter
3 Tbsp. mayonnaise
3 Tbsp. chopped green onions
salt and black pepper
dash of Tabasco sauce

Preheat broiler.

Place fish in a buttered baking dish. Brush with lemon juice and let stand.

Meanwhile, combine cheese, butter, mayonnaise, green onions, salt, pepper and Tabasco sauce.

Broil fillets 3–4 inches from preheated broiler for about 5 minutes. Spread with cheese mixture and broil for another 2–3 minutes being careful not to burn.

Nan O'Connor

Sea Bass with Lemon Nut Crust

Easy
Serves: 4
Preparation: 15 min.
Cooking: 10 min.
Can be made ahead

2   lg. eggs

½   cup pecans

½   cup dry bread crumbs

1   Tbsp. grated lemon zest

4   6-oz. sea bass fillets, about 1" thick

salt and pepper

flour

4   Tbsp. butter, divided

½   cup finely chopped parsley

2   Tbsp. fresh lemon juice

Preheat oven to 400°.

Place eggs in a shallow bowl and beat to blend. Finely grind pecans, bread crumbs and lemon peel in a food processor. Transfer nut mixture to a shallow bowl. Sprinkle fish with salt and pepper. Coat each fillet with flour, then eggs, then seasoned crumbs. Transfer the fish to a waxed paper lined plate. Can be prepared 3 hours ahead and refrigerated at this point.

Over medium high heat, melt 2 table-spoons of butter in a large ovenproof skillet. Add fish and sauté until brown, about 1 minute per side. Place the skillet in the oven and bake until the fish is opaque in the center and just firm to the touch, about 8 minutes.

Meanwhile, melt remaining 2 table-spoons of butter in a small skillet, over medium low heat and cook until the butter begins to foam. Mix in the parsley and lemon juice. Season with salt and pepper.

Transfer the fish to plates and spoon the butter sauce over it, dividing evenly. Serve.

Mary Lee Parrington

Mustard Glazed Halibut
"Try it with salmon also"

Easy
Serves: 4
Preparation: 15 min.
Cooking: 10 min.

½ cup Dijon mustard

½ cup olive oil

1 tsp. minced garlic

½ cup finely chopped
    fresh dill

6 Tbsp. golden brown
    sugar, packed

4 8-oz. halibut steaks

salt and pepper

Preheat oven to 350°.

Mix the mustard, olive oil, garlic, dill, and brown sugar. Brush the halibut steaks with the sauce, season with salt and pepper and bake for about 10 minutes.

Good served with roasted red skin potatoes that have been mixed with some of the brown sugar sauce.

Jane Ellen Rabe

Tuna with Fresh Mango and Red Pepper Salsa
"A headliner"

Easy
Serves: 4
Preparation: 15 min.
Marinate: 1 hr.
Cooking: 10 min.

1 lg. ripe mango, peeled,
    chopped

1 med. red pepper,
    chopped

1 med. onion, finely
    chopped

¼ cup finely chopped
    cilantro

juice of 1 lime

salt and pepper

4 6-oz. tuna steaks

olive oil

Preheat grill.

To make the salsa, combine mango, pepper, onion, cilantro and lime juice in a nonreactive bowl. Season with salt and pepper and refrigerate for at least 1 hour. Can be made ahead to this point.

Brush tuna steaks with a little olive oil and grill for approximately 10 minutes over high heat. Serve topped with a little of the mango salsa.

Peggy Finnegan
WPXI TV

Grilled Swordfish with Tomatillo Salsa

"The snappy salsa appeals to the eye and the palette"

Easy
Serves: 4
Preparation: 25 min.
Cooking: 10 min.

Salsa:

6   **fresh tomatillos**

1   **sm. red onion, cut into chunks**

2   **cloves garlic, minced**

1   **large fresh Anaheim chile or other mild chile, halved, seeded, cut into pieces**

½   **fresh red or green jalapeño chile, seeded, cut into pieces**

¼   **cup fresh cilantro sprigs**

salt

4   **6–8-oz. swordfish steaks, about 1" thick**

2   **Tbsp. vegetable oil**

salt and freshly ground black pepper

Preheat grill.

Salsa:
Remove and discard the papery husks from the tomatillos. Chop them coarsely. In a food processor fitted with the metal blade, combine the tomatillos, onion, garlic, Anaheim and jalapeño chiles and the cilantro. Process just until coarsely chopped and transfer to a bowl. The ingredients may be coarsely chopped by hand and then combined in a bowl. Season with salt to taste and set aside.

Rub the fish steaks with oil and sprinkle with salt and pepper. Grill, turning once or twice, for about 10 minutes. Remove to a warmed platter. Place a spoonful of the salsa on each steak. Serve with remaining salsa.

Daniel J. Dooley
Executive Chef
Penn Brewery

Seviche

"Terrific when the temperature rises"

Easy
Serves: 4
Preparation: 1 hour
Marinate: 2 days
Make ahead

3 cups (about 1½-2 lbs.) raw white fish fillets without skin or bones

⅔ cup lemon juice

1 cup spicy tomato juice

½ cup olive oil

½ cup chopped white onion

4 jalapeños, seeded, chopped

6 large tomatoes, chopped

¼ cup chopped red pepper

2 cloves garlic, minced

½ tsp. dried thyme

1 Tbsp. dried parsley

1 Tbsp. coriander, or several sprigs of cilantro, finely chopped

Use cod or other similar white fish fillets. Cut into bite size pieces.

Mix lemon juice, tomato juice and olive oil and pour over the fish. Fish should be submerged in this marinade. Marinate fish overnight to "cook" the fish. Stir occasionally. Next morning, add the vegetables and seasonings to the fish marinade; marinate in the refrigerator for at least 6 to 8 hours. The longer this marinates, the better the flavor and the more "cooked" the fish will be.

Serve on Bibb lettuce with soft bread sticks or individual baguettes. Accompany with lemon wedges, olives, tomato slices and potato salad.

Great as a light luncheon or as a first course.

Susan A. DePree

119

Spicy Coconut Shrimp
"Serve with rice and a cold beer"

Easy
Serves: 4
Preparation: 20 min.
Cooking: 20 min.

¼ cup (½ stick) unsalted butter, divided

1 lb. lg. or med. shrimp, shelled, deveined

½ tsp. salt

3 jalapeño peppers, seeded and minced

3 cloves garlic, minced

½ cup sliced green onions

1 lg. red pepper, chopped

1 cup heavy cream

¼ cup chicken broth

1 Tbsp. fresh lime juice

½ cup finely chopped fresh cilantro

⅓ cup shredded coconut

In a skillet, melt 3 tablespoons of butter. Add shrimp, season with salt and sauté until pink, about 2 minutes. Transfer to a bowl and keep warm.

Melt remaining butter in the skillet. Add jalapeño peppers, garlic, green onions and red pepper. Cook until softened.

Add cream and broth; bring to a boil. Reduce heat and simmer until the sauce is slightly thickened. Stir in the lime juice and coriander. Spoon sauce on a platter, top with shrimp, and sprinkle with coconut. Serve with rice.

Kate Sawyer

Shrimp with Feta

Easy
Serves: 4
Preparation: 30 min.
Cooking: 20 min.

2 Tbsp. olive oil

1 14-oz. can diced tomatoes

1 red or yellow pepper, pureed

1 red or yellow pepper, julienned

1–2 Tbsp. minced garlic

1 16-oz. bag frozen uncooked lg. shrimp

2 Tbsp. finely chopped fresh herbs (tarragon, thyme, basil, oregano)

3 dashes hot pepper sauce

salt and pepper

1 cup crumbled feta cheese

Heat oil in a skillet over medium high heat. Add tomatoes, pureed pepper, julienne pepper and garlic. Sauté 5 minutes or until the pepper is tender. Add shrimp and sauté until cooked through, about 2 minutes. Stir in the herbs and hot pepper sauce. Season with salt and pepper. Remove from heat, stir in the feta cheese and serve.

Jack Ansaldi

Spicy Shrimp William
"A fresh flavorful sauté"

Easy
Serves: 2
Preparation: 30 min.
Cooking: 15 min.

1   Tbsp. butter
1   Tbsp. olive oil
1   Tbsp. finely chopped celery
1   Tbsp. finely chopped onions
1   clove garlic, minced
⅛   tsp. red pepper flakes
½   cup diced, seeded tomatoes
¼   cup chopped red pepper
1   tsp. finely chopped cilantro
16 lg. shrimp, uncooked, shelled, deveined

2   Tbsp. white wine
1   Tbsp. fresh lemon juice
salt and pepper
2   finely chopped parsley sprigs
cooked rice

Melt butter and olive oil in a skillet. Add celery, onion, garlic, red pepper flakes, tomatoes, red pepper and cilantro. Sauté until the vegetables are very tender. Add shrimp, wine and lemon juice. Sauté the mixture until the shrimp lose transparency. Season with salt and pepper, then sprinkle with parsley.

Serve shimp and sauce over rice.

William Ward
Butler Country Club

Sea Bass and Scallops
"A robust seafood medley"

Easy
Serves: 4
Preparation: 15 min.
Cooking: 20 min.

2   Tbsp. olive oil
2   sm. onions, finely chopped
4   cloves garlic, minced
1   16-oz. can crushed tomatoes
½   cup white wine
2   cups chicken broth
1   bay leaf
1   tsp. dried thyme
¼   cup finely chopped parsley
1   Tbsp. chili powder

1   6.5-oz. can minced clams, juice reserved
1   lb. sea bass cut into 2" pieces
½   lb. sea scallops
¼   cup chopped cilantro

Heat oil in a large skillet. Add onion and garlic and sauté until soft. Add tomatoes, wine, broth, bay leaf, thyme, parsley and juice from clams. Bring to a boil, then simmer, covered, for 5 minutes. Add chili powder and simmer an additional 5 minutes. Stir in clams, sea bass and scallops. Simmer until fish is cooked, about 5 minutes. Serve in bowls over rice, and garnish with cilantro.

Emilie Szakach

Baked Stuffed Shrimp Imperial
"Indulge yourself"

Easy
Serves: 4–6
Preparation: 40 min.
Cooking: 20 min.
Can be made ahead

Imperial Mayonnaise:
1 cup mayonnaise
½ tsp. Tabasco sauce
½ tsp. fresh lemon juice
½ tsp. Worcestershire sauce
½ tsp. Old Bay Seasoning

Stuffing:
1 lb. crab meat
1 cup Imperial Mayonnaise
¼ cup bread crumbs
¼ tsp. salt
¼ cup finely chopped red pepper
4 tsp. finely chopped chives

16 jumbo shrimp, uncooked, shelled and deveined
2 Tbsp. butter
¼ cup white wine
2 Tbsp. fresh lemon juice

Preheat oven to 350°.

Imperial Mayonnaise:
Mix first 5 ingredients to make mayonnaise.

Stuffing:
Mix all the ingredients with the Imperial Mayonnaise until well blended.

Split the shrimp in half lengthwise so the shrimp rests flat. Spoon the stuffing on top of each shrimp. Sprinkle with lemon juice and white wine. Dot with butter.

Bake for 15 to 20 minutes, or until the stuffing is lightly browned.

Great with baked potatoes, salad or sourdough bread.

Dodie Schaffer

Shrimp and Scallop Casserole
"A magnificent meal"

Easy
Serves: 10–12
Preparation: 30 min.
Cooking: 25 min.

12 oz. thin noodles, cooked and drained
1 cup (2 sticks) butter, divided
1 lb. shrimp
2 lbs. scallops
6 Tbsp. flour
½ tsp. salt
4 cups milk
½ cup sherry
1 cup sour cream
¾ lb. mushrooms, sliced
8 oz. sharp cheese, shredded

1 onion, chopped
1 green pepper, chopped

Preheat oven to 350°.

Sauté scallops in 4 tablespoons butter, about 3 to 4 minutes. Cook shrimp for 2–3 minutes in simmering salted water and peel. Combine noodles, scallops and shrimp in a 4-quart casserole.

In a saucepan, melt 6 tablespoons butter. Blend in flour and salt. Add milk. Cook until thickened and add sherry. Pour into noodle mixture. Stir in sour cream.

Sauté mushrooms in remaining butter; add to casserole. Top with shredded cheese, chopped onion and green pepper. Bake for 25 minutes.

123

Debbie Darby

Grilled Scallops Mediterranean

Moderately difficult
Serves: 2
Preparation: 20 min.
Cooking: 10 min.

1 cup olive oil
1 Tbsp. dried basil
¼ tsp. dried oregano
8 oz. lg. sea scallops
2 Tbsp. olive oil
1 Tbsp. minced garlic
10 oz. med. diced plum tomatoes
1 4-oz. pkg. frozen spinach, thawed, drained
1 cup Kalamata olives, pitted, halved

Preheat grill.

In a medium nonreactive mixing bowl combine 1 cup olive oil, basil, oregano and sea scallops. Set aside.

Heat 2 tablespoons of olive oil in a large sauté pan. Add garlic and cook for 1 minute. Add tomatoes and cook 1 minute. Stir in spinach, cook 5 minutes and add olives. Remove from heat and set aside.

Take scallops out of the marinade, and shake off excess oil. Place scallops into a grill basket or thread on wooden skewers. Grill, rotating frequently, until they are cooked. Place spinach in center of a platter and surround with scallops.

Michael Geiger

Maryland Crab Cakes with Cajun Remoulade Sauce

Easy
Serves: 4
Preparation: 20 min.
Cooking: 20 min.
Can be frozen

8   oz. lump crabmeat, drained and shredded

⅛   cup Dijon mustard

½   cup bread crumbs

¼   cup each finely diced red, yellow and green pepper

⅛   cup finely chopped onion

⅛–¼ cup mayonnaise

1   egg

½   cup (1 stick) butter

Cajun Remoulade Sauce:
½   cup mayonnaise

¼   cup finely diced tomatoes

2   Tbsp. finely diced green onions

1   Tbsp. sweet relish

1   Tbsp. mustard, stone ground

3   Tbsp. sour cream

½   tsp. chopped capers

¼   tsp. cayenne pepper

1   tsp. Worcestershire sauce

salt

Preheat oven to 325°.

Combine crabmeat, mustard, bread crumbs, peppers, onion, mayonnaise and egg. Mix well. Divide and shape the batter into 8 patties and flatten.

Heat the butter in a large nonstick skillet. Add the crab cakes, 4 at a time, and brown lightly on each side. Place the browned crab cakes on an oven-proof dish in a single layer. Bake for approximately 5 minutes. Serve with Remoulade Sauce.

Cajun Remoulade Sauce:
Combine all the ingredients, adding salt to taste. Chill until ready to serve.

This sauce is also good with baked potatoes.

Sallie Lux

Saffron Fish Stew
"A sensational crowd pleaser"

Easy
Serves: 6
Preparation: 15 min.
Cooking: 25 min.
Can be made ahead

¼   **cup olive oil**
2   **cups finely chopped onions**
4   **lg. garlic cloves, minced**
1   **green pepper, finely chopped**
5   **cups finely chopped tomatoes**
1   **cup diced fennel**
3   **cups clam juice**
2   **cups dry white wine**
1   **bay leaf**
2   **Tbsp. finely chopped fresh basil**
1   **Tbsp. finely chopped fresh thyme**
1   **4"x1" strip orange rind**
¼   **tsp. saffron threads**
1   **tsp. red pepper flakes**
½   **tsp. black pepper**
1   **cup pasta shells or orzo**
20   **clams**
1   **lb. cleaned squid, cut into ¼" rings**
1   **lb. firm-flesh fish (Bass, Tilapia, etc.)**
1   **lb. raw shrimp, shelled, deveined**
½   **cup finely chopped parsley for garnish**
salt and pepper

Heat the oil in a large sauté pan. Add the onion, garlic and green pepper. Sauté over low heat for 5 minutes, stirring occasionally. Add the next 12 ingredients, tomatoes through pasta, and bring to a boil. Reduce the heat and allow the liquid to simmer for about 15 minutes.

Add clams. Cover the pan and continue cooking just until the clams are open. Add the remaining fish and cook 2 minutes more. Do not overcook. Season with salt and pepper to taste.

Serve in a large soup tureen garnished with minced parsley. Delicious served with crusty bread.

Gaynor Grant

125

Franco's Immaculate Lasagna

"Enjoy a piece of Pittsburgh history"

Easy
Serves: 6–8
Preparation time: 30 min.
Cooking time: 1 hr.
Can be frozen

3   lg. cloves garlic, minced
1   lb. ground beef
1   1 lb. 13-oz. can tomato puree
1   lg. onion, quartered
1   6-oz. can tomato paste
6   oz. water
½   tsp. dried oregano
¼   tsp. dried basil
¼   cup red wine
2   tsp. salt
½   cup grated Romano cheese
1   lb. lasagna noodles, cooked and drained
1   lb. ricotta cheese
8   oz. mozzarella cheese

Preheat oven to 350°.

Lightly grease a 13"x9" pan.

In a large skillet, brown garlic and meat. Drain.

Combine puree and onion in a blender until smooth. Add to meat along with the other ingredients, except noodles and cheeses. Cover and simmer 10 minutes.

To assemble the lasagna, cover the bottom of the dish with ⅓ of the meat mixture. Put ½ of the Romano evenly over this. Lay 5 noodles lengthwise and 1 crosswise at top to fill the pan. Spread ½ of the ricotta evenly over the noodles. Grate ½ of the mozzarella over the top. Repeat, ending with the meat sauce and Romano. Cover tightly with foil and bake 1 hour. Remove from oven and let stand 5 minutes before serving.

Franco Harris

Rigatoni with Vodka Cream Sauce

"Prosciutto enhances this piquant sauce"

Easy
Serves: 4–6
Preparation: 20 min.
Cooking: 20 min.

2   Tbsp. olive oil
1½ cups chopped shallots
¼   tsp. red pepper flakes
1   cup vodka
1½ cups whipping cream
1½ cups canned tomato
    sauce
1   lb. rigatoni, cooked and
    drained
4–6 oz. prosciutto, chopped
3   Tbsp. finely chopped
    parsley
4   Tbsp. finely chopped
    fresh basil

1   cup grated Parmesan
    cheese, divided

Heat oil in a large pan. Add shallots and red pepper flakes; sauté over low heat for 5 minutes. Add the vodka and ignite using a long match. Simmer until the flames subside. Add the cream; boil until the mixture thickens, about 3 to 5 minutes. Add the tomato sauce and simmer a few minutes more.

Toss sauce with cooked rigatoni, proscuitto, parsley, basil and ¹/₂ cup of the Parmesan cheese.

Serve with remaining Parmesan cheese.

Mark Zappala

127

Fettuccine with Shitake Mushroom Sauce

"Incredibly creamy and complex flavor"

Easy
Serves: 6
Preparation: 30–40 min.
Cooking: 10 min.

2   oz. dried shitake
    mushrooms
⅔   cup dry white wine
4   oz. prosciutto, cut into
    thin strips
Alfredo Sauce:
½   cup (1 stick) butter
6–8 cloves garlic, minced
1   tsp. chopped fresh basil
1   tsp. chopped fresh
    oregano
6   oz. grated Parmesan
    cheese
2   cups whipping cream

1   lb. fettucine, cooked
    and drained

Rinse mushrooms and drain. Cover with white wine and let stand 30 minutes. Drain, reserving ⅓ cup wine. Slice mushrooms into ¼" pieces.

Alfredo Sauce:
Place all ingredients in a heavy saucepan and simmer until hot and sauce begins to thicken. Do not boil.

Cook mushrooms over medium heat in reserved wine. Add to Alfredo Sauce. Add prosciutto and heat through.

Toss with cooked fettuccine and serve.

Lynn B. Popovich

Café Georgio's Boursin Ravioli
"Intoxicating"

Easy
Serves: 8 (as a first course)
Preparation: 30 min.
Cooking: 5 min.
Can be made ahead

Boursin Filling:
12 oz. cream cheese
4 oz. crumbled Gorgonzola cheese, room temperature
2 oz. grated Asiago cheese, room temperature
2 oz. grated Romano cheese, room temperature
½ tsp. minced garlic
1 Tbsp. finely chopped fresh parsley
1 Tbsp. finely chopped fresh basil
1 Tbsp. finely chopped fresh oregano
salt and pepper
1 Tbsp. chopped capers
¼ cup roughly chopped oil packed sun dried tomatoes
1 pkg. large wonton skins
1 lb. fresh spinach, sautéed
½ cup roasted red peppers, diced
1 egg, beaten (for egg wash)
marinara or pesto sauce
fresh chopped herbs for garnish

In a large mixing bowl, cream together the cheeses. Add the remaining ingredients through the sun dried tomatoes, and mix well.

To assemble the ravioli, place one wonton skin on waxed paper. Paint the outer edges of the wonton with the egg wash. Put 1 tablespoon of the Boursin cheese mixture in the center and flatten slightly.

Place a spinach leaf and a little roasted pepper on top. Paint the outer edges of another wonton with the egg wash and place on top, painted side facing down. Press the moistened edges together with fork tines. Repeat with remaining wontons.

Cook assembled ravioli in boiling water until transparent, about 4 to 5 minutes. Drain well. Top with desired choice of sauce and fresh chopped herbs.

Café Georgio

London Chop House Red Pepper and Chicken Fettuccine
"A velvety smooth sauce"

Moderately difficult
Serves: 6
Preparation: 20 min.
Marinate: 3 hrs.
Cooking: 1 hr.

Chicken Marinade:
½ cup olive oil
½ cup chopped fresh basil
3 Tbsp. fresh lemon juice
1 Tbsp. crushed red pepper
2 tsp. minced garlic
4 chicken breasts, boned and skinned

Sauce:
1 red pepper
1 yellow pepper
3 Tbsp. margarine
½ cup dry white wine
½ cup chicken broth
2 cups heavy cream

4 oz. sliced mushrooms
½ tsp. salt
12 oz. fettuccine noodles, cooked and drained
½ cup grated fresh Parmesan cheese
¼ cup finely chopped fresh basil

Chicken marinade:
Combine all marinade ingredients. Cut chicken breasts into bite-sized pieces and mix with marinade. Cover and refrigerate for at least 3 hours.

Sauce:
Peel both peppers (using a potato peeler) and save skins. Cut peppers into thin strips and refrigerate. In a small saucepan, melt 1½ tablespoons margarine; add pepper skins and cook for 2 minutes. Stir in wine and chicken broth. Reduce for about 5 minutes, until only 2 tablespoons of liquid remain. Cool. Stir in cream. On low heat, reduce sauce to about half. Pour cream sauce through a sieve. Sauce can be made ahead and refrigerated at this point.

Using a slotted spoon, remove chicken from marinade. In large skillet, sauté chicken and mushrooms until brown. Add pepper strips and simmer until warm. Season with salt.

Heat sauce but do not boil.

Mix fettuccine with hot chicken and sauce. Add Parmesan cheese and basil.

Ginny Z. Monroe

129

Chicken on Pasta with Spicy Asian Sauce

"Asian cuisine with a kick"

Moderately difficult
Serves: 4–6
Preparation: 30 min.
Cooking: 45 min.

3 Tbsp. vegetable oil, divided

6 garlic cloves, minced

3 jalapeño chiles, seeded and minced

1½ cups canned, unsweetened coconut milk

⅓ cup creamy peanut butter

⅓ cup soy sauce

2 Tbsp. fresh lime juice

2 Tbsp. sesame oil

2 Tbsp. fresh peeled, minced ginger

1 Tbsp. honey

1½ tsp. Tabasco

salt and pepper

¾ cup diced red peppers

½ cup sliced mushrooms

½ cup chopped green onions

1 lb. chicken breast, boned and skinned and cut into ⅓" wide strips

1 lb. linguini, cooked and drained

Heat 2 tablespoons oil in a large saucepan over medium heat. Add garlic and jalapeños. Sauté until softened, but not brown, about 3 minutes. Add coconut milk, peanut butter, soy sauce, lime juice, sesame oil, ginger, honey and Tabasco; whisk until smooth. Bring to a simmer. Remove from heat. Season with salt and pepper. Sauce can be made 1 day ahead. Cover and refrigerate.

Heat remaining oil in a large skillet over medium high heat. Add peppers, mushrooms and green onions and sauté 3 minutes. Add chicken and sauté until cooked through, about 3 minutes. Add sauce.

Bring sauce mixture to simmer. Pour over pasta and toss well.

Diane Dolan

Chicken and Pasta Romanesque

"Quick and colorful"

Easy
Serves: 4–6
Preparation: 15 min.
Cooking: 20 min.

½ cup olive oil

1–1½ lbs. chicken breasts, boned, skinned and cubed

4 cloves garlic, minced

1 bunch fresh spinach, cleaned, stems removed, chopped into med. sized pieces

2 10½-oz. cans chicken broth, divided

1 lb. colored pasta spirals or rotini

6–8 oz. oil packed sun dried tomatoes, drained, cut into julienne strips

1 10-oz. jar marinated artichoke hearts, drained

6 green onions, thinly sliced

1 tsp. finely chopped fresh basil

4 oz. grated Romano cheese

In a large skillet, heat oil. Add chicken and garlic. Cook over medium heat until done. Set aside. In a large saucepan, cook the spinach in 1 can of the chicken broth until tender, about 5 minutes. Drain. Add the remaining can of chicken broth and the cooked chicken to the pan, and cook over low heat for 2 to 3 minutes.

Cook the pasta according to package directions and drain. Add to the chicken mixture along with sun dried tomatoes, artichokes and green onions. Place on a serving platter and sprinkle with basil and Romano.

Toss lightly and serve.

Lynn B. Popovich

131

Fettuccine with Shrimp, Artichokes and Red Chile Pepper

"Simple and elegant"

Easy
Serves: 2
Preparation: 10 min.
Cooking: 25 min.

1   **10-oz. can artichokes hearts, drained**

2   **lg. shallots, finely chopped**

½   **cup chicken broth**

2   **tsp. finely chopped fresh thyme**

½   **tsp. crushed red pepper**

salt

1¼ **lbs. raw shrimp, peeled, deveined, with tails intact**

½   **cup whipping cream**

1   **Tbsp. butter**

2   **Tbsp. fresh lemon juice**

¾   **tsp. freshly grated lemon peel**

8   **oz. fettuccine, cooked and drained**

lemon wedges

cracked pepper

Cut artichokes into quarters. In a large skillet, combine artichokes, shallots, broth, thyme, red pepper and salt to taste. Bring to a boil and simmer for 5 minutes. Remove vegetables from skillet with a slotted spoon. Set aside. Add shrimp to skillet and cook for 2–3 minutes. Transfer shrimp to vegetable mixture.

Reduce liquid to about 1 tablespoon. Add cream and cook until thickened. Stir in butter, lemon juice and peel. Add shrimp and vegetable mixture to sauce. Pour over cooked fettuccine and gently toss.

Serve with lemon wedges and cracked pepper.

Sharon Schaefer

Linguini with Clams and Sun Dried Tomatoes

Serves: 3–4
Easy
Preparation: 15 min.
Cooking: 15 min.

2   6½-oz. cans chopped or
    minced clams

1   med. onion, chopped

2   cloves garlic, minced

¼   tsp. crushed red pepper

2   Tbsp. olive oil

½   cup dry white wine

⅓   cup oil packed sun
    dried tomatoes,
    drained, cut into strips

2   Tbsp. finely chopped
    fresh parsley

8   oz. linguini, cooked and
    drained

Drain clams, reserving liquid. In a medium saucepan over low heat, cook onion, garlic and red pepper in the olive oil until the onion is translucent. Stir in wine and reserved clam liquid. Bring to a boil; cook 10 minutes, or until the sauce is reduced to 1 cup.

Stir in the clams, tomatoes and parsley. Heat through and spoon over the linguini.

Kathy Winberg

133

Pasta with Anchovies and Bread Crumbs
"Make this for your favorite anchovy lover"

Easy
Serves: 4–6
Preparation: 15 min.
Cooking: 6 min.

½   cup extra virgin olive
    oil, divided

1   cup plain bread crumbs

5–6 cloves garlic, minced

1   2-oz. can anchovies, in
    olive oil

1   bunch broccoli florets,
    lightly steamed

1   lb. linguine, cooked and
    drained

Heat ¼ cup olive oil in a large skillet. Add bread crumbs; sauté over low to medium heat. Stir to absorb oil. Continue to cook until lightly toasted. Remove from heat.

Heat ¼ cup olive oil in a large skillet. Add garlic, being careful not to burn. Once garlic begins to brown, remove it from oil; add the can of anchovies with oil. Over low to medium heat, using a fork, mash anchovies and continue to stir. Add anchovy mixture to drained pasta. Add bread crumbs to pasta, then broccoli florets. Toss well and serve.

Jennifer Otto Giotto

Oriental Noodles
"A wonderful picnic item served with fruit salad"

Easy
Serves: 6–8
Preparation: 25 min.
Can be made ahead

2   chicken breasts, boned, skinned, poached, cooled, and cut into strips
5   oz. sliced baked ham, cut into strips
1   bunch green onions, chopped
½   cup chopped walnuts
1   lb. thin vermicelli, cooked al dente, drained, rinsed, cooled
1   cup vegetable oil
2½ Tbsp. sesame seeds
¾   cup soy sauce
1   tsp. hot chile oil

Put first 5 ingredients into a large bowl and set aside. In a smaller bowl, make the dressing by mixing the next four ingredients. Pour the dressing over the mixture in the larger bowl. Use just enough dressing to coat the vermicelli. Refrigerate. This is best done the day ahead and tossed periodically. Serve cold.

For variety, heat the oils and seeds in a pan over medium heat until the seeds are lightly browned, cool 5 minutes, then add the soy sauce. Try adding more chicken to the recipe to create an entrée.

Joyce A. Scalercio

Sesame Pasta
"Smooth and spicy"

Easy
Serves: 6
Preparation: 20 min.
Cooking: 15 min.
Can be made ahead

3   cloves garlic, minced
1   Tbsp. red wine vinegar
1   Tbsp. brown sugar
6   Tbsp. creamy peanut butter
¼   cup soy sauce
6   Tbsp. sesame oil
2   Tbsp. hot chile oil
1   lb. linguine, cooked and drained
8   Tbsp. sesame seeds, toasted, divided
6   green onions, chopped

Place garlic, vinegar, brown sugar, peanut butter and soy sauce in food processor. Process for 1 minute. With the motor running, slowly add the sesame and hot chile oils through the feed tube. Process until well blended.

Toss sauce with the linguine. Add 6 tablespoons of the sesame seeds, tossing to coat well. Sprinkle with remaining 2 tablespoons of sesame seeds and green onions. Serve at room temperature.

Sheila M. Fillip-Gordon

Penne with Tomatoes and Two Cheeses
"Make the sauce ahead, and you have a deliciously rich main dish in no time."

Moderately difficult
Serves: 6
Preparation: 10 min.
Cooking: 1 hr. 50 min.
Can be made ahead

6 Tbsp. olive oil

1 onion, chopped

1 clove garlic, minced

3 28-oz. cans Italian plum tomatoes, drained

2 tsp. dried basil

1½ tsp. crushed red pepper

2 cups chicken broth

salt and pepper

1 lb. penne pasta, cooked and drained

2½ cups grated Havarti cheese

⅓ cup pitted brine cured olives, halved

⅓ cup grated Parmesan cheese

Preheat oven to 375°.

Heat oil in a Dutch oven. Add onion and garlic and sauté over medium heat for about 5 minutes. Mix in the tomatoes, basil, red pepper and broth; bring to a boil. Break up the tomatoes. Lower heat and simmer until the mixture begins to thicken and is reduced to about 6 cups, about 1 hour. Season with salt and pepper. The sauce can be made ahead to this point, and will keep in the refrigerator for about 2 days.

Reheat sauce on low heat and toss with pasta. Add the Havarti cheese and toss again. Transfer pasta to a 13"x9" glass baking dish, sprinkle with olives and Parmesan cheese and bake about 30 minutes.

Mary Jo Hottenstein

135

Pasta with Asiago Cheese and Spinach

Easy
Serves: 8
Preparation: 45 min.
Cooking: 15 min.

3   **cups boiling water**

4   **oz. sun dried tomatoes, packed without oil**

2   **Tbsp. extra virgin olive oil**

⅛   **tsp. salt**

pepper

2   **cloves garlic, minced**

12   **oz. penne or fusilli, cooked and drained**

1   **10-oz. bag fresh spinach, torn**

¾   **cup grated Asiago cheese**

½   **cup finely grated Parmesan cheese**

Combine boiling water and sun dried tomatoes in a bowl; let stand 30 minutes. Drain and chop.

Combine tomatoes, oil, salt, pepper and garlic in a large bowl. Add the pasta and spinach and gently toss. Sprinkle with the cheeses and toss gently again.

Serve with crusty bread or as a side dish.

Cheryl Dea Kaufman

Pasta with Uncooked Tomatoes, Basil and Mozzarella
"Make this in the summer with your garden tomatoes"

Easy
Serves: 6–8
Preparation: 15 min.
Cooking: 15 min.
Must be made ahead

1½   **lbs. (about 3 cups) tomatoes, chopped**

3   **cloves garlic, minced**

½   **cup fresh basil, coarsely chopped**

1   **cup diced mozzarella cheese**

½   **cup extra virgin olive oil**

2   **Tbsp. red wine vinegar**

salt and pepper

crushed pepper, optional

1   **lb. pasta**

Combine all ingredients except pasta in a bowl. Season to taste. Cover and let stand 1 to 4 hours.

Cook and drain pasta. Toss with tomato mixture and serve.

Mary Lou Scarfone

Linguine with Macadamia Pesto
"The macadamia nuts give this pesto pizzaz"

Moderately difficult
Serves: 8
Preparation: 30 min.
Cooking: 25 min.
Can be made ahead

3　cups basil leaves

1　cup olive oil

¾　cup roasted macadamia
　　nuts

6　garlic cloves, peeled

1¼ cups freshly grated
　　Parmesan cheese

salt and pepper

2　lg. red peppers

2　lbs. linguine

2　Tbsp. olive oil

chopped macadamia nuts
for garnish

grated Parmesan cheese
for garnish

To prepare the pesto, puree the basil, olive oil, macadamia nuts and garlic in a processor. Add the Parmesan cheese and process until well incorporated. Season with salt and pepper to taste.

Roast the red peppers over a gas flame or under a broiler until the skin is blackened. Place in a paper bag and let steam for 15 minutes. Remove the skins and seeds and discard. Cut the peppers into thin slices.

Cook and drain linguine. Add 2 tablespoons of olive oil.

To serve, spoon the pasta into individual bowls, drizzle with pesto and top with red peppers.

Garnish with chopped macadamia nuts and grated Parmesan.

Allison M. Miller

137

Orzo with Red Pepper and Mushrooms
"Wonderful with veal or chicken"

Easy
Serves: 4
Preparation: 10 min.
Cooking: 15 min.

1   Tbsp. olive oil
1   tsp. butter
½   cup chopped onion
½   cup chopped red pepper
8   oz. sliced mushrooms
2   cups chicken broth
1   cup orzo
3   Tbsp. toasted pine nuts
2   Tbsp. finely chopped fresh basil or Italian parsley
salt and pepper

Heat oil and butter in a large saucepan. Add the onion, peppers and mushrooms; sauté until tender, about 10 minutes. Add chicken broth and bring to a boil. Stir in the orzo and reduce heat to medium low. Be careful not to burn. Cover and simmer until the orzo is tender and all the liquid is absorbed, stirring occasionally, about 15 minutes.

While the orzo is cooking, toast the pine nuts in a sauté pan over medium low heat. Do not burn.

Remove the orzo from the heat and stir in the nuts and minced basil or parsley. Season with salt and pepper to taste, and serve.

Jane Ellen Rabe

Spinach and Cannellini Bean Pasta
"Hearty and healthy"

Easy
Serves: 6
Preparation: 15 min.
Cooking: 15 min.
Can be made ahead

1   Tbsp. olive oil
1   Tbsp. butter
1   med. onion, thinly sliced
8   cloves garlic, minced
2   lbs. fresh spinach, cleaned, stems removed
1   rounded tsp. chicken base
1   14½-oz. can cannellini beans, undrained
salt and pepper
½   tsp. dried basil
2   tsp. dried parsley
¼   cup Romano cheese
1   lb. pasta, cooked and drained

Heat olive oil and butter in a sauté pan. Add onion and garlic and sauté until soft. Add the spinach and cook until wilted. Add the chicken base, beans, salt and pepper; simmer for 10 minutes. Stir in the Romano cheese. Spoon over the prepared pasta and serve.

Sunni P. Jenkins

Mediterranean Pie

"A light dish with a robust flavor"

Moderately difficult
Serves: 6
Preparation: 40 min.
Cooking: 50 min.
Can be made ahead

Pie Crust:
2½ cups flour

1 tsp. dried Herbes de Provence

¼ tsp. salt

¾ cup (1½ sticks) chilled butter, cut into ½" cubes

8–12 Tbsp. ice water

Filling:

1 Tbsp. olive oil

1 lg. yellow onion, diced

2 cloves garlic, minced

2 Tbsp. tomato puree

2 Tbsp. ready made pesto

12 oz. feta cheese, sliced

1 12-oz. pkg. frozen, chopped spinach, thawed, drained

2 Tbsp. capers

4 oil packed, sun dried tomatoes, sliced

2 Tbsp. pine nuts

2 tomatoes, sliced

1 egg yolk mixed with a little milk

Preheat oven to 400°.

Pie Crust:
Place flour, herbs and salt in the bowl of a food processor and process for a few seconds. Add chilled butter and process until the mixture resembles coarse meal. Add enough ice water so that when you process, a ball will just begin to form on the blade. Remove and shape into a ball. Wrap tightly with plastic wrap and refrigerate for 15 minutes. Divide the dough in half and roll each into a round. Place one round in the bottom of a deep tart pan with removable bottom, or deep pie plate. Bake for 5 minutes and remove from the oven.

Filling:
Heat oil in a large skillet; sauté onion and garlic over medium heat until soft, about 3 minutes. Transfer to a bowl. Mix spinach, capers, sun dried tomatoes and pine nuts into onion mixture. Set aside. In another bowl, mix pesto and tomato puree together; spread half over crust. Spread half of onion mixture, top with layer of half the tomatoes and half of the feta slices. Repeat layers and place remaining round of piecrust over top, sealing edges. Brush with egg yolk mixture.

Bake 40 to 50 minutes.

Amanda Dunn

Tomato and Basil Pie

"A gift from the summer garden"

Easy
Serves: 4–8
Preparation: 20 min.
Cooking: 40 min.

1 **9" prepared pie crust, unbaked**

1½ **cups shredded mozzarella cheese, divided**

5 **plum, or 4 med. tomatoes**

1 **cup loosely packed fresh basil leaves**

4 **cloves garlic**

½ **cup mayonnaise**

¼ **cup grated Parmesan cheese**

⅛ **tsp. ground white pepper**

additional basil for garnish

Preheat oven to 375°.

Unfold the pie crust, and place in a 9" quiche or pie plate. Flute the edges or press with fork tines. Pre-bake according to the package directions. Remove from oven and sprinkle with ½ cup of the mozzarella cheese. Cool on a wire rack.

Cut tomatoes into wedges, and drain on paper towels. Arrange the wedges on top of the melted cheese in the baked shell. In a food processor, combine the basil and garlic, processing until coarsely chopped. Sprinkle over the tomatoes.

In a medium mixing bowl, combine the remaining mozzarella cheese, mayonnaise, Parmesan and pepper.

Spoon cheese mixture over basil mixture, spreading to evenly cover the top.

Bake for 35 to 40 minutes, or until the top is golden and bubbly. Serve warm garnished with basil leaves.

Laurel E. Echavarria

140

Sweet Onion Pie
"Inhale the heavenly aroma"

Easy
Serves: 6
Preparation: 30 min.
Cooking: 30 min.
Can be made ahead

1   9" prepared pie crust, unbaked

4   onions, Vidalia if available, thinly sliced

1   Tbsp. olive oil

3   Tbsp. butter

2   eggs

1   cup half-and-half

2   Tbsp. flour

1   tsp. salt

⅛   tsp. pepper

pinch of nutmeg

2   oz. grated Swiss cheese, divided

Preheat oven to 375°.

Place pie crust into a flan dish and prick the bottom and sides with a fork. Line pastry with aluminum foil. Fill with dried beans to keep pastry flat. Bake for 15 minutes; remove foil and bake additional 10 minutes, until pastry is lightly browned. Set aside.

Sauté onions in oil and butter. In a bowl beat the eggs, half-and-half, flour, salt, pepper and nutmeg. Add onions and half of the grated cheese. Pour this mixture into the prepared crust and sprinkle with the remaining cheese. Bake for 25 to 30 minutes, or until filling is set.

Kitty Gross

141

Cindy's Delicious Garden Quiche

Easy
Serves: 6
Preparation: 20 min.
Cooking: 25 min.

1   sm. eggplant, chopped into ½" pieces
1   cup chopped onion
1   clove garlic, minced
3   Tbsp. oil
1   sm. zucchini, sliced
1   tsp. dried oregano
½   tsp. salt
½   tsp. pepper
3   ripe tomatoes, seeded, chopped
3   eggs
8   oz. mozzarella cheese, grated, divided
¼   cup grated Parmesan cheese

Preheat oven to 375°.

Butter a 9" pie plate.

Heat oil in a large skillet. Add eggplant, onion and garlic. Cook until soft, about 10 minutes. Stir in the zucchini, oregano, salt, pepper and tomatoes. Cook over medium heat until all liquid has evaporated.

Beat the eggs and stir in the vegetable mixture and half the mozzarella cheese. Spoon into the prepared pie plate and top with the remaining mozzarella and Parmesan cheese.

Bake for 25 minutes until filling is golden and center is set. Let rest for 10 minutes before slicing.

Cindy Capo

Roasted Vegetable Tarts
"Beautiful and delicious"

Easy
Serves: 6
Preparation: 30 min.
Cooking: 20–25 min.

1   **med. eggplant, sliced ¼" thick**

2   **med. portobello mushrooms, caps only, sliced**

2   **med. shallots, thinly sliced**

1   **med. red pepper, cut into ½" dice**

1   **med. zucchini, sliced crosswise, ¼" thick**

2   **Tbsp. olive oil**

salt and pepper

4   **oz. Roquefort or blue cheese, crumbled**

3   **oz. cream cheese, softened**

1   **lg. egg**

1   **Tbsp. Parmesan cheese**

2   **9" prepared pie crusts**

Preheat oven to 450°.

Use 2 baking sheets.

In a large roasting pan, toss the vegetables with olive oil, salt and pepper. Roast vegetables for 12–14 minutes, stirring occasionally, until softened.

Using a handheld mixer, beat crumbled cheese and cream cheese until smooth. Add egg and Parmesan. Beat until blended.

Place 1 pie crust on each baking sheet. Unfold and pinch together any tears. Divide cheese mixture between the crusts and spread over tops. Arrange roasted vegetables on top. Fold the dough up to partially cover the filing, crimping to seal the edges. Bake for 20–25 minutes.

Nathalie and Mario Lemieux
Pittsburgh Penguins

143

Breakfast Casserole

Easy
Serves: 10–12
Preparation: 30 min.
Cooking: 50–55 min.
Must be prepared ahead

2½ cups seasoned croutons

1   lb. sausage roll

4   eggs

2¼ cups milk

1   10-oz. can condensed cream of mushroom soup

1   10-oz. pkg. frozen chopped spinach, thawed and squeezed dry

1   4-oz. can mushrooms, drained and chopped

1   cup shredded sharp Cheddar cheese

1   cup shredded Monterey Jack cheese

¼   tsp. dry mustard

Preheat oven to 325°.

Grease a 13"x9" baking dish.

Spread croutons on bottom of baking dish. Crumble sausage in a skillet. Cook until browned, stirring occasionally. Drain off grease. Spread sausage over croutons.

Whisk eggs and milk until blended. Stir in soup, spinach, mushrooms, cheeses and mustard. Pour mixture over sausage and croutons. Refrigerate overnight.

Bake casserole for 50–55 minutes, or until set and lightly browned.

Betty

Turkey Omelet Casserole
"Wake up and bake it"

Easy
Serves: 6–8
Preparation: 20 min.
Cooking: 45–50 min.
Must be made ahead

2   lbs. turkey sausage

1   24-oz. pkg. frozen hash brown potatoes

2   cups grated Cheddar cheese

6   eggs

2   cups skim milk

1   tsp. salt

1   tsp. dry mustard

½   tsp. pepper

Preheat oven to 350°.

In a large skillet, brown turkey sausage. Coat a 13"x9" pan with cooking spray. Arrange potatoes on bottom. Cover with sausage and sprinkle with grated cheese.

In a blender, mix eggs, milk and spices. Pour mixture over cheese and refrigerate overnight.

Bake for 45–50 minutes.

Joanne Hyatt Striebel

144

Gorgonzola Cheesecake
"Don't deny yourself this sumptuous dish"

Easy
Serves: 6–8
Preparation: 30 min.
Cooking: 1 hr.

¾ cup toasted bread crumbs

¾ cup toasted walnuts, finely chopped

3 Tbsp. unsalted butter, melted

¾ lb. Gorgonzola cheese, crumbled

1¼ lb. cream cheese, room temperature

4 eggs

1 med. garlic clove, minced

¼ tsp. finely chopped fresh or dried tarragon

Preheat oven to 350°.

Butter and flour an 8" springform pan.

Mix bread crumbs, walnuts and butter. Press into the bottom and sides of the prepared pan. Set aside.

Using an electric mixer, beat the Gorgonzola with the cream cheese until smooth. Add eggs one at a time, beating after each addition. Add garlic and tarragon. Combine well. Pour into the springform pan. Bake 60 minutes.

The cake should be golden and set in the center. Remove from oven and let stand for 30 minutes before serving.

Lucille B. Cardone

145

Blintz Loaf
"This makes brunch a breeze"

Easy
Serves: 8
Preparation: 15 min.
Cooking: 40 min.

½ cup (1 stick) butter, melted

1 lb. cottage cheese

½ cup Bisquick

3 Tbsp. sugar

3 eggs

Preheat oven to 350°.

Grease a 9"x5" loaf pan.

Using an electric mixer, combine melted butter with cheese. Slowly add Bisquick, followed by sugar. Add eggs one at a time.

Pour into a prepared pan and bake for 40 minutes.

David Johnson
WPXI TV

Light Entrees

Cheese Cake Kugel

"Wonderful for brunch, or a sensational side dish"

Easy
Serves: 8
Preparation: 20 min.
Cooking: 1 hr. 10 min.

cooking spray

2 8-oz. pkg. cream cheese, softened

2 cups small curd cottage cheese

1 cup sugar

1 pt. sour cream

1 tsp. vanilla

6 eggs

¼ cup (½ stick) butter, softened

1 lb. fine noodles, cooked and drained

Topping:
1 cup graham cracker crumbs

3 Tbsp. butter, melted

1 Tbsp. powdered sugar

Preheat oven to 350°.

Coat 13"x9" glass pan with cooking spray.

Mix all cake ingredients in a mixer. Fold the noodles into the ingredients. Place in pan and bake for 1 hour.

Topping:
Mix all ingredients and spread on top of kugel. Bake for 10 minutes more.

Dolly Landay

The Reese's Cheese Fondue

"Great fun for family and friends"

Easy
Serves: 6
Preparation: 10 min.
Cooking: 20 min.

⅓ cup margarine

¼ cup flour

1 tsp. sweet hot mustard

1 tsp. Worcestershire sauce

dash of salt

12 oz. beer

½ lb. Swiss cheese, grated

½ lb. Cheddar cheese, grated

bread cubes for serving

In a heavy saucepan, melt margarine and stir in flour. Add mustard, Worcestershire sauce and salt. Gradually add beer and continue stirring until mixture thickens and comes to a boil. Add cheese a handful at a time. Stir until melted and smooth.

Serve in a fondue pot with bread cubes for dipping.

Virginia L. Reese

146

Manicotti

Moderately difficult
Serves: 6
Preparation: 30 min.
Cooking: 25 min.

Crepes:
1   cup flour
½   cup water
½   cup milk
¼   tsp. salt
4   eggs
Filling:
1   lb. ricotta cheese
salt and pepper
chopped parsley to taste
grated Romano cheese, to taste
mozzarella, cut into thin strips
your favorite tomato sauce

Preheat oven to 350°.

Blend all crepe ingredients until smooth. Lightly grease an 8" non-stick skillet or crepe pan. Set over medium low heat. Pour in just enough batter to make a thin pancake, swirling to spread batter evenly. When the center is firm, lift by the edge and turn to cook on the second side for a few seconds. Pancakes are just cooked, not browned. Using a sheet of waxed paper between each crepe, stack on a plate and refrigerate until ready to fill.

Mix ricotta, salt, pepper and parsley. Spread a heaping tablespoon of ricotta mixture in the center of a pancake. Place two or three strips of mozzarella on top, sprinkle with Romano cheese and roll up, forming a tube. Spread tomato sauce on the bottom of a 13"x9" baking dish. Fill the pan with the rolled up manicotti, pour more sauce on top, sprinkle with grated Romano and bake for about 25 minutes.

Chris Fennimore
WQED TV

147

Grilled Portobello Sandwich

"A lucious lunch or a light supper"

Easy
Preparation: 15 min.
Serves: 1
Marinate: 24–36 hrs.
Cooking: 5 min.

4   oz. balsamic vinegar
16 oz. Italian dressing
5   oz. portobello mushrooms
3   ¼" slices zucchini
3   ¼" slices yellow squash
4   ½" slices tomato
1   focaccia bread, 6" long 4" wide, cut in half horizontally
3   slices Fontinella cheese, 3" long and ½" wide each

Preheat grill on high.

Mix vinegar and Italian dressing. Add mushrooms, zucchini and yellow squash. Marinate for 24–36 hours.

Remove marinated vegetables from dressing and wipe off excess. Reserve marinade. Add tomato slices to reserved marinade. Place vegetables in a grill basket and grill until lightly browned on both sides. Remove cooked vegetables and grill tomato slices in the same way.

Cover the focaccia with alternate layers of vegetables, followed by cheese slices and tomato slices.

Michael Geiger

Cheese, Walnut and Pear Tea Sandwiches

"The pears and cheese were made for each other"

Moderately difficult
Serves: 4–6
Preparation: 20 min.

½   cup walnuts
4   Tbsp. cream cheese
2   Tbsp. blue cheese
6   thin slices of 7 grain bread, crusts removed
2–3 Tbsp. butter
½   pear, cored and sliced into 12 thin slices

Preheat broiler.

Toast walnuts under broiler and chop finely. Place both cheeses in a small bowl and mash with a fork until they are soft and combined. Spread each slice of bread with a thin coating of butter. Divide the cheese equally among 3 slices of bread. Gently spread the cheese.

Sprinkle a heaping tablespoon of walnuts over the cheese on each slice. Place 4 slices of pear on each sandwich. Top with the remaining bread slices and press down firmly. Cut each sandwich into 4 sections.

Theresa T. Newell

Lamb Sandwich with Feta and Cucumbers

Easy
Serves: 6
Preparation: 40 min.
Cooking: 30 min.

6   oz. feta cheese

3   Tbsp. extra virgin oil, divided

2   Tbsp. fresh lemon juice

salt and freshly ground pepper

1   cucumber, peeled, halved lengthwise, seeded and finely chopped

½   sm. red onion, finely chopped

1   Tbsp. finely chopped fresh mint

1   Tbsp. finely chopped fresh parsley

1   Tbsp. fresh dill

1½–2 lb. boneless leg of lamb, butterflied

6   pita breads, 5" in diameter, cut in half

salt and pepper

Preheat broiler or grill.

To make the salad, crumble feta into a bowl; add 2 tablespoons olive oil, lemon juice and salt and pepper to taste. Using a fork, mash thoroughly. Stir in the cucumber, onion, mint, parsley and dill. Set aside.

Brush lamb with 1 tablespoon olive oil. Place on grill rack or broiler pan. Grill or broil 4" from heat until brown on one side, about 15 minutes. Turn and cook until brown on the other side, about 15 more minutes. A thermometer inserted into the thickest portion should register 130°–135° for medium rare, or until meat is slightly pink when cut with a knife. Transfer the lamb to a cutting board, cover with aluminum foil and let rest for 10 minutes before carving.

Preheat oven to 350°.

Wrap pita halves in aluminum foil, place in oven and heat until warm, about 10 minutes. Slice the meat diagonally against the grain. Season to taste with salt and pepper. Open pita pockets and evenly distribute lamb and feta and cucumber salad among the halves. Place 2 half sandwiches on each plate and serve immediately.

Daniel J. Dooley
Executive Chef
Penn Brewery

149

Grilled Chicken and Pepper Sandwich

"A savory summer sandwich"

Moderately difficult
Serves: 6
Preparation: 1 hr.
Marinate: 6 hrs.
Cooking: 45 min.

6   chicken breasts, boned and skinned

5   Tbsp. olive oil, divided

1   Tbsp. cracked black pepper

2   Tbsp. chopped fresh thyme

2   red peppers

Sauce:

½   cup mayonnaise

¼   cup Dijon mustard

1   tsp. Worcestershire sauce

1   tsp. red wine vinegar

dash of salt

3   tomatoes, sliced

1   bunch arugula leaves

6   Kaiser rolls

Preheat grill.

Preheat oven to 500°.

Rub chicken breasts with 3 tablespoons olive oil, pepper and thyme. Cover and refrigerate at least 6 hours, preferably overnight. Remove from refrigerator 1 hour before cooking.

Grill or broil chicken breasts 6–10 minutes each side. Transfer to a platter and let cool slightly.

Place peppers directly on the oven rack and roast. Turn peppers occasionally until the skins are charred, about 20–30 minutes. Place peppers in a paper bag and seal top until cool. Remove the skins with your fingers. Core, seed and slice into ¼" strips. Toss peppers with the remaining olive oil and store in a glass container until ready to use.

Sauce:

Mix mayonnaise, mustard, Worcestershire sauce, vinegar and salt. Refrigerate until needed.

To assemble sandwich, spread a liberal amount of the sauce on one side of a Kaiser roll. Slice the breasts diagonally and place each breast on a roll. Top with roasted pepper strips, slices of tomato and arugula, and top with roll.

Debra Gibbs

Zesty Dijon Marinade

"This, versatile, fat-free marinade is a great way to perk up your favorite fish"

Easy
Serves: 4
Preparation: 5 min.
Cooking: 15 min.

1   **cup balsamic vinegar**
½   **cup Dijon mustard**
½   **tsp. ground black pepper**
¼   **tsp. salt**
2   **cloves garlic, minced**

Combine all ingredients in a glass or plastic bowl. Stir well.

Great used on swordfish or blue fish. Marinate for 1 hour before broiling or grilling.

Tom and Megan Barrasso
Pittsburgh Penguins

Dijon Mustard Sauce

"Perfect with pork"

Easy
Preparation: 10 min.
Cooking: 15 min.

½   **cup half-and-half**
½   **cup sour cream**
6   **Tbsp. Dijon mustard**
1   **tsp. Worcestershire sauce**
½   **tsp. salt**
1   **tsp. pepper**
1   **tsp. cayenne pepper**
1   **tsp. finely chopped, fresh basil or ½ tsp. dried**

Combine all ingredients in a saucepan. Stir frequently over low heat until thickened. Simmer but do not boil.

Jane Ellen Rabe

Hot Mustard Sauce

"Sweet, savory and spicy"

Easy
Makes: 1½ cups
Preparation: 20 min.
Cooking: 10–15 min.
Must be made ahead

½ cup dry mustard

⅓ cup sugar

½ cup cider vinegar

2 eggs

2 Tbsp. unsalted butter, softened

Combine mustard and sugar in top of double boiler. Add vinegar. Add eggs one at a time. Remove from heat and beat in butter using a wire whisk.

Serve chilled with ham or filet.

Marta R. McDonald

Horseradish Sauce

152

Easy
Makes: 1 cup
Preparation: 5 min.
Must be made ahead

1 cup sour cream

2 Tbsp. mayonnaise

4 Tbsp. horseradish

1 Tbsp. finely chopped parsley

Combine all ingredients. Chill for 1 hour. Serve with beef.

Marta R. McDonald

Mint Sauce for Lamb

Easy
Cooking time: 15 min.
Can be made ahead

½ cup (1 stick) butter

1 cup currant jelly

3 Tbsp. mint sauce

¾ cup chili sauce

Melt butter in a double boiler. Add the currant jelly, mint sauce and chili sauce. Heat for approximately 10 minutes. May be kept in the refrigerator for a few weeks.

Frances M. Rollman

Tomato Coulis

Easy
Serves: 10
Preparation: 20 min.
Cooking: 20 min.
Can be frozen

1 tsp. olive oil
1 tsp. minced garlic
2 med. shallots, minced
1 tsp. finely chopped
    fresh basil
1 tsp. finely chopped
    fresh chives
3 med. tomatoes, peeled,
    seeded and chopped
1 roasted red pepper,
    chopped

½ cup tomato sauce
1 cup chicken broth
1 Tbsp. sugar
1 Tbsp. red wine vinegar
salt and pepper

Place olive oil in a medium pot and sauté garlic, shallots, basil and chives. Let simmer for a few minutes. Add the tomatoes, red pepper, tomato sauce, chicken broth, sugar, and red wine vinegar and simmer 15 to 20 minutes.

Put the sauce in a food processor and puree until smooth. Season to taste.

Guy Chappie
Green Oaks Country Club

153

Mango and Avocado Salsa
"Fresh and flavorful for chicken or fish"

Easy
Serves: 6
Preparation: 15 min.
Can be made ahead

2 lg. mangos, halved,
    pitted, peeled, diced
1 ripe avocado, halved,
    pitted, peeled, diced
½ fresh jalapeño pepper,
    seeded, minced
⅓ cup diced red onion
¼ cup fresh cilantro,
    finely chopped
3 Tbsp. fresh lime juice
¼ cup orange juice
2 Tbsp. olive oil
salt and pepper

Combine all ingredients and mix well. Season to taste with salt and pepper.

Spoon over fish or chicken just prior to serving. Salsa will keep in the refrigerator for up to a week.

Tom and Megan Barrasso
Pittsburgh Penguins

Real Texas Salsa

"Spoon this mixture over almost anything"

Easy
Serves: 30
Preparation: 15 min.
Can be made ahead

5   lbs. Italian plum
    tomatoes
4   tsp. seasoned salt
4   lg. green onions
2½ tsp. ground cumin
1   Tbsp. fresh oregano, or
    1 tsp. dried
¼   tsp. fresh ground
    pepper
¾   cup fresh cilantro,
    firmly packed
2   Tbsp. fresh parsley, or
    2 tsp. dried
3   fresh jalapeño peppers
juice of 1 lemon
salt and pepper
4   cloves garlic
½   cup oil

154

Place all ingredients, except oil, in food processor and process on pulse until finely chopped. Pour in the oil. Adjust seasonings to taste. Serve or refrigerate.

Use as a sauce over fish, chicken, pork or beef.

Sunni P. Jenkins

Spiced Peaches

Easy
Serves: 12
Preparation: 30 min.
Cooking: 5 min.
Must be made ahead

2   lg. cans peach halves
½   cup vinegar
2–3 sticks cinnamon
¼   tsp. whole allspice
¼   cup sugar
4   whole cloves

Drain peaches, reserving syrup.

Bring vinegar, cinnamon sticks, allspice, sugar and cloves to a boil in a saucepan and cook 5 minutes. Put the peaches in a quart jar with the vinegar mixture, pouring enough liquid over them to come to within ¼" of the rim of the jar. You may need to add some reserved syrup. Refrigerate. Best if made at least 24 hours ahead of serving.

The Reverend Laura Y. Theis

Cranberry Chutney

"Use this as a sauce or side dish"

Easy
Makes: 4 cups
Preparation: 10 min.
Cooking: 30 min.
Can be made ahead

1   lb. cranberries
1   cup seedless raisins
1⅔ cups sugar
1   Tbsp. cinnamon
1½ tsp. ginger
¼   tsp. cloves
1   cup water
1   med. apple, peeled, chopped
½   cup thinly sliced celery
1   med. onion, chopped

Combine cranberries, raisins, sugar and spices with water. Cook for 15 minutes, or until cranberries pop. Stir in the apple, celery and onion and simmer 15 minutes more, or until the mixture thickens. Cool and refrigerate.

Carolyn S. Hammer

155

Curried Fruit
"Delicious over chicken and rice"

Easy
Serves: 6
Preparation: 15 min.
Cooking: 1 hr.
Can be made ahead

- ¼ cup (½ stick) butter
- 1 tsp. curry powder
- ¾ cup brown sugar
- 1 15-oz. can pineapple chunks, drained
- 1 15-oz. can peach halves or slices, drained
- 1 15-oz. can pear halves or slices, drained
- 1 sm. jar of maraschino cherries

Preheat oven to 350°.

Melt the butter in a saucepan. Add the curry and sugar and simmer until they are completely dissolved.

Arrange the drained fruit in an oven-proof baking dish. Pour the butter mixture over the fruit. Bake for 1 hour.

Pamela Wright

156

John Heinz's Stuffing

Easy
Preparation: 20 min.

- ¼ cup (½ stick) butter
- 5 cloves garlic, minced
- 1 lg. onion, chopped
- ½ cup chopped celery
- pinch of thyme, marjoram, sage and pepper
- 6–8 cups bread cubes
- 2 cups vegetable broth
- ½ cup toasted pine nuts
- ½ cup apple, chopped
- ½ cup water chestnuts
- ½ cup dried apricots

Melt butter in a heavy skillet. Sauté garlic, onion and celery. Add herbs. Mix in remaining ingredients.

Use to stuff poultry or pork.

Theresa Heinz

Vegetables & Side Dishes

Stuffed Zucchini
"Snappy taste"

Easy
Serves: 6–8
Preparation: 30 min.
Cooking: 30 min.

4   med. zucchini
¼   cup chopped onion
1   Tbsp. butter
¼   tsp. dried basil
1   tsp. salt
⅛   tsp. pepper
1   egg, beaten
2   Tbsp. butter, melted
1½ cups crushed crisp rice cereal
½   cup Parmesan cheese

Preheat oven to 350°.

Cut the zucchini in half and steam for about 5 minutes. Cool, scoop out the flesh, chop and set aside. Save shells. While the zucchini are cooking, sauté onion in butter and add seasonings. Add the chopped zucchini to the onion mixture along with the beaten egg. Put this filling in the zucchini shells.

Mix melted butter with cereal and cheese and sprinkle on top of the zucchini boats. Bake for 30 minutes, or until the cereal is golden brown.

Mary South Gaab

Zucchini Fritters
"Terrific as a side dish or an entree"

Easy
Serves: 8
Preparation: 25 min.
Cooking: 10 min.
Can be made ahead

2   zucchini, shredded
½   cup ricotta cheese
½   cup Parmesan cheese
3   eggs
2–3 Tbsp. flour to bind ingredients
1   clove garlic, minced
1   tsp. lemon zest
black pepper to taste
1–2 Tbsp. olive oil

Combine all ingredients except oil. Heat a little olive oil in a skillet. Drop large spoonfuls of zucchini batter into the pan, as you would for pancakes, and cook until golden brown.

Serve with lemon, marinara sauce or alone.

Lucy Shoupp

Baked Zucchini and Cheese James
"Try this when zucchini are abundant"

Easy
Serves: 6–8
Preparation: 30 min.
Cooking: 50 min.

3   slices lean bacon, finely chopped

¾   lb. zucchini, coarsely grated (about 3 cups)

1   lg. onion, finely chopped

1   cup grated Cheddar cheese

1   cup self-rising flour

½   cup vegetable oil

5   eggs, lightly beaten

¾   tsp. salt

½   tsp. pepper

Preheat oven to 350°.

Grease an 8"x8" pan.

Fry bacon slowly until transparent. Drain on paper towels.

In a medium bowl, combine the zucchini, onion and bacon. Gently stir in the Cheddar cheese, flour, oil, eggs, salt and pepper. Mix well. Turn into the prepared pan and bake for 40 to 50 minutes, or until golden brown.

Mrs. James H. Alexander

Onion Zucchini Bake

159

"A tasty alternative to potatoes"

Easy
Serves: 4
Preparation: 15 min.
Cooking: 30 min.
Can be frozen

2   lg. sweet onions, thinly sliced

1   Tbsp. oil

4   eggs

1   cup milk

½   cup grated Parmesan cheese

1   med. zucchini, shredded

2   cups chicken flavored stuffing

Preheat oven to 350°.

Grease an 8"x8" pan.

Sauté onions in oil until tender. Do not brown.

In a bowl, mix eggs and milk until blended. Add remaining ingredients, including the onions. Place in the prepared pan. Bake for 30 minutes, or until top is browned.

Monica L. Narr

Balsamic Spaghetti Squash
"Light and tangy"

Easy
Serves: 8
Preparation: 30 min.
Cooking: 10 min.
Can be made ahead

1   med. spaghetti squash
1   med. tomato, chopped
5   Tbsp. finely chopped
    fresh basil

Vinaigrette:
¼   cup balsamic vinegar
3   garlic cloves, minced
2   Tbsp. olive oil
salt and pepper
freshly grated Parmesan
cheese

To cook the squash, pierce in four or five places. Microwave until soft, about 10–12 minutes. Scrape out the cooked squash with a fork, making long strands, and put into a bowl. Add the tomato and basil. Can be made ahead to this point.

Vinaigrette:
Combine vinegar, garlic, oil and salt and pepper to taste. Pour over the squash mixture and gently stir. Sprinkle with cheese and serve at room temperature.

Genny Mozolak

Mexican Squash
"A quick, colorful, casserole"

160

Easy
Serves: 6
Preparation: 25 min.
Cooking: 30 min.
Can be made ahead

5–8 med. yellow squash
4   Tbsp. chopped onion
10 Tbsp. butter, divided
1½ cups shredded Cheddar
    cheese
1   10-oz. can tomatoes
    with green chiles,
    drained
salt and pepper
¾   cup coarsely ground
    cracker crumbs

Preheat oven to 350°.

Butter a 2 qt. casserole.

Peel and slice squash. Sauté squash and chopped onion in 4 tablespoons butter, until tender. Drain squash well and add 4 tablespoons of the butter, cheese, tomatoes with chiles, and salt and pepper to taste.

Stir lightly. Place in the casserole. Melt the remaining 2 tablespoons of butter and toss with the cracker crumbs. Place this mixture on top of the squash and bake for 30 minutes.

Susan D. Brantley

Eggplant Roulades
"Enticing and mouthwatering"

Moderately difficult
Serves: 8
Preparation: 2½ hrs.
Cooking: 20 min.
Can be frozen

1–2 lg. eggplants, peeled, cut into ½" slices, lengthwise

salt

1   15-oz. container part skim ricotta cheese

¼   cup grated Parmesan cheese

2   Tbsp. finely chopped fresh parsley

½   cup shredded mozzarella cheese

cooking spray

1   26-oz. jar marinara sauce

½   cup grated mozzarella cheese

finely chopped parsley

1–1½ lbs.cooked pasta

Preheat oven to 400°.

Sprinkle eggplant slices with salt and layer in a strainer. Weigh down with a plate and let stand 2 hours. Rinse and pat dry with paper towels.

Lightly brush both sides of the eggplant slices with olive oil. Arrange the slices in a single layer on a large baking sheet. Bake until bottoms are lightly browned, about 15 minutes. Remove from oven and cool.

In a small bowl, combine the ricotta, Parmesan, parsley and mozzarella. Spread over each of the cooled eggplant slices and loosely roll from the small end to the large end.

Coat a 13"x9" baking dish with cooking spray. Cover the bottom of the dish with marinara sauce. Gently lay eggplant rolls in the dish. Cover with remaining marinara sauce. Sprinkle with grated mozzarella and parsley. Bake for 20 minutes, or until heated through.

Serve with prepared pasta.

Sunni P. Jenkins

161

Asparagus Soufflé

"For a pretty presentation, save a few tips for garnish"

Easy
Serves: 4
Preparation: 30 min.
Cooking: 30 min.

1   lb. asparagus, trimmed, peeled
½   cup heavy cream
3   eggs
salt to taste

Preheat oven to 400°.

Grease a 6 cup soufflé dish or individual molds..

Steam asparagus for 25 minutes, or until very soft. Place in a food processor with remaining ingredients and puree until smooth. Place in prepared soufflé dish (or individual dishes) and bake for 30 minutes, or until set. Unmold and serve immediately.

Mary Jo Hottenstein

Broccoli Casserole

"Quick and delicious on a busy day"

Easy
Serves: 6–8
Preparation: 20 min.
Cooking: 30 min.
Can be frozen

2   Tbsp. butter, melted
2   Tbsp. flour
¼   tsp. salt
1   3-oz. pkg. cream cheese, softened
¼   cup crumbled blue cheese
1   cup milk
2   10-oz. pkg. frozen chopped broccoli, cooked and drained
⅓   cup finely crushed Ritz crackers (about 10)

Preheat oven to 350°.

Place the melted butter in a medium saucepan. Add flour, salt and cheeses and mix well.

Gradually whisk in the milk. Bring to a boil, stirring constantly, then add broccoli. Pour into buttered casserole dish; top with crackers. Bake 30 minutes.

Ian and Britta Moran
Pittsburgh Penguins

Roasted Lemon Broccoli
"Broccoli at its best"

Easy
Serves: 4
Preparation: 10 min.
Cooking: 15 min.

1¼ lb. head of broccoli to
    yield 1 lb. florets
2 Tbsp. olive oil
salt and pepper
2 Tbsp. pine nuts
2 Tbsp. unsalted butter
1 tsp. minced garlic
½ tsp. grated lemon zest
1–2 Tbsp. fresh lemon
    juice

Preheat oven to 500°.

In a large bowl, toss broccoli florets with olive oil, and salt and pepper to taste. Arrange the broccoli in a single layer on a baking sheet and roast about 12 minutes, turning once.

Meanwhile, toast pine nuts in a dry skillet for 3 minutes. Set aside. Melt 2 tablespoons butter over low heat, then add garlic and lemon zest. Heat about 1 minute, stirring. Let cool slightly and stir in lemon juice.

Place the broccoli in a serving dish, pour lemon butter over it, sprinkle with pine nuts and gently toss. Serve immediately.

Betty B. Kramer

Cauliflower Potato Puree
"Smooth and satisfying"

163

Easy
Serves: 8
Preparation: 20 min.
Cooking: 30 min.

1¼ lbs. cauliflower, cut
    into pieces
1 med. boiling potato,
    peeled, cut into pieces
½ cup whipping cream
½ cup grated Parmesan
    cheese
3 Tbsp. unsalted butter
salt and pepper to taste
lg. pinch of nutmeg

Preheat oven to 325°.

Butter a 2 qt. casserole.

Steam the cauliflower and potatoes until soft, about 12 minutes. Transfer to a food processor. Add cream, Parmesan, butter, salt, pepper and nutmeg. Process until completely smooth. Pour into the prepared casserole and bake for 30 minutes, or until completely heated through.

Betty Ann Morgan

Spinach Cheese Casserole
"This couldn't be easier"

Easy
Serves: 6–8
Preparation: 10 min.
Cooking: 45 min.

Preheat oven to 350°.

Grease a 10" round or 9"x9" square casserole.

2   eggs

6   Tbsp. flour

2   10-oz. pkg. frozen spinach, chopped, cooked and drained well

2   cups cottage cheese

2   cups grated, sharp Cheddar cheese

salt and pepper

Beat eggs to blend and gradually mix with flour. Add spinach, cottage cheese and Cheddar cheese. Mix. Add salt and pepper to taste and mix again. Pour into the prepared casserole and bake for 45 minutes.

Howard and Jean May

Spinach with Shitake Mushrooms
"Full of fresh flavor"

Easy
Serves: 6
Preparation: 30 min.
Cooking: 20 min.

½   tsp. sesame seeds

1½ tsp. unsalted butter

1   Tbsp. olive oil

4   oz. Shitake mushrooms, stems discarded and caps thinly sliced

¼   tsp. salt

2   lbs. spinach, stems trimmed, leaves washed but not dried

salt

freshly ground pepper

In a large skillet, toast sesame seeds over moderate heat, stirring until golden, about 5 minutes.

In a large skillet, melt butter and olive oil over moderately high heat. Add mushrooms, season with salt and cook until softened, about 5 minutes. Remove from skillet. Wipe out skillet with a paper towel. Add the spinach, season with salt and pepper and cook, stirring until all the water has evaporated, about 7 minutes. Stir in the mushrooms. Transfer spinach to a serving dish and sprinkle with toasted sesame seeds. Serve immediately.

Marlene A. Wohleber

Fennel and Mushroom Sauté
"A welcome change of pace"

Easy
Serves: 6
Preparation: 15 min.
Cooking: 15 min.

1   lg. fennel bulb
2   Tbsp. olive oil
2   Tbsp. butter
2   garlic cloves, split in half
1   14½ oz. can Italian plum tomatoes, drained and chopped
¼   cup chicken broth
1   tsp. dried thyme
1   tsp. salt

pepper to taste

1   lb. mushrooms, thinly sliced
2   Tbsp. fine bread crumbs

Parmesan cheese to taste

Cut off upper stalks of the fennel. Slice off bottom of bulb and remove outer layer. Slice the bulb vertically and remove the center core using a V cut. Slice thinly lengthwise and cut slices into 1½" lengths.

In a large sauté pan, heat oil over medium heat, then add butter. To infuse oil, add the garlic, sauté until golden, remove and discard. Add fennel, tomatoes, broth, thyme, salt and pepper. Cover the pan and cook on low, about 10 minutes. Uncover, turn heat to high and add the mushrooms.

Cook, uncovered, stirring constantly, until mushrooms just start to exude juices, about 1 minute. Add the bread crumbs and continue cooking, stirring constantly, until little moisture is left in the bottom of the pan, about 1 minute. Transfer to a platter and serve immediately. Sprinkle with Parmesan cheese, if desired.

Elise Keely Smith

165

Portobello Mushrooms in Sherry Sauce
"Heavenly aroma and flavor"

Easy
Serves: 4
Preparation: 20 min.
Cooking: 10 min.

4   med. portobello
    mushrooms, cleaned
    and stemmed
¼   cup (½ stick) butter
⅔   cup water
2   oz. sliced pimentos
    (roasted red peppers
    may be substituted)
1   cup shredded Asiago
    cheese
¼   cup cream sherry

Preheat oven to 350°.

Butter a small casserole.

In a 12" skillet over medium heat, sauté the portobello mushrooms with the butter and water until they are almost tender. Top the mushrooms with pimentos and Asiago cheese. Add the sherry, cover and simmer until the cheese is melted. Transfer the mushrooms to a casserole and pour sherry sauce on top. Place in the oven, uncovered, and cook until the cheese is golden brown, about 5–10 minutes. Remove and serve.

Nate Kurek

Baked Carrot and Apple Casserole
"Lovely on a crisp, fall evening"

Easy
Serves: 6
Preparation: 30 min.
Cooking: 35 min.
Can be made ahead

6   apples, cored and
    peeled
6   med. carrots, peeled
1   Tbsp. margarine
⅓   cup brown sugar
⅛   tsp. cinnamon
1   Tbsp. flour
½   cup orange juice

Preheat oven to 325°.

Grease a 1½ qt. casserole.

Cut the apples into thin slices and set aside. Cut the carrots diagonally into slices. Melt the margarine and partially cook the carrots over low heat until just tender. Do not overcook. Remove and set aside.

Layer the apples and carrots in the prepared casserole. Blend the brown sugar, cinnamon, flour and orange juice and pour over the layers. Bake uncovered for 35 minutes.

Susan D. Craig

Paillasson
"A tantalizing trio"

Easy
Serves: 8
Preparation: 20 min.
Cooking: 30 min.

2 cups julienned potatoes
2 cups julienned parsnips
1 cup julienned carrots
¼ cup (½ stick) melted butter
½ tsp. salt
¼ tsp. pepper
dash nutmeg

Preheat oven to 450°.

In a large bowl, combine all ingredients and toss well. Turn into a 10" nonstick ovenproof skillet and press with the back of a spoon to level. Cook over medium heat for 10 minutes, or until vegetables begin to brown. Place in the oven and bake 25 to 30 minutes. Invert onto a platter and serve.

Carolyn S. Hammer

Celery Au Gratin with Almonds

Easy
Serves: 6–8
Preparation: 15 min.
Cooking: 30 min.
Can be made ahead

2 Tbsp. butter
2 Tbsp. flour
1 cup chicken broth
¼ cup light cream
salt and pepper
2 cups cut celery, parboiled
¼ cup blanched almonds
grated American cheese
bread crumbs

Preheat oven to 350°.

Butter a small casserole.

In a saucepan, melt the butter; then stir in the flour. Cook for 2–3 minutes, until mixture foams and lightens, then gradually add broth to make a smooth sauce. Add the cream, and salt and pepper to taste, stirring constantly.

Add the celery and almonds. Place the mixture in the prepared casserole and top with cheese and bread crumbs. Bake about 30 minutes, or until brown.

Joan H. Loper

167

Parsnip and Carrot Puree

Easy
Serves: 6
Preparation: 1 hr.
Cooking: 35 min.
Can be frozen

4½ cups, about 1½ lbs. parsnips, peeled

4½ cups, about 1½ lbs. carrots, peeled

2 Tbsp. brown sugar

¼ scant cup apple or orange juice

2 Tbsp. butter

½ tsp. nutmeg

salt and pepper to taste

Topping:
1½ cups fresh bread crumbs

½ cup chopped pecans

¼ cup (½ stick) melted butter

2 Tbsp. finely chopped parsley

Preheat oven to 350°.

Butter a 2 qt. casserole.

Slice the parsnips and carrots thinly and boil until tender, about 30 minutes. Drain very well then process in a food processor with the next five ingredients.

Topping:
In a small bowl, combine all the topping ingredients. Place parsnip mixture in a casserole and cover with topping. Bake for 20 minutes, covered, then 15 minutes uncovered.

Patricia A. Mackay

Sonja'sBeans
"Delicously rich"

Easy
Serves: 4
Preparation: 10 min.
Cooking: 6 min.

1 lb. green beans

5 slices bacon, cut into ¼" strips

1 cup walnuts, roughly chopped

salt and pepper to taste

4 oz. Roquefort or blue cheese

Cook beans until tender but not limp. In a skillet, brown bacon, reserving drippings.

Mix all ingredients well (including some or all of bacon drippings). Toss and serve.

Sonja Bayly

Onion Cornbread

"A hearty, satisfying side dish"

Easy
Serves: 12
Preparation: 15 min.
Cooking: 35–40 min.

2   lg. sweet onions, sliced
¼   cup (½ stick) butter
8   oz. sour cream
½   tsp. dill seed or parsley
¼   tsp. salt
1   cup grated sharp Cheddar cheese, divided
1   15-oz. can creamed corn
⅓   cup milk
1   8½-oz. pkg. corn muffin mix
1   egg, slightly beaten
1   10-oz. can diced tomatoes & green chiles
⅔   cup seasoned bread crumbs

Preheat oven to 400°.

Grease a 13"x9" baking dish.

In a large skillet, sauté onions in butter until transparent. Stir in sour cream, dill or parsley, salt and half the cheese. In a large bowl, combine corn, milk, muffin mix, egg and tomatoes.

Pour corn mixture into prepared dish. Spread onion mixture over top and sprinkle with remaining cheese. Cover with seasoned bread crumbs. Bake for 35–40 minutes.

Serve as a side dish, or with a salad as a light entree.

Dolores M. Zitterbart

169

Grilled Vegetables

Easy
Serves: 4–6
Preparation: 20 min.
Marinate: 1 hr.
Cooking: 15 min.

2   lg. yellow squash cut into ¾" slices

1   lg. zucchini, cut into ¾" slices

2   lg. green, red or yellow peppers, cut into 1" cubes

¾   lb. mushrooms, peeled

¼   cup olive oil

2   Tbsp. tarragon vinegar

1   clove garlic, minced

¼   tsp. ground thyme

salt and pepper to taste

Preheat grill.

Combine all ingredients in a large nonreactive bowl and marinate at least 1 hour, tossing occasionally. Skewer vegetables, putting all squash together, all zucchini together, etc. Place on a hot grill, cover and cook for about 15 minutes, turning frequently. Remove vegetables from skewers, toss together and serve.

Paula A. Doebler

Oven Roasted Vegetables

Easy
Serves: 6–8
Preparation: 20 min.
Cooking: 50 min.

1   lb. red skin potatoes cut into 1" pieces

1   16-oz. bag peeled baby carrots

1   med. onion, sliced

3   garlic cloves, minced

2   Tbsp. dried oregano

2   Tbsp. finely chopped fresh basil

1   tsp. salt

1   tsp. pepper

½   cup olive oil

3   Tbsp. fresh lemon juice

1   zucchini, cut into ½" wide strips

1   lg. red pepper, cut into ½" strips

1   lg. green pepper, cut into ½" strips

Preheat oven to 450°.

In a 13"x9" pan, combine the potatoes, carrots and onion. Mix all the spices, oil and lemon juice and drizzle over vegetables. Toss to coat. Bake, uncovered, for 30 minutes, turning occasionally.

Remove from oven and add remaining vegetables. Return to the oven and bake for an additional 15 to 20 minutes. If vegetables are too dry, add more olive oil and toss.

Lynn B. Popovich

Potato Baskets
"Something new for Sunday dinner"

Moderately difficult
Serves: 6–8
Preparation: 10 min.
Cooking: 35 min.
Can be made ahead

Baskets:
2   potatoes, peeled

2   Tbsp. butter, melted

salt

Filling:
2   cups mashed potatoes
     (about 4 med.
     potatoes)

¼   cup sour cream

¼   cup (½ stick) butter,
     melted

1   egg yolk

½   tsp. salt

¼   tsp. garlic powder

1   Tbsp. finely chopped
     fresh chives, optional

Preheat oven to 425°.

Baskets:
Grate potatoes and press into bottoms and sides of 12 greased muffin cups. Bake for 10 minutes. Brush with melted butter, sprinkle with salt and bake for 15 minutes more, until brown and crispy.

Filling:
Mash potatoes and add remaining ingredients. If mixture is too stiff, add more sour cream. Spoon or pipe into baskets.

Heat in oven for 10 minutes and serve.

Gretchen A. Wimer

171

Roasties
"Leaves you free to enjoy your guests"

Easy
Serves: 8–10
Preparation: 15 min.
Cooking: 2 hrs. 5 min.

4   lbs. baking potatoes

½   cup (1 stick) butter,
     melted

½   tsp. salt

¼   tsp. freshly ground
     black pepper

¼   tsp. sweet paprika

2   cloves garlic, minced

½   cup chicken broth

flour for dusting

Preheat oven to 350°.

Butter a 13"x9" baking dish.

Peel potatoes and quarter them lengthwise. Place in baking dish. Add all ingredients except chicken stock. Turn potatoes to coat.

Bake for 1 hour. Add chicken stock and bake for an additional hour, turning occasionally. Dust with flour near the end of cooking time. Place under broiler until nicely browned.

Judy B. Scioscia

Roasted Potatoes with Goat Cheese

"Gourmet made easy"

Easy
Serves: 6
Preparation: 10 min.
Marinate: 30 min.–2 hrs.
Cooking: 45 min.
Can be made ahead

Marinade:

¼ cup olive oil

½ cup balsamic vinegar

2 cloves garlic, minced

finely chopped fresh
rosemary, to taste

salt and pepper

6 lg. russet potatoes,
washed and cubed
(skins left on)

4–6 oz. goat cheese,
crumbled

Preheat oven to 425°.

Prepare marinade and soak potatoes for 30 minutes–2 hours.

Drain marinade and bake potatoes for 45 minutes, turning occasionally.

Toss with goat cheese and serve.

Cindy Dyer

Artichoke Mashed Potatoes

Easy
Serves: 2
Preparation: 10 min.
Cooking: 20 min.

4 frozen artichoke
hearts, defrosted

2 med. russet potatoes,
peeled and quartered

2 garlic cloves, peeled

2 Tbsp. butter

¼ cup milk

2 tsp. finely chopped
fresh parsley

salt and pepper

Steam the artichoke hearts until tender, about 10 minutes. Cool. Slice artichoke hearts lengthwise.

Cover potatoes and garlic with water and bring to a boil. Cook until potatoes are tender. Drain.

While potatoes are draining, heat butter and milk in a separate pan.

Mash potatoes and garlic, then gradually stir in the milk mixture. Gently stir in the artichokes and chopped parsley. Season with salt and pepper to taste.

Barbara Laman Gaudio

Horseradish Mashed Potatoes Supreme

"Will keep you warm on a cold, winter's night"

Easy
Serves: 10
Preparation: 10 min.
Cooking: 45 min.
Can be frozen

9   med. potatoes, peeled and quartered

½   cup (1 stick) butter

2   Tbsp. horseradish

⅔   cup warm milk

1   Tbsp. finely chopped parsley

1   tsp. caraway seeds (optional)

1½ tsp. salt

pepper

1½ cups grated Cheddar cheese

1   cup heavy cream, whipped

Preheat oven to 350°.

Boil potatoes in salted water until tender. Drain and beat in a large bowl with electric mixer until fluffy. Add butter, horseradish, parsley, caraway seeds, salt and pepper to taste. Turn into a buttered casserole. Fold cheese into whipped cream. Spread on top of potatoes. Bake for 25 minutes until golden brown.

Susan Vogelgesang

173

Tim Todd Potatoes

Easy
Serves: 6–8
Preparation: 30 min.
Cooking: 1½–2 hrs.

2   med. onions, finely chopped

½   cup (1 stick) butter

6–8 med. potatoes

8   oz. cream cheese

pinch garlic powder

1   cup heavy cream

2   eggs, lightly beaten

dash pepper

Preheat oven to 325°.

Butter a 2 qt. casserole.

Sauté onions in butter. Peel, quarter, boil and mash potatoes.

While potatoes are hot, add cream cheese and pinch of garlic powder; beat at high speed with electric mixer. Add onions and butter; beat again. Add cream and beat. Add eggs and blend thoroughly. Season with dash of pepper. Transfer to prepared casserole and bake for 1–1½ hours, until top is golden brown.

Mary Louise Fowkes

Scalloped Redskins

Easy
Serves: 8
Preparation: 20 min.
Cooking: 1 hr.
Can be made ahead

2   Tbsp. butter
⅓   cup chopped green onions
⅓   cup chopped red pepper
1   clove garlic, minced
¼   tsp. ground red pepper
¾   cup milk
2   cups whipping cream
salt and pepper
2½ lbs. sm. red skin potatoes, sliced, unpeeled
2   cups shredded Swiss cheese
½   cup grated Parmesan cheese

Preheat oven to 350°.

Grease a medium casserole.

Sauté green onions, red pepper, garlic and ground red pepper in butter. Cook for 2 minutes. Add milk, whipping cream, and salt and pepper to taste and mix thoroughly. Add potato slices and cook over medium heat until almost tender, about 15 minutes. Transfer to prepared baking dish and top with the grated cheeses. Bake for 45 minutes, or until bubbly and golden.

Allow to stand for 15 minutes before serving.

Diane Verdish

Potato Gratin with Mustard and Dill

"A classic with a contemporary twist"

Easy
Serves: 8–10
Preparation: 30 min.
Cooking: 1 hr.
Can be made ahead

3½ lbs. russet potatoes,
   peeled, cut into
   ⅛" slices

salt and pepper

1 Tbsp. snipped fresh
   dill, divided

3 cups Swiss cheese,
   grated, divided

1½ cups whipping cream

1 14-oz. can chicken
   broth

¼ cup Dijon mustard

Preheat oven to 400°.

Grease 13"x9" baking dish.

Overlap ⅓ of potatoes in dish. Season with salt and pepper to taste and ⅓ dill, then sprinkle with 1 cup of cheese. Repeat layering twice. Whisk cream, broth and mustard together and pour over potatoes.

Bake until potatoes are tender and crusty on top, about 1 hour.

Jane Ellen Rabe

Sweet Potato Casserole

"Great for the holidays"

Easy
Serves: 6–8
Preparation: 15 min.
Cooking: 20–30 min.
Can be made ahead

1 29-oz. can yams,
   drained

1 egg, beaten

1 Tbsp. melted butter

½ cup sugar

½ tsp. cinnamon

Topping:
1 cup crushed Ritz
   crackers

½ cup chopped walnuts

½ cup (1 stick) butter,
   melted

½ cup brown sugar

Preheat oven to 350°.

In a 2 qt. casserole, mix yams, egg, butter, sugar and cinnamon. Set aside.

In small bowl, prepare topping by mixing all the remaining ingredients. Sprinkle topping over yam mixture. Bake for 20–30 minutes.

Dee Sacco

Perfect Rice
"The name says it all"

Easy
Serves: 6–8
Preparation: 10 min.
Cooking: 17 min.

2½ Tbsp. butter, divided
2 Tbsp. minced onion
¼ tsp. minced garlic
1 cup rice
2¼ cups chicken broth
2 sprigs parsley
1 sprig fresh thyme, or
   ¼ tsp dried
½ bay leaf
⅛ tsp. cayenne pepper

Preheat oven to 400°.

Melt 1 tablespoon butter in a heavy casserole. Add onions and garlic, stirring occasionally. Cook until onion is translucent, about 5 minutes. Add rice and stir briefly over low heat until grains are coated with butter. Stir in chicken broth, making sure there are no lumps in the rice. Add parsley, thyme, bay leaf and cayenne. Cover with a close-fitting lid and place in oven, or cook on top of stove for exactly 17 minutes.

Remove and discard parsley, thyme sprig and bay leaf. Using a two-prong fork, stir in remaining butter.

Mrs. Dorothy Dufala

Eastern Rice
"Goes well with lamb or chicken"

Easy
Serves: 4
Preparation: 10 min.
Cooking: 20 min.

1 Tbsp. butter
2 Tbsp. chopped onion
1 clove garlic, minced
1 14-oz. can chicken
   broth
¼ cup water
1 cup long-grain rice
1 tsp. curry powder
⅛ tsp. ground cinnamon
pinch of ground cloves
⅓ cup golden raisins

Melt butter in a 2 qt. saucepan. Add onion and garlic; sauté for 2–3 minutes, being careful not to let them brown. Add broth and water; bring to a boil.

Mix rice with curry, cinnamon and cloves; add to the boiling broth. Reduce heat to low and cook for 20 minutes. If the liquid evaporates too quickly, add a little more water. Stir in raisins and serve.

Kitty Gross

Wild Rice Casserole
"Full of flavor"

Easy
Serves: 4
Preparation: 30 min.
Cooking time: 20 min.
Can be frozen

1   box Uncle Ben's Long
    Grain and Wild Rice

1⅓ cups water

1   cup orange juice

½   cup chutney (apple or
    apricot)

½   cup almonds, sliced, or
    pine nuts

2   Tbsp. finely chopped
    Italian parsley

freshly grated Parmesan
cheese

Preheat oven to 350°.

Cook rice according to instructions on package, using the orange juice and water for the cooking liquid. Remove from heat and add the remaining ingredients. Pour into a casserole, cover, and heat for 20 minutes in oven.

Sprinkle with Parmesan and serve.

Sally M. Wood

Herbed Bulgar Pilaf

177

Easy
Serves: 6
Preparation: 5 min.
Cooking: 20 min.
Can be frozen

½   cup orzo

2   Tbsp. olive oil

1   cup bulgar wheat,
    coarse

2   cups chicken or
    vegetable broth

½   cup chopped onion

1   tsp. oregano

2   Tbsp. finely chopped
    parsley

Sauté orzo in 2 tablespoons of olive oil, until golden. Add bulgar wheat and sauté 1 minute more. Slowly add 2 cups of broth. Stir in onions and herbs and bring to a boil. Cover and simmer for 20–25 minutes. Remove from heat and fluff with a fork.

Carole S. Russell

Couscous with Grilled Vegetables

Easy
Serves: 6
Preparation: 45 min.
Can be made ahead

2   peppers (red, orange or yellow)
1   jalapeño pepper
1   sm. eggplant, cut crosswise into ¼ inch slices
1   zucchini, cut crosswise into ¼ inch slices
6   Tbsp. olive oil, divided
1½ cups couscous
2   lg. red tomatoes, diced
¼   cup fresh cilantro, chopped
2   Tbsp. finely chopped parsley
6   Tbsp. fresh lemon juice
3   cloves garlic, minced
salt and pepper

Preheat grill or broiler.

Cut all peppers in half lengthwise and remove skins and stems. Place halves under broiler until skin is black and blistered. Remove from heat, cover with foil and allow to steam for 10 minutes. When cool, peel off skin; cut peppers into bite-sized pieces. Mince jalapeños and set aside.

While peppers are steaming, brush eggplant and zucchini slices on both sides with 2–3 tablespoons of olive oil. Place on grill rack or under broiler. Grill until golden brown and tender, turning occasionally (approximately 6–8 minutes for zucchini and 8–12 minutes for the eggplant). Grilled vegetables may be prepared ahead of time.

Prepare couscous according to package instructions. Place in a large bowl. Add chopped peppers, zucchini, eggplant, diced tomatoes, cilantro and parsley.

In a small bowl, whisk remaining 4 tablespoons of olive oil, lemon juice, garlic, and salt and pepper to taste. Drizzle over couscous and toss to mix. Serve at room temperature.

Tom and Megan Barrasso
Pittsburgh Penguins

Salads

Crunchy Romaine Toss
"A hint of the Orient"

Easy
Serves: 10–12
Preparation: 45 min.

1   pkg. ramen noodles,
    uncooked

1   cup walnuts, chopped

4   Tbsp. unsalted butter

1   head Romaine lettuce,
    washed

1   bunch broccoli,
    coarsely chopped

4   green onions, chopped

1   cup sweet-and sour
    dressing

Sweet-and-Sour Dressing:
1   cup vegetable oil

1   cup sugar

½   cup white vinegar

3   tsp. soy sauce

salt and pepper to taste

Discard flavor packet from noodles. In a sauté pan, brown walnuts and noodles in butter. Cool on paper towels.

Tear lettuce into bite-sized pieces. In a large bowl, combine the walnut mixture with broccoli, lettuce and onions. Set aside.

Dressing:
In a separate bowl, whisk all the dressing ingredients. Pour one cup of dressing over the Romaine mixture and serve.

Patricia A. Almes

Spring Green Salad
"Beautiful in its simplicity and flavor"

Easy
Serves: 4
Preparation: 10 min.

Dressing:
juice of 1 lemon
⅓ cup olive oil
1 tsp. Dijon mustard
1 clove garlic, minced

Salad:
1 bag baby spring mixed greens
¼ cup chopped pecans
1 cup grated Romano or Parmesan cheese

½ cup sun dried tomatoes, oil packed, or fresh strawberries
coarsely ground black pepper

Dressing:
Place all dressing ingredients in a small bowl and whisk until well blended.

Just before serving, toss the salad ingredients and coat well with dressing. Add extra cheese and coarsely ground pepper to taste.

Nancy H. Boland

Baked Goat Cheese Salad
"Savory goat cheese transforms these simple greens"

Easy
Serves: 4
Preparation: 15 min.
Marinate: 2–3 hrs.
Cooking: 5 min.

½ cup olive oil
1 tsp. dried thyme or 4 fresh sprigs, finely chopped
1 bay leaf, crumbled
2 4-oz. logs of mild goat cheese, cut into ½" slices
1 cup toasted fresh white bread crumbs
3 Tbsp. balsamic vinegar
salt and pepper
8 cups assorted baby salad greens

Preheat oven to 450°

Combine the first three ingredients in a small bowl. In a small glass baking dish, arrange the cheese rounds in a single layer. Pour the oil mixture over the cheese and turn cheese to coat. Cover and refrigerate for several hours or overnight.

181

Remove cheese from the oil, reserving oil, and coat cheese with toasted breadcrumbs, pressing gently to make sure they adhere. Arrange them on a lightly oiled baking sheet and bake until lightly bubbling and golden, about 5 minutes.

Whisk vinegar into reserved oil and season with salt and pepper to taste. Place greens in a bowl and lightly coat with vinaigrette. Check seasoning. Top salad with hot cheese and serve.

Dana Graff

Spinach Salad Supreme

Easy
Serves: 4
Preparation: 30 min.

6   strips of bacon
1   tsp. prepared mustard
½   tsp. sugar
1   sm. onion, grated
1   cup mayonnaise
¼   cup vegetable oil
¼   cup white wine vinegar
¼   cup Parmesan cheese
1   lb. fresh spinach,
    cleaned and broken
    into bite-sized pieces

In a sauté pan, fry the bacon. Allow to cool, then crumble. Make the dressing by whisking remaining ingredients together. When ready to serve, toss the spinach with desired amount of dressing, top with bacon and add additional Parmesan.

Susan N. Cockrell

Mandarin Orange Spinach Salad

Easy
Serves: 6
Preparation: 1 hr.
Cooking: 10 min.

½   cup sliced almonds
¼   cup sugar
½   cup chopped green
    onions
1   11-oz. can mandarin
    oranges, drained
1   head Romaine lettuce,
    cleaned and broken
    into bite-sized pieces
1   bunch spinach, cleaned
    and broken into bite-
    sized pieces

Dressing:
½   cup sugar
1   tsp. celery seed
½   cup cider vinegar
1   cup olive oil

In a small skillet, cook almonds with sugar until caramelized. Remove from heat and place in a serving bowl. Add green onions, mandarin oranges, lettuce and spinach.

Dressing:
In a separate bowl, whisk dressing ingredients, mixing well. Pour over salad just before serving, making sure to toss well.

Jean Whitehill Schnatterly

Apple and Walnut Salad

"Add this to a slice of quiche for a lovely luncheon"

Easy
Serves: 6
Preparation: 20 min.

1   head Romaine lettuce
1   Red Delicious apple, chopped
1   Golden Delicious apple, chopped
4   oz. Gorgonzola cheese
½   cup chopped walnuts, toasted

Dressing:
2   tsp. Dijon mustard
2   cloves garlic, minced
¼   cup white wine vinegar
¼   tsp. salt
¼   tsp. pepper
⅓   cup olive oil

Line a salad bowl or platter with a few lettuce leaves. Tear the rest into bite-sized pieces and combine with the apples, cheese and walnuts.

Whisk the dressing ingredients in a small bowl and pour over the salad.

Joyce Michaels

Lois's Bean Salad

Easy
Serves: 8–10
Preparation: 30 min.
Cooking: 10 min.
Can be made ahead

2   lbs. green beans
1   cup walnuts chopped
1   cup sliced red onion
1   cup crumbled feta cheese
½   cup mint leaves

¼   cup white wine vinegar
¾   tsp. salt
½   tsp. pepper
½   cup olive oil

Steam beans. Cut beans into bite-sized pieces. Add remaining ingredients. Toss, chill and serve.

Patricia Kendall

183

Strawberry Salad

Easy
Serves: 6–8
Preparation: 45 min.

¼ cup sliced almonds

1 Tbsp. plus 1 tsp. sugar

⅓ head of lettuce, torn into bite-sized pieces

⅓ bunch Romaine lettuce, torn in bite-sized pieces

2 med. stalks celery, chopped

2 green onions, thinly sliced

1 11-oz. can mandarin oranges, drained

2½ cups fresh strawberries, sliced

Sweet-and-Sour Dressing:

¼ cup vegetable oil

2 Tbsp. sugar

dash of pepper

½ tsp. salt

2 Tbsp. white wine vinegar

dash of red pepper sauce

In a small skillet, over medium heat, cook almonds and sugar. Stir constantly, until the sugar is melted and the almonds are coated. Cool on waxed paper and break apart.

Dressing:
Whisk all the dressing ingredients in a small bowl.

Place lettuce in a large bowl with the celery, onions, mandarin oranges and strawberries. Toss with dressing and sprinkle with almonds.

Patricia A. Almes

Tomatoes with Parsley Pesto

Easy
Serves: 6
Preparation: 15 min.

1   **cup parsley**
¼   **cup snipped fresh chives**
1   **clove garlic**
¼   **tsp. salt**
dash of pepper
3   **Tbsp. olive oil**
2   **Tbsp. cider or red wine vinegar**
3   **med. tomatoes, cut into wedges**

In a blender or food processor, combine parsley, chives, garlic, salt and pepper. Process until finely chopped. Add oil and vinegar and mix well. Transfer to a bowl, cover and refrigerate.

When ready to serve, add tomatoes, tossing gently to coat.

Betty Kramer

Fennel Salad

"A new addition to your salad repertoire"

Easy
Serves: 4
Preparation: 5 min.
Can be made ahead

1   **lg. fennel bulb**
lettuce leaves
1   **cup shaved Reggiano Parmesan cheese**
vinaigrette or fresh lemon juice and olive oil
freshly ground black pepper

Cut off upper stalks of fennel bulb. Using a vegetable peeler, lightly peel the outside of the bulb to remove strings. Using a V cut, slice the bulb vertically to remove the center core. Slice thinly.

Arrange a few lettuce leaves on individual serving plates. Lay sliced fennel over the lettuce. Top with several shavings of the cheese. Dress lightly with vinaigrette, or squeeze lemon juice and a little olive oil over each plate. Season with freshly ground black pepper.

Elise Keely Smith

185

Sweet Corn and Red Pepper Salad

Easy
Serves: 5–6
Preparation: 20 min.
Marinate: 1 hr.

⅓ cup sherry vinegar

1 Tbsp. Dijon mustard

¾ cup extra virgin olive oil

½ tsp. salt

freshly ground black pepper

3 cups fresh sweet corn kernels

1 red pepper, seeded and diced

1 yellow pepper, seeded and diced

1 lb. Sonoma Jack cheese or Provolone, diced

½ cup finely chopped cilantro

4 whole green onions, thinly sliced

Whisk vinegar, mustard, olive oil, salt and pepper in a large bowl. Add corn, peppers, cheese, cilantro and green onions and gently toss. Cover the bowl and let the ingredients marinate for at least one hour. Toss before serving.

Kaisa Hall

Colorful Black Bean, Corn and Pepper Salad
"Perfect for a picnic"

Easy
Serves: 8
Preparation: 10 min.
Can be made ahead

1 15–oz. can black beans, rinsed

1 10–oz. pkg. frozen corn, thawed, drained

2 Tbsp. chopped pimento

2 Tbsp. finely chopped cilantro

2 green onions, chopped

½ yellow pepper, chopped

½ orange pepper, chopped

bottled or homemade vinaigrette

Mix all ingredients in a large bowl. Add dressing to taste. Serve chilled.

Linda L. Lednak

New Potato and Green Bean Salad

Easy
Serves: 6
Preparation: 30 min.
Cooking : 20 min.

Dressing:
¼ cup balsamic vinegar
2 Tbsp. Dijon mustard
2 Tbsp. fresh lemon juice
1 clove garlic, minced
dash of Worcestershire sauce
½ cup extra virgin olive oil
salt and pepper

Salad:
1½ lbs. sm. red skin potatoes
¾ lbs. green beans, trimmed
1 sm. red onion, coarsely chopped
¼ cup chopped fresh basil

Dressing:
Whisk together the first five ingredients in a medium bowl. Gradually incorporate the oil. Season with salt and pepper to taste.

Salad:
Cook potatoes until tender. Cool, then cut into quarters. Cook the green beans in a large pot of boiling water until crisp but tender, about 5 minutes. Cut the beans in half. Combine beans, potatoes, onion and basil in a large bowl. Use the desired amount of dressing to coat all ingredients and toss well.

Jane Birnie

Home-Style Potato Salad

"Bring this bountiful salad to your next barbecue"

Easy
Serves: 8–10
Preparation:
Can be made ahead

4   lbs. red skin potatoes

5   cups chicken broth

3   Tbsp. Dijon mustard

3   Tbsp. red wine vinegar

1   tsp. fresh lemon juice

½   tsp. celery salt

½   tsp. sugar or honey

pepper

½   cup olive oil

½   cup mayonnaise

¼   cup chopped parsley
    leaves

2   Tbsp. snipped fresh dill

½   cup chopped red onion

3   green onions, thinly
    sliced

¾   cup chopped celery

1   cup assorted, chopped
    bell peppers

½   cup chopped sweet
    gherkins

Optional:
2   hard-boiled eggs,
    chopped

⅓   cup chopped black
    olives

⅓   cup pimento stuffed
    olives, chopped

Wash the potatoes and cut into 1"
pieces. Place them in a large kettle
with the broth and, if necessary,
enough water to cover them. Simmer,
covered, for 8 to 10 minutes, or until
potatoes are just tender. Drain and
cool.

In a large bowl, whisk the mustard,
vinegar, lemon juice, celery salt,
sugar or honey and pepper to taste.
Add oil in a stream, whisking continuously until the dressing has emulsified. Whisk in mayonnaise, parsley
and dill. Add this dressing to the
potatoes and toss well. Add the red
onion, green onion, celery, peppers,
gherkins and, if using, the eggs and
olives to the potatoes. Toss the salad
well before serving.

Bill Behan

Wild Rice with Dried Cranberries

"Enliven your table with this colorful, crunchy accompaniment"

Easy
Serves: 8–10
Preparation: 20 min.
Cooking: 30 min.
Can be made ahead

4   cups salted water

1   cup uncooked wild rice

½   cup diced celery

½   cup diced red pepper

½   cup diced yellow pepper

½   cup chopped pecans, toasted

¾   cup dried cranberries

Dressing:
6   Tbsp. balsamic vinegar

½   tsp. salt

2   Tbsp. brown sugar

1   tsp. Dijon mustard

½   cup vegetable oil

½   cup olive oil

salt and pepper

To cook rice, bring salted water to a boil, add the rice and stir. Bring back to a boil and lower heat to medium. Cover and simmer for about 25–30 minutes, or until rice is tender. Drain any excess water and cool.

Combine wild rice with the celery, peppers, pecans and cranberries.

Dressing:
Whisk the vinegar, salt, brown sugar and mustard in a small bowl. Slowly whisk in the oils until well emulsified.

Dress the salad with enough dressing to coat and flavor well. Season with salt and pepper, if desired.

Rania Harris

189

Tabouleh with Feta Cheese

Moderately difficult
Serves: 14–16
Preparation: 65 min.
Must be made ahead

- 2 **lbs. fine grain bulgur wheat**
- 1¾ **cups fresh lemon juice, divided**
- 6 **cups hot water**
- 8 **oz. feta cheese, coarsely crumbled**
- 3 **cups parsley, finely chopped**
- 2 **sm. cloves garlic, minced**
- 6 **med. tomatoes, seeded, finely chopped**
- 1 **med. red onion, finely chopped**
- 4 **sm. cucumbers, seeded, finely chopped**
- 5 **Tbsp. finely chopped fresh mint**
- 1½ **cups olive oil (or as needed)**
- **salt and pepper**

Put bulgur wheat, 1½ cups lemon juice and hot water into a large bowl. Let stand 45 minutes, until the wheat is tender. Drain.

Add feta cheese, parsley, garlic, tomatoes, onion, cucumber and mint to the bulgur wheat. Toss.

Dress with enough oil and the remaining ¼ cup of lemon juice to just moisten mixture.

Season with salt and pepper to taste. Refrigerate several hours. Serve cold with pita bread.

Joyce A. Scalercio

Panzanella Salad

"Last night's bread becomes today's sumptuous salad"

Easy
Serves: 6–8
Preparation: 1 hr.
Marinate: 30 min.
Must be made ahead

5   cups coarsely cubed, French or peasant bread

3   lg. beefsteak tomatoes, seeded, diced into ½" pieces

2   cucumbers, peeled, halved, seeded, cut on sharp diagonal into ¼" slices

1   yellow pepper, cut into julienne strips

1   red onion, cut into thin rings

2   Tbsp. capers, drained

½   cup black olives, pitted, coarsely chopped

⅔   cup extra virgin olive oil

¼   cup balsamic vinegar

coarse salt and pepper

½   cup shredded fresh basil

Cube the bread and let sit out so that it becomes a bit dry, preferably overnight.

In a large mixing bowl, combine tomatoes, cucumbers, yellow pepper strips, onion rings, capers and olives. Toss with oil and vinegar. Season with coarse salt and pepper. Let sit 30 minutes at room temperature to marinate. Toss bread and basil with the marinated vegetables and let sit another hour, until the bread absorbs the dressing and vegetable juices. If salad is too dry, drizzle with a bit more olive oil.

Serve at room temperature.

Catherine M. Dunn

191

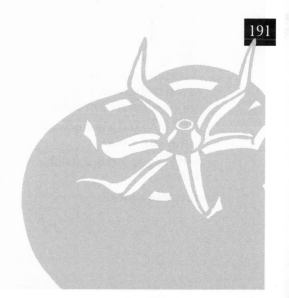

Mahi-Mahi Pasta Salad

Easy
Serves: 4
Preparation: 20 min.
Marinate: 30 min.
Cooking: 20 min.

1   lb. Mahi-mahi

soy sauce

¾   lb. tomatoes, chopped

2   lg. red peppers, seeded, chopped

¼   lb. crumbled feta cheese

½   cup olive oil

½   cup Kalamata olives

¼   cup fresh lemon juice

2   Tbsp. white wine vinegar

1   Tbsp. dried thyme

6   green onions, chopped

3   lg. garlic cloves, minced

1   12-oz. pkg. cheese tortellini, freshly cooked

Marinate mahi-mahi in soy sauce for 30 minutes. Broil or grill and cut into bite-sized pieces.

Combine the next ten ingredients (tomatoes through garlic cloves) in a very large bowl. Add the warm tortellini and the mahi-mahi just off the grill. Toss and serve.

Cathy Kelly

Curried Shrimp Salad

"A splash of sophistication"

Easy
Serves: 4
Preparation: 15 min.

1–2 Tbsp. curry powder

½   cup mayonnaise

1½ lbs. med. shrimp, cooked, peeled and deveined

1   cup white seedless grapes, halved, or 1 cup honeydew melon balls

½   cup slivered almonds or chopped nuts

watercress or lettuce (Bibb or Boston)

watermelon pickle

Mix curry powder with mayonnaise. Add shrimp, and grapes or honeydew balls. Sprinkle with nuts. Chill well before serving.

Serve on watercress or lettuce, with watermelon pickle on the side.

Sally Wiggin
WTAE-TV

Almond Chicken Pasta Salad
"Great with croissants for a brunch or shower"

Easy
Serves: 6
Preparation: 45 min.

3　cups cooked, cubed chicken

2　med. apples, (2 cups) cored and coarsely chopped

6　oz. corkscrew pasta, cooked and drained

1　8½-oz. can pineapple chunks, drained

½　cup halved seedless grapes

⅓　cup chopped celery (1 stalk)

¼　cup thinly sliced green onion

Dressing:
¾　cup mayonnaise

⅓　cup low fat plain yogurt

1　Tbsp. sesame seeds

1　tsp. finely shredded lime zest

2　Tbsp. lime juice

1　Tbsp. honey

2　tsp. peeled, grated fresh ginger

2　tsp. salt

To Serve:
lettuce leaves

½　cup sliced almonds

lime slices, avocado and red pepper rings for garnish

In a large bowl, mix chicken, apples, pasta, pineapple, grapes, celery and onion.

Dressing:
In a small bowl, combine mayonnaise, yogurt, sesame seeds, lime zest, lime juice, honey, ginger and salt. Pour over the pasta mixture and toss gently to combine. Cover and chill.

To serve:
Toss pasta and chicken mixture. Serve on lettuce lined plates, topped with almonds. If desired, garnish with lime slices, avocado and red pepper rings.

Shelia Hyland
Fox 53 TV

193

Chicken Salad with Apricot Salsa
"A fresh approach"

Easy
Serves: 4
Preparation: 30 min.
Cooking: 15 min.
Can be made ahead

4   chicken breasts, boned and skinned

salt and pepper

¼   cup plain yogurt

¼   cup mayonnaise

1   clove garlic, minced

1½ tsp. curry powder

1   tsp. peeled, grated fresh ginger

Salsa:
2   Tbsp. fresh lime juice

2   Tbsp. olive oil

¼   tsp. salt

⅛   tsp. coarsely ground black pepper

6   fresh (or canned) apricots, diced

½   cup diced red onion

½   cup diced red pepper

lettuce for plates

Place chicken in a large pot of water. Season with salt and pepper, cover and bring to a boil. Reduce heat and simmer until the chicken is tender. Drain, cool and chop the chicken.

Stir the yogurt and next four ingredients until blended. Pour over chicken and toss gently. Cover and chill.

Salsa:
Whisk lime juice, olive oil, salt and pepper until blended. Stir in apricots, onions and red pepper. Cover and chill.

Serve the chicken mixture on lettuce lined plates. Top with the apricot salsa.

Susan S. Harvey

Grilled Chicken on Baby Greens
"Pretty on the palate and the plate"

Easy
Serves: 4
Preparation: 20 min.
Marinate: 2 hrs.
Cooking: 10 min.

Citrus Marinade:
1   tsp. grated orange zest
½   cup fresh orange juice
⅓   cup fresh grapefruit juice
1   tsp. grated lime zest
2   Tbsp. fresh lime juice
2   Tbsp. vegetable oil
1   Tbsp. white wine vinegar
1   tsp. white wine Worcestershire sauce
½   tsp. Dijon mustard
¼   tsp. ground red pepper
Salad:
4   chicken breasts, boned and skinned
¾   cup plus 2 Tbs. citrus marinade, divided
cooking spray
8   cups mixed baby salad greens
1   med. orange, peeled, sectioned
1   med. grapefruit, peeled, sectioned
1   sm. red onion, thinly sliced, separated into rings

Preheat grill.

Citrus Marinade:
Combine all ingredients in a medium bowl; stir well. Use immediately or store in the refrigerator.

Salad:
Place the chicken in a large resealable plastic bag and add ½ cup of the marinade. Seal the bag and marinate in the refrigerator for 2 hours. Reserve the remaining marinade for the salad dressing.

Coat a grill rack with cooking spray. Remove chicken from marinade, discarding liquid. Grill, covered, for 4 to 5 minutes on each side, or until done. Cut the chicken into thin slices.

Place 2 cups of the greens on each salad plate. Arrange the orange and grapefruit sections and onion rings over the greens. Top each salad with chicken slices. Drizzle with remaining ¼ cup plus 2 tablespoons of the citrus marinade.

Mary Lee Parrington

195

Fresh Asparagus Vinaigrette

Easy
Serves: 4-6
Preparation: 20 min.
Can be made ahead

1½ lbs. fresh asparagus
2   hard-boiled eggs, chopped
¾   cup olive oil
¼   cup white wine vinegar
2   Tbsp. Dijon mustard
1   Tbsp. finely chopped chives
2   Tbsp. finely chopped green onions
2   Tbsp. finely chopped fresh parsley
1   tsp. finely chopped fresh tarragon, or ½ tsp. dried

Cook asparagus until just tender. Chill.

Combine remaining ingredients. Pour over asparagus and serve.

Can be used as a first course.

Melissa Doyle

Festival Salad Dressing

"These ingredients will surprise you"

Easy
Yields: 1 qt.
Preparation: 5 min.
Must be made ahead

1   10-oz. can tomato soup
1   cup oil
¾   cup sugar
1   tsp. salt
¼   tsp. pepper
1   cup vinegar
1   tsp. paprika
1½ tsp. dry mustard
1   oz. crumbled blue cheese
2   cloves garlic, minced

Combine all ingredients and mix well. Refrigerate overnight. Serve with green salad.

Irene Gates

Southwestern Salad Dressing
"Spice up your salad"

Easy
Yields: ½ cup
Preparation: 10 minutes
Can be made ahead

3   Tbsp. sugar
⅓   cup olive oil
3   Tbsp. fresh lime juice
3   Tbsp. white wine vinegar
¼   cup finely chopped fresh cilantro
½   tsp. salt
¼   tsp. pepper
¼   tsp. chili powder
1   clove garlic, minced

In a bowl, whisk all ingredients together thoroughly. Toss with lettuce.

Good with a lettuce, black bean, corn and cheese salad.

Christine C. Sunderman

Pacific Rim Vinaigrette

Easy
Yields: ⅓ cup
Preparation: 10 min.
Must be made ahead

2   green onions
2   cloves garlic
2   Tbsp. sesame oil
2   Tbsp. soy sauce
2   Tbsp. rice vinegar
2   Tbsp. peeled, finely chopped, fresh ginger
2   Tbsp. honey
¼   cup canola oil

Blend first 7 ingredients in a food processor. With the machine running, gradually add the oil and process until well blended. May be prepared one day in advance. Cover and refrigerate. Let stand 30 minutes at room temperature before serving.

Serve with green salad.

Sally W. Bruce

197

Ice House Dressing
"Zesty and smooth"

Easy
Makes: 1 qt.
Preparation: 5 min.
Can be made ahead

Combine all ingredients in medium bowl and mix well. Cover tightly and refrigerate until serving time.

Serve with crisp salad greens.

Penny C. Lawrence

2 **cups mayonnaise**

1¼ **cups sour cream**

½ **cup finely chopped Italian parsley**

⅓ **cup capers**

¼ **cup minced green onion**

1 **Tbsp. dried tarragon, soaked in white wine vinegar for 15 minutes**

2 **Tbsp. fresh lemon juice**

1 **anchovy fillet, minced**

1 **clove garlic, minced**

198

Sweets

Clark Bar Cheesecake

"A creamy candy delight"

Easy
Serves: 12
Preparation: 20 min.
Cooking: 1 hr.
Must be made ahead

Crust:
2   lg. Clark Bars
1   pkg. honey graham crackers
⅛   tsp. ground ginger
6   Tbsp. (¾ stick) butter, melted
2   Tbsp. sugar

Filling:
3   8-oz. pkg. cream cheese, room temperature
5   eggs
¾   cup sugar
2   Tbsp. Amaretto
3   lg. Clark Bars, coarsely ground

Topping:
1   pt. whipping cream
1   lg. Clark Bar, coarsely ground

Preheat oven to 350°.

Crust:
In a food processor, mix the Clark Bars, graham crackers and ginger until finely processed. Remove and place in a large bowl. Add melted butter to the graham cracker mixture along with the sugar. Mix well. Press evenly and firmly onto the base of a 9" or 10" springform pan. Chill.

Filling:
Using an electric mixer, beat cream cheese until smooth. Add eggs one at a time. Add sugar, mixing until smooth. Add Amaretto and ground Clark Bars. Pour into the chilled crust and bake for approximately 1 hour, or until set.

Remove cake from oven and cool in pan on rack for one hour. Cover and place in refrigerator to chill thoroughly, at least 4 hours.

Topping:
When ready to serve, top with whipped cream and coarsely ground Clark Bar pieces.

John Birch

Estelle's New York Style Cheesecake

"Everyone asks for this recipe"

Moderately difficult
Serves: 12
Preparation: 20 min.
Cooking: 1½–2 hrs.
Must be made ahead
Can be frozen

Crust:
1   cup flour, sifted
¼   cup sugar
½   cup (1 stick) butter
1   slightly beaten egg yolk
¼   tsp. vanilla

Filling:
5   8-oz. pkg. cream
    cheese, softened
1¾ cups sugar
3   Tbsp. flour
¼   tsp. salt
¼   tsp. vanilla
5   eggs
2   egg yolks
¼   cup heavy cream

Preheat oven to 400°.

Crust:
Combine flour and sugar in a bowl. Cut in butter until mixture is crumbly. Add egg yolk and vanilla. Blend thoroughly. Pat ⅓ of mixture on bottom of a lightly greased 9" or 10" springform pan with the sides removed. Bake for about 6 minutes, or until golden. Cool. Butter sides of pan and attach to the bottom. Pat remaining mixture evenly on sides to a height of 2 inches.

Raise oven to 500°.

Filling:
Using an electric mixer, beat softened cream cheese until fluffy. In a separate bowl, combine sugar, flour, salt and vanilla. Gradually blend into cheese. Add eggs and egg yolks one at a time, beating well after each addition. Gently stir in heavy cream and pour into crust-lined pan. Bake in oven for 5–8 minutes, or until top edge of crust is golden. Reduce heat to 200°. Bake for 1½–2 hours. Remove from oven. Cool in pan for about 3 hours. Remove sides of pan. Refrigerate or freeze.

Dee Rifenburgh

White Chocolate Raspberry Cheesecake
"Luscious elegance"

Easy
Serves: 8–10
Preparation: 20 min.
Cooking: 55–60 min.
Must be made ahead

Crust:
1½ cups graham cracker crumbs

½ cup sugar

½ cup (1 stick) butter, melted

1 tsp. cinnamon

Filling:
1 8-oz. pkg. cream cheese, softened

1 cup sugar

3 eggs

4 oz. white chocolate, melted

2 Tbsp. cornstarch

½ cup whipping cream

1 tsp. vanilla

1 pt. fresh raspberries

Topping:
½ cup sugar

2 cups sour cream

1 tsp. vanilla

Preheat oven to 350°.

Crust:
Mix crust ingredients and press into a 9" or 10" springform pan.

Filling:
Using an electric mixer, cream cream cheese and sugar together. Add eggs one at a time, beating well. Add melted white chocolate, cornstarch, whipping cream and vanilla; mix well at low speed. Pour half the mixture into the springform pan. Add raspberries, then cover with remaining cream cheese mixture, making sure raspberries are covered. Bake for 55–60 minutes. Let stand for 10 minutes.

Topping:
Mix topping ingredients and spread over cheese. Bake for 5 minutes more. Chill well before serving.

Connie Stumbras

Maple Pumpkin Cheesecake
"This is definitely a winner"

Easy
Serves: 6–8
Preparation: 25 min.
Cooking: 1 hr. 15 min.
Must be made ahead
Can be frozen

1¼ cups graham cracker
crumbs

¼ cup sugar

¼ cup (½ stick) butter,
melted

Filling:
3 8-oz. pkg. cream
cheese, softened

1 14-oz. can sweetened
condensed milk

1 16-oz. can pumpkin

3 eggs

¾ cup pure maple syrup

1½ tsp. ground cinnamon

1 tsp. nutmeg

¼ tsp. salt

Maple Walnut Raisin
Glaze:

2 Tbsp. water

4 tsp. cornstarch

2 Tbsp. butter, melted

½ cup pure maple syrup

½ cup raisins

½ cup chopped walnuts

Preheat oven to 300°.

Crust:
Combine crumbs, sugar and butter. Press firmly on bottom of a 9" spring-form pan.

Filling:
Using an electric mixer, beat cream cheese until fluffy. Gradually beat in milk until smooth. Add pumpkin, eggs, syrup, cinnamon, nutmeg and salt. Mix well. Pour into prepared pan. Bake for 1 hour 15 minutes, or until edge springs back when lightly touched. Center will be slightly soft.

Maple Walnut Raisin Glaze:
In a small saucepan, combine the water and cornstarch. Stir until dissolved. Add the melted butter, syrup, raisins and walnuts. Cook, stirring constantly, until slightly thickened. Cool. Spoon over cheesecake.

Jackie F. Bowman

Apricot and Peach Cobbler
"Also wonderful with other favorite fruits"

Moderately difficult
Serves: 8
Preparation: 1 hr.
Cooking: 30 min.
Can be made ahead
Can be frozen

½　cup granulated sugar

2　Tbsp. cornstarch

1　1 lb. 13-oz. can sliced peaches, drained, juice reserved

1　10½- oz. can apricot halves, drained, juice reserved

1　Tbsp. butter

½　tsp. cinnamon

¼　tsp. nutmeg

¼　tsp. ground ginger

½　tsp. butternut flavoring

Topping:
½　cup flour

½　cup sugar

¾　tsp. baking powder

pinch of salt

2　Tbsp. butter, softened

1　egg

1　cup heavy cream

2　Tbsp. honey, room temperature

½　tsp. cinnamon

Preheat oven to 350°.

In a medium saucepan, mix sugar and cornstarch. Stir in ½ cup each of reserved peach and apricot juices. Cook over medium heat, stirring constantly, until mixture thickens. Remove from heat. Stir in butter, cinnamon, nutmeg, ginger and butternut flavoring. Add peaches and apricots. Spoon fruit mixture into a 1½ qt. casserole.

Topping:
Mix flour, sugar, baking powder, salt, butter and egg. Spoon topping over fruit mixture. Bake cobbler 30 minutes, or until topping is golden brown. Cool on a rack.

Whip the cream, slowly adding the honey and cinnamon. Serve on warm cobbler.

Virginia Syrylo

Pumpkin Cobbler

"As easy as pie and some like it better"

Easy
Serves: 10–12
Preparation: 15 min.
Cooking: 1 hr 20 min.

1   28-oz. can pumpkin
4   eggs, beaten
1½ cups sugar
1   tsp. salt
1   tsp. ginger
½   tsp. cloves
2   tsp. cinnamon
1   13-oz. can evaporated milk
1   yellow cake mix
1   cup (2 sticks) butter, melted
2   Tbsp. brown sugar
½   cup slivered almonds or chopped walnuts

Preheat oven to 350°.

Grease a 13"x9" pan.

Using an electric mixer, blend pumpkin, eggs, sugar, salt, ginger, cloves, cinnamon and evaporated milk. Pour into prepared pan. Sprinkle dry cake mix over top of mixture. Drizzle melted butter over dry cake mix. Sprinkle brown sugar over butter, then sprinkle nuts on top. Bake 1 hour and 20 minutes. Serve warm.

Nancy V. Walker

Peach And Blueberry Crumble

"Make this when summer fruit is at its best"

Easy
Serves 10
Preparation: 30 min.
Cooking: 40–45 min.
Can be made ahead

Fruit mixture:
6–8 lg. peaches, peeled and thinly sliced (about 6 cups)
1   cup blueberries
¼   cup sugar
1   Tbsp. fresh lime or lemon juice

Topping:
1   cup flour
¾   cup old fashioned rolled oats
¾   cup packed dark brown sugar
½   tsp. cinnamon
¼   tsp. salt
½   cup pecans or walnuts, chopped, optional
½   cup (1 stick) cold butter, cut into sm. pieces

Preheat oven to 375°.

Gently mix peaches, blueberries, sugar and juice together. Place into an 11"x7" baking dish. Combine flour, oats, brown sugar, cinnamon, salt and nuts (if desired). Add butter and work with fingers until crumbly. Sprinkle crumb mixture over fruit and bake 40–45 minutes, or until bubbly and browned. Cool on rack until ready to serve.

Susanne S. Harvey

205

Nick Malgieri's Apple And Rhubarb Crisp

"Try this with blackberries when rhubarb isn't available"

Easy
Serves 6
Preparation: 30 min.
Cooking: 45 min.
Can be made ahead

Apple Mixture:

2½ lbs. tart apples, such as Granny Smith

1 lb. fresh rhubarb

1 cup raisins

½ cup light brown sugar

½ cup sugar

1 tsp. cinnamon

½ cup water

Topping:

¾ cup (1½ sticks) butter

½ cup light brown sugar

¼ cup sugar

1½ cups all-purpose flour

1 tsp. cinnamon

1 tsp. baking powder

1 cup pecans, chopped

Preheat oven to 375°.

Apple Mixture:
Peel, halve, core and slice the apples into wedges. Rinse and string the rhubarb. Cut it into 2" lengths. Combine apples, rhubarb and remaining mixture ingredients. Place into a 13"x9" baking dish.

Topping:
Melt the butter and pour into a bowl. Stir in sugars. Combine flour with cinnamon and baking powder, stir to mix. Stir into butter and sugar mixture. Stir in pecans. Separate the topping mixture into large crumbs and distribute over the top of the apple mixture. Bake at 375° about 45 minutes or until bubbling and well browned. Serve warm or at room temperature.

Nick Malgieri

Giant Apple Popover

"There's no debate over this dish—it's a bi-partisan winner"

Moderately difficult
Serves: 8–10
Preparation: 15 min.
Cooking: 5–10 min.

6   **eggs**
1½ **cups flour**
½   **tsp. salt**
1   **Tbsp. sugar**
1½ **cups milk**
¾   **cup (1½ sticks) butter**
3   **lg. apples, peeled,
     cored, thinly sliced**
juice of ½ lemon
¾   **cup sugar**
2   **Tbsp. cinnamon**

Preheat oven to 425°.

Place eggs, flour, salt, sugar and milk in a blender and process until blended.

Divide butter and melt in two 9" oven-proof skillets.

Sprinkle apple slices with lemon juice and divide between the two pans. Divide sugar and cinnamon over apples and sauté until glazed and golden.

Divide the batter and pour over apples. Bake 5–10 minutes, until puffed and golden brown. Serve at once.

Arlen Specter
United States Senate

Blueberry Kuchen

Easy
Serves: 8–10
Preparation: 10 min.
Cooking: 1 hr.
Can be made ahead

Crust:
1   **cup flour**
pinch salt
1   **Tbsp. sugar**
½   **cup (1 stick) butter**
1   **Tbsp. white vinegar**
Filling:
1   **cup sugar**
2   **Tbsp. flour**
dash cinnamon
3   **cups blueberries,
     divided**
powdered sugar

Preheat oven to 400°.

Crust:
Place crust ingredients in a food processor and blend until crumbled. Press into bottom and sides of a 9" springform pan.

Filling:
Mix first three ingredients with 2 cups of blueberries. Pour into crust and bake for 1 hour. Remove kuchen from oven. Add last cup of blueberries, pressing them into the tart while still hot.

Cool and dust with powdered sugar.

Norma W. Sproull

207

Desserts

Peach Charlotte
"This would be beautiful at a summer luncheon"

Moderately difficult
Serves: 8–10
Preparation: 30 min.
Must be made ahead

12 ladyfingers
3 envelopes unflavored gelatin
½ cup sugar
1 cup water
1 cup heavy cream
¼ tsp. almond extract
1 qt. soft peach ice cream or yogurt
2 cups sliced peaches

Currant Raspberry Sauce:
2 Tbsp. cornstarch
½ cup water
¼ cup currant jelly
1 10-oz. pkg. frozen raspberries, partially thawed, undrained

Cut ½" from ladyfingers, reserving the ends. Line the sides of a 9" springform pan with ladyfingers.

In a small saucepan, mix gelatin, sugar and water. Stir constantly over low heat until dissolved.

In a large bowl, using an electric mixer, whip cream and almond extract to soft peaks. Add ice cream or yogurt and beat until smooth and well blended. With beater at high speed, gradually add gelatin mixture. Fold in reserved ladyfingers and pour into pan. Chill until firm. Remove springform and decorate with peaches. Serve with currant raspberry sauce.

Sauce:
Blend cornstarch, water and jelly. Stir over heat until thickened. Stir in raspberries and chill.

Janet Chace

Strawberry White Chocolate Tiramisu

Moderately difficult
Serves: 10–12
Preparation: 45 min.
Must be made ahead

Filling:
2   6-oz. pkg. white
    chocolate baking bars
1½ cups whipping cream,
    divided
1   3-oz. pkg. cream
    cheese, softened

Crust:
3   3-oz. pkg. (36)
    ladyfingers, split
1¼ cups espresso or strong
    coffee, cooled
2   Tbsp. brandy, optional
2   pts. fresh strawberries,
    stemmed and divided

Filling:
Melt white chocolate baking bars with ¼ cup of whipping cream in the top of a double boiler over hot, not boiling, water. Stir until smooth. Cool to room temperature. Using an electric mixer, beat cream cheese in a large bowl until fluffy. Stir in white chocolate mixture. Whip remaining 1¼ cups cream to form soft peaks. Gradually whisk into cream cheese mixture and set aside.

Crust:
Line the sides of a 9" springform pan with ladyfinger halves, flat sides facing towards center of pan. In a small bowl, combine coffee and brandy. Arrange half the remaining ladyfingers on bottom of springform pan. Brush with half of the coffee mixture. Cover with half the filling. Slice one pint of strawberries and layer over filling. Repeat ladyfinger, coffee and filling layers.

Cover and refrigerate at least 4 hours, or overnight. Remove sides of pan. Halve remaining strawberries and arrange decoratively on top.

Barbara Laman Gaudio

209

Cinnamon Swirl Raisin Bread Pudding
"Sweet simplicity"

Easy
Serves 8–10
Preparation: 30 min.
Cooking: 1 hr.
Can be made ahead
Can be frozen

1   16-oz. loaf cinnamon bread
1   qt. milk
3   eggs
2   cups sugar
2   tsp. vanilla
1   Tbsp. butter (optional)

Preheat oven to 350°.

Butter a 13"x9" baking dish.

Tear bread into 2" pieces, drop into large mixing bowl and add milk. Let soak for 15 minutes. Using an electric mixer, beat eggs and sugar until thick and light yellow. Add vanilla and pour over soaked bread. Mix until evenly coated.

Transfer mixture to prepared baking dish. Place uncovered in large pan filled with 1½" water. Bake until set and knife inserted comes out clean, about 1 hour. Dot with butter before baking for a less crusty pudding.

Jane Ellen Rabe

Dessert Bruschetta
"A new twist on Bruschetta"

Easy
Serves 6
Preparation: 5 min.
Cooking: 30 seconds

6   ¾" slices Italian or crusty sourdough bread
½   cup chocolate hazelnut spread
3   Tbsp. hazelnuts, chopped
3   Tbsp. brown sugar
3   med. bananas, thinly sliced
2   Tbsp. butter, melted
chocolate curls, optional

Preheat broiler.

Toast bread and cool. Spread with chocolate hazelnut spread and place on a baking sheet.

In a mixing bowl, combine nuts and sugar. Set aside.

Layer banana slices on top of chocolate hazelnut spread. Brush with butter. Top with 1 tablespoon of the nut mixture. Broil bruschetta 5" from heat for about 30 seconds. Decorate with chocolate curls and serve.

Linda D. Orsini

Chocolate Bread and Butter Pudding

Moderately difficult
Serves: 8
Preparation: 30 min.
Cooking: 30–35 min.
Must be made ahead

9–12 slices, ¼" thick white
    bread
5   oz. dark continental
    chocolate with 70% of
    cocoa solids, chopped
2   cups whipping cream
4   Tbsp. dark rum
½   cup superfine sugar
3   Tbsp. butter
3   extra lg. eggs
chilled whipping cream

Preheat oven to 350°.

Lightly butter an 11"x7" pan.

Remove crusts from bread and cut each slice into 4 triangles. Place chocolate, whipping cream, rum, sugar and butter in a bowl over a pan of barely simmering water. Heat until butter and chocolate have melted and sugar has dissolved. Remove from heat and stir well. Cool slightly.

Place eggs in a separate bowl, add chocolate mixture and whisk until thoroughly blended.

Spread ⅓ of the chocolate mixture over the bottom of the dish; cover with half the bread triangles in overlapping rows. Cover with second ⅓ of the chocolate, then arrange the remaining bread triangles on top and cover with the last ⅓ of chocolate mixture. Using a fork, press bread gently down to absorb chocolate mixture. Cover the dish with plastic wrap and allow to stand at room temperature for 2 hours before transferring to the refrigerator for a minimum of 24 hours (preferably 48 hours).

Remove plastic wrap and bake near top of oven for 30–35 minutes. Top will be crunchy and inside soft.

Let stand for 10 minutes before serving with whipped cream.

Lorraine Baker

211

"Watermelon" Sherbet

"This will entertain everyone at your backyard barbecue"

Easy
Serves: 10–12
Preparation: 20 min.
Must be made ahead
Must be frozen

1 **pt. lime sherbet, softened**

1 **pt. pineapple sherbet, softened**

1 **qt. raspberry sherbet, softened**

1 **cup miniature chocolate chips**

Line a large bowl with foil. Press softened lime sherbet against the bottom and sides of the lined bowl. Freeze uncovered until firm, about 1 hour. Press softened pineapple sherbet into frozen lime sherbet. Freeze about 30 minutes. Stir chocolate chips into raspberry sherbet and fill the center of the lime and pineapple bowl. Freeze 8 hours. Invert carefully onto serving dish. Remove foil and slice like watermelon.

Marilyn J. Sittig

Pecan Custard

Easy
Serves: 4
Preparation: 15 min.
Cooking: 45 min.
Can be made ahead

1 **egg**

2 **egg whites**

½ **cup brown sugar**

½ **cup light corn syrup**

1 **Tbsp. butter, melted**

½ **tsp. vanilla**

dash of salt

½ **cup pecans, coarsely chopped and lightly toasted**

Preheat oven to 400°.

Combine egg and egg whites in a medium bowl and beat slightly. Add brown sugar, corn syrup, melted butter, vanilla and salt. Stir to blend thoroughly. Add the pecans.

Pour into individual custard cups and place in a deep ovenproof pan. Add hot water to the pan, making sure it comes halfway up the sides of the custard cups . Bake for 10 minutes. Lower the temperature to 350° and bake for 35 minutes or until set. Cool on a rack for at least 15 minutes. Serve warm or at room temperature.

Spero A. Maginas

Chocolate Almond Torte

"No last minute fuss for this fabulous dessert"

Moderately difficult
Serves: 10–12
Preparation: 45 min.
Cooking: 45–50 min.
Must be made ahead

1⅔ cups semi-sweet
   chocolate chips
6 Tbsp (¾ stick) butter
2 Tbsp. brandy
¾ cup whole blanched
   almonds, ground
6 Tbsp. flour
4 eggs, separated
¾ cup sugar
¼ tsp. almond extract
pinch of salt
Topping:
½ cup whipping cream
⅔ cup chocolate chips
sliced almonds, optional

Preheat oven to 325°.

Butter a 9" springform pan, line with waxed paper and butter again.

Melt chocolate chips with butter in a double boiler over low heat. Stir in brandy and cool.

Combine almonds and flour in a food processor. Using an electric mixer, beat egg yolks and sugar for 1 minute. Gradually add chocolate mixture and almond extract to the egg yolks and sugar.

Beat egg whites and salt until they form soft peaks. Fold ⅓ of the egg whites into the chocolate mixture. Fold in remaining egg whites. Gently fold in almond and flour mixture.

Pour into prepared pan and smooth top. Bake for 45–50 minutes, or until moist crumbs cling to a toothpick. Cool on rack for 10 minutes. Remove sides of pan and cool for 1 hour. Remove waxed paper.

Topping:
Heat cream to simmer. Remove from heat and add chocolate chips, stirring until smooth. Cool until slightly thickened, 15–30 minutes. Pour topping over cake, spreading to coat. Let stand until set. Decorate with almond slices. Must be made 1–2 days ahead.

Carolyn S. Hammer

213

Sunburst Fruit Tart
"Like a slice of sunshine"

Moderately difficult
Serves: 12
Preparation: 40 min.
Cooking: 15 min.
Must be made ahead

Crust:
¼ cup ground almonds
½ cup (1 stick) butter, softened
½ cup sugar
1½ cups flour
1 egg yolk
1 tsp. vanilla
1 tsp. almond extract

Filling:
8 oz. cream cheese, softened
3 Tbsp. sugar
4 tsp. Amaretto
1 tsp. vanilla
½ tsp. almond extract

Apricot glaze:
½ cup apricot preserves
1 Tbsp. butter
1 Tbsp. fresh lemon juice
2 Tbsp. Amaretto

Topping:
3–4 cups fresh soft fruit, (strawberries, raspberries, kiwi, peaches, bananas)

Preheat oven to 375°.

Crust:
In food processor or mixing bowl, combine almonds, butter, sugar and flour. Add egg yolk and extracts. Blend until dough holds together. Press onto bottom and sides of 11" tart pan with removable bottom. Bake for about 15 minutes, until golden brown. Cool.

Filling:
Using an electric mixer, blend all filling ingredients until smooth; spread on cooled tart crust. Chill until firm, at least 30 minutes.

Glaze:
Mix all ingredients in a small saucepan. Heat over low heat until melted. Cool and set aside.

To assemble tart:
Arrange fruits in a circular pattern on filling 1–2 hours before serving. Brush fruit with glaze. Remove rim before serving slightly chilled or at room temperature.

Nan V. O'Connor

French Apple Tart

Difficult
Serves: 8
Preparation: 1 hr. 30 min.
Cooking: 45 min.
Can be made ahead

2   cups flour, sifted

½   cup sugar, divided

1   cup (2 sticks) unsalted
     butter, chilled and cut
     into pieces

pinch of salt

¼   cup orange juice,
     chilled

3   lg. Granny Smith
     apples

1¼ cups apricot preserves

3   tsp. rum

Preheat oven to 375°.

In a food processor, blend flour, ¼ cup sugar, butter and a pinch of salt until the mixture resembles coarse oatmeal. Add orange juice and pulse 3–4 times. Turn the mixture out onto a work surface; press into 2 balls, one larger than the other. Wrap in plastic and chill for 30 minutes.

On a lightly floured surface, roll the larger ball into a 14" round. Transfer to an 11" tart pan with removable rim. Trim the edges, leaving a ½" overhang.

Sprinkle the bottom of the shell with the remaining ¼ cup sugar. Peel, core and thinly slice the apples. Arrange them in the shell in overlapping concentric circles.

In a small saucepan, cook the preserves and rum over a moderately low heat, stirring until the mixture comes to a boil. Strain the mixture through a fine sieve into a small bowl. Brush all but ¼ cup of the preserve mixture over the apples.

On a lightly floured surface, roll out the remaining dough to ⅛" thick. Cut into ½" wide strips and arrange the strips in a lattice pattern over the apples. Press the overhanging dough gently back over the strips.

Bake the tart for 45 minutes, or until the crust is golden. Let tart cool for 5 minutes. Remove rim.

Let tart cool for 30 minutes more on a rack, then brush with remaining ¼ cup preserves.

Ingrid Arsuaga

215

Pear Tart
"Delightfully rich pear flavor"

Easy
Serves: 8
Preparation: 30 min.
Cooking: 25 min.
Can be made ahead

parchment paper

4 oz. cream cheese

½ cup (1 stick) unsalted butter

1 cup flour

1 cup sugar, plus 3 Tbsp., divided

¼ tsp. salt

4 Tbsp. fresh lemon juice

4 Tbsp. pear brandy

3–4 Bosc or Red Bartlett pears, unpeeled

sugar

½ tsp. cinnamon

whipped cream

Preheat oven to 400°.

Grease and flour a baking sheet, or line with parchment paper.

Combine cream cheese and butter in a food processor. Add flour, 1 cup sugar and salt. Process until combined. Dough will be sticky. Turn dough out onto prepared baking sheet. With lightly floured fingers, pat dough onto the baking sheet. Refrigerate.

In a medium bowl, combine remaining 3 tablespoons sugar with lemon juice and brandy. Halve pears lengthwise and core. Cut lengthwise into ¼" slices. Transfer to lemon juice mixture and coat well.

Place pears in a strainer to drain liquid. Arrange slices around the border of the dough, overlapping slightly. Arrange remaining slices in the center. Sprinkle tart with sugar, then dust with cinnamon. Bake until golden, about 25 minutes. Serve warm or at room temperature, with whipped cream.

Susan Jones

Peach Of A Pie
"A sweet creamy treat"

Easy
Serves: 8
Preparation Time: 30 min.
Cooking: 5 min.
Must be made ahead

1   9" baked pie shell
8   oz. cream cheese
¼   cup sugar
⅛   tsp. salt
1   Tbsp. milk
½   tsp. vanilla
1   lb. pkg. frozen strawberries
2   Tbsp. cornstarch
1   Tbsp. fresh lemon juice
¼   cup sugar
1   2½ lb. can sliced peaches

Using an electric mixer, blend cream cheese, sugar, salt, milk and vanilla. Spread onto baked pie shell.

Defrost frozen strawberries and push through strainer into a bowl. Combine cornstarch, juice and sugar in a small saucepan and cook for about 3 minutes. Cool.

Pour half the strawberry mixture on top of cheese mixture. Drain peaches and layer on top of strawberry mixture. Top with remaining strawberry mixture. Refrigerate for at least an hour before serving.

Melissa Strong

Blueberry Crumb Pie
"Tastes like a summer day"

Easy
Serves: 8–10
Preparation: 30 min.
Cooking: 40 min.
Will freeze

2   cups fresh blueberries
¾   cup sugar
3   tsp. quick cooking tapioca
pinch of salt
1   Tbsp. Grand Marnier
1   9" prepared graham cracker crust
⅔   cup flour
⅓   cup dark brown sugar
½   cup butter

Preheat oven 400°.

Lightly mix blueberries, sugar, tapioca, salt and Grand Marnier. Spread evenly in pastry shell.

Blend flour, brown sugar and butter with a fork until mixture is crumbly. Sprinkle evenly over blueberries.

Bake for 40 minutes, or until golden brown.

Cool before serving.

June C. Kinne

217

Blueberry Pie

Easy
Serves: 6
Preparation: 5 min.
Must be made ahead

1   pt. blueberries, washed
    and patted dry
1   9" prepared graham
    cracker crust
1   jar currant jelly
½   cup plain yogurt
½   cup sour cream
fresh mint leaves

Put blueberries in bottom of crust. Melt currant jelly and pour over blueberries. Refrigerate for a few hours.

Mix yogurt and sour cream. Spread cream mixture over the pie. Decorate with mint leaves before serving.

Frances M. Rollman

Rhubarb Zucchini Pie
"A surprising combination of flavors"

Easy
Serves: 6–8
Preparation: 35 min.
Cooking: 40 min.

Pie:
1½ cups sugar
1   tsp. cinnamon
1   tsp. nutmeg
½   tsp. ginger
1½ Tbsp. flour
2   cups rhubarb, cut into
    ½" pieces
2   cups zucchini peeled,
    quartered, with seeds
    discarded and cut in ¼"
    slices
1   unbaked 9" pie shell
Topping:
¾   cup flour
¾   cup crushed crisp rice
    cereal
½   cup brown sugar
1   Tbsp. butter

Preheat oven to 425°.

Pie:
Mix sugar, cinnamon, nutmeg, ginger and flour. Add rhubarb and zucchini; mix well. Pour into pie shell.

Topping:
Mix flour, rice cereal and sugar. Cut in the butter until crumbly. Sprinkle topping over pie, covering completely. Bake for 15 minutes, then reduce heat to 350° and continue baking for another 25 minutes. Serve warm.

Arleen Einloth

Rhubarb Torte

Easy
Serves: 6
Preparation: 15 min.
Cooking: 35–40 min.
Can be made ahead

1   cup flour

½   cup (1 stick) unsalted
    butter

5   Tbsp. powdered sugar

2   eggs, beaten

¼   tsp. salt

¾   tsp. baking powder

¾   cup sugar

1   tsp. vanilla

1   tsp. grated lemon rind

3   cups diced rhubarb

whipped cream

Preheat oven to 350°.

Using an electric mixer, cream flour, butter and powdered sugar. Press into the bottom only of an 8" or 9" greased, straight sided, tart pan and bake for 8–10 minutes.

Combine remaining ingredients and spread over crust. Return to oven and bake for an additional 30 minutes, or until the center has set.

Serve warm or at room temperature, topped with whipped cream.

Nan V. O'Connor

Streusel Concord Grape Pie
"A little extra effort for an extraordinary dessert"

Moderately Difficult
Serves: 8
Preparation: 1 hr.
Cooking: 35–40 min.

Oat Streusel:
½   cup quick cooking
    rolled oats

½   cup brown sugar

¼   cup flour

¼   cup (½ stick) butter

1   unbaked 9" pie shell

4½ cups Concord grapes

1   cup sugar

¼   cup flour

2   tsp. fresh lemon juice

⅛   tsp. salt

Preheat oven 425°.

Streusel:
Combine oats, brown sugar and ¼ cup flour. Cut in butter to distribute evenly. Set aside.

Wash grapes and remove skins by pinching at end opposite stem. Reserve skins. Place pulp in saucepan and bring to a boil. Cook until pulp is soft. Put through strainer or food mill, while hot, to remove seeds. Mix strained pulp with reserved skins. Stir in sugar, flour, lemon juice and salt. Place grape mixture in pie shell. Sprinkle with oat streusel. Bake for 35–40 minutes, or until center of pie is bubbling slightly.

Karen Flam

Strawberry Cookie Pie

"This sweet crunchy crust is almost good enough to eat on its own"

Moderately difficult
Serves: 8–10
Preparation: 20 min.
Cooking: 10–15 min.
Must be made ahead

1   cup flour

⅓   cup brown sugar

½   cup chopped nuts

½   cup (1 stick) butter, melted

8   oz. cream cheese

½   cup powdered sugar

2   cups sliced fresh strawberries

3   cups crushed fresh strawberries

⅓   cup cornstarch

1   cup sugar

1   cup whipped cream

Preheat oven to 375°.

Grease a 10" springform pan.

Mix flour, brown sugar, nuts and melted butter. Press into prepared pan. Bake for 10–15 minutes, until light brown. Cool crust completely. Remove side of pan.

Thoroughly mix cream cheese and powdered sugar. Spread over cooled crust. Arrange sliced strawberries on top.

Cook crushed strawberries, cornstarch and sugar until thick. Cool. Pour over sliced strawberries. Serve with whipped cream.

Sylvia Shuty

Schmierkase Pie

Easy
Serves: 6–8
Preparation: 10 min.
Cooking: 50 min.
Can be made ahead

24   oz. cottage cheese

2   Tbsp. evaporated milk

1½ cups sugar

¾   tsp. salt

3   eggs

1½ tsp. vanilla

3   Tbsp. flour

⅜   tsp. nutmeg

1   9" unbaked pie shell

cinnamon

Preheat oven to 450°.

Thoroughly hand mix the first 8 ingredients in a large bowl. Pour into the pie shell. Sprinkle lightly with cinnamon.

Bake for 10 minutes. Reduce heat to 350° and bake for 40 minutes more, until set. It may be necessary to cover the crust edges to keep them from getting too brown.

Optional: A little chopped apple, pineapple, raisins or nuts may be added.

Erma M. Henry

Ozark Pie

"When dinner is done, your dessert will be waiting for you in your freezer"

Easy
Serves: 8
Preparation: 20 min.
Cooking: 25 min.
Must be frozen

1   egg
¾   cup sugar
¼   cup flour
⅛   tsp. salt
1½ tsp. baking powder
½   cup chopped apples
½   cup chopped pecans
1   qt. vanilla ice cream
2   Heath Bars, crushed

Preheat oven to 350°.

Grease a 10" pie plate.

Mix the first 5 ingredients thoroughly, then add apples and pecans.

Pour into prepared pan and bake for 25 minutes. Allow to cool slightly. Top with ice cream and then Heath Bars. Freeze.

Remove from the freezer 15 minutes before serving.

Susan D. Brantley

Fudge Pie

"Simply scrumptious"

Easy
Serves: 8–10
Preparation: 20 min.
Cooking: 30 min.
Must be made ahead

12 oz. chocolate chips
1½ tsp. instant coffee
    granules
¼   cup (½ stick) margarine
1   cup brown sugar
3   eggs
¼   cup flour
1   cup pecans, roughly
    chopped
1   9" unbaked pie shell

Preheat oven to 325°.

Melt chocolate in a double boiler over gently simmering water. Add instant coffee.

Cream margarine and sugar. Add eggs, one at a time, beating well after each addition.

Beat chocolate mixture into egg mixture. Stir in flour and nuts and pour into pie shell. Bake for 30 minutes. Allow to cool before serving.

Melissa Strong

221

Snickers Pie
"A creamy candy creation"

Moderately difficult
Serves: 8
Preparation: 30 min.
Cooking: 40 min.
Must be made ahead

1　9" unbaked pie crust

Fudge layer:
½　cup unsalted butter
4　oz. semi-sweet chocolate, chopped
½　cup sugar
1　egg
1　egg yolk
1　tsp. vanilla
6　Tbsp. flour
½　tsp. baking powder

Snickers layer:
2　cups Snickers Bars broken into 2" pieces (about 12 oz.)

Cream Cheese layer:
8 oz. cream cheese
⅓　cup sugar
1　egg
1　tsp. vanilla

Topping:
2　oz. milk chocolate, chopped
3　Tbsp. whipping cream

Preheat oven to 350°.

Place pie crust in 9" pan, prick base and bake for 6 minutes. Remove from oven.

Fudge Layer:
Melt butter and chocolate in double boiler over low heat until smooth. Cool. In medium bowl, using an electric mixer, beat sugar, egg and egg yolk. Add cooled chocolate and vanilla. In another bowl, sift flour and baking powder; beat into chocolate mixture. Pour into crust and bake 17 minutes. Cool 10 minutes.

Snickers Layer:
Place Snickers on top of fudge layer.

Cream Cheese Layer:
In a small bowl using an electric mixer, beat all ingredients. Spread over Snickers. Bake for 15 minutes.

Topping:
Combine milk chocolate and whipping cream in a double boiler over low heat until chocolate is melted, stirring to mix well. Drizzle on top of cream cheese layer after it is baked. Chill before serving.

Cheryl Dea Kaufman

Chocolate Pecan Pie
"A little bit of heaven"

Easy
Serves: 8
Preparation: 15 min.
Cooking: 45–55 min.
Must be made ahead

4   eggs, beaten
½   cup melted butter
1   cup light corn syrup
½   cup sugar
1   tsp. vanilla
1   cup pecans, chopped
½   cup semi-sweet chocolate chips
1   9" unbaked pie shell
whipped cream

Preheat oven to 350°.

Mix eggs, butter and corn syrup. Add sugar and blend well. Stir in vanilla, pecans and chocolate chips. Pour into pie shell. Bake for 45–55 minutes, or until softly set in the middle. Cool and place pie in refrigerator to set completely, preferably overnight.

Serve with whipped cream.

Melissa A. Doyle

Southern Pecan Pie
"A rich tradition"

Easy
Serves: 5–6
Preparation: 15 min.
Cooking: 40 min.
Can be made ahead

3   eggs, beaten
1   cup light brown sugar
1   cup dark corn syrup
1   Tbsp. flour
1   Tbsp. butter, melted
1   tsp. vanilla
⅔   cup pecan halves
1   9" unbaked pie crust

Preheat oven to 450°.

Place all ingredients, except pecans and pie shell, in a bowl; mix thoroughly, using an electric mixer. Pour into unbaked pie shell. Place pecans carefully on top, starting at the rim and circling to the center.

Bake for 10 minutes; then reduce temperature to 350° for 30 minutes longer, or until the filling shakes like gelatin. Cool and serve.

Nancylee N. Mohler

Oatmeal Coffee Cake

"The broiled topping makes this a cut above the rest"

Moderately difficult
Serves: 16
Preparation: 40 min.
Cooking: 45–55 min.
Can be frozen

Cake:

1½ cups boiling water

1 cup quick cooking rolled oats

½ cup (1 stick) butter, softened

1 cup brown sugar

1 cup white sugar

2 eggs

1 tsp. vanilla

1½ cups flour

1 tsp. baking soda

1 tsp. baking powder

½ tsp. salt

1 tsp. cinnamon

½ cup chopped walnuts

½ cup raisins

Topping:

6 Tbsp. (¾ stick) butter melted

¼ cup evaporated milk

1 tsp. vanilla

1 cup coconut

⅔ cup brown sugar

½ cup chopped walnuts

Preheat oven to 350°.

Butter a 13"x9" pan.

Pour boiling water over oats and let stand for 20 minutes.

Using an electric mixer, cream butter and sugars in a large bowl; add to oat mixture. Add remaining ingredients, stirring after each addition. Mix well. Bake in buttered pan for 40–50 minutes.

Preheat broiler.

Mix topping ingredients and spread over cake. Broil for 3–5 minutes. Cool before serving.

Doris G. Sofaly

Irish Coffee Cake

"All leprechauns agree, it's magically delicious"

Easy
Serves: 10
Preparation: 3¼ hrs.
Cooking: 35–40 min.
Must be made ahead

Cake:
½   **cup (1 stick) butter, softened**
½   **cup sugar**
2   **eggs**
2   **Tbsp. strong coffee**
1   **cup flour**
1   **tsp. baking powder**

Syrup:
⅔   **cup strong coffee**
½   **cup sugar**
3   **Tbsp. Irish whiskey**

Icing:
1   **cup whipping cream**
1   **Tbsp. powdered sugar**
1   **Tbsp. Irish whiskey**

Preheat oven to 350°.

Butter and flour an 8" tube pan.

Cake:
Using an electric mixer, cream butter and sugar in a large bowl, then add eggs and beat until mixed. Stir in coffee. Sift flour and baking powder; gradually add to egg mixture. Pour into prepared pan and bake for 35–40 minutes. Test with cake tester. Remove from oven and let stand 10 minutes. Turn onto a wire rack to cool.

Syrup:
In a saucepan, heat coffee and sugar until dissolved; boil one minute. Remove from heat and add whiskey. Return cake to clean tube pan and prick the entire surface with a fork. Pour syrup over cake and let stand for 2–3 hours.

Icing:
Whip cream until stiff, then fold in sifted powdered sugar and whiskey. Turn cake onto a serving plate and cover with whipped cream. Chill 1 hour before serving.

Cel McCabe

"Pinch Me" Cake

Easy
Serves 8
Preparation: 15 min.
Cooking: 45-50min.

1½ cups brown sugar

½ cup sugar

1 tsp. vanilla

1½ tsp. cinnamon

1 cup (2 sticks) butter, softened

1 cup chopped nuts

3 cans refrigerated biscuits (8 in each)

Preheat oven to 350°.

Grease a 6 cup bundt pan.

Using an electric mixer, combine sugars, vanilla, cinnamon, butter and nuts in a medium bowl.

Layer 1 can of biscuits in a bundt pan and cover with half the sugar mixture. Repeat layering, ending with a biscuit layer.

Bake for 45–50 minutes. Turn out onto platter and serve immediately.

Carol S. Metzger

Grandma's Spice Cake

Easy
Serves: 8
Preparation: 10 min.
Cooking: 35–40 min.

¼ cup (½ stick) butter

1 cup sugar

1 tsp. baking soda

1½ cups flour

dash salt

2 tsp. cinnamon

1 tsp. ground cloves

1 tsp. nutmeg

1 10½-oz. can condensed tomato soup

1 cup raisins

Preheat oven to 375°.

Grease an 8"x8" pan.

Using an electric mixer, cream the butter and sugar. Sift together the dry ingredients and combine with soup, raisins, creamed butter and sugar. Mix well. Place in the prepared pan and bake for 35–40 minutes.

Sandy Clem

Raspberry Cream Cheese Coffee Cake

Easy
Serves: 16
Preparation: 15 min.
Cooking: 45–55 min.

2¼ cups flour
1 cup sugar, divided
¾ cup (1½ sticks) butter
½ tsp. baking powder
½ tsp. baking soda
¼ tsp. salt
¾ cup sour cream
2 eggs, divided
1 tsp. almond extract
8 oz. cream cheese, softened
½ cup raspberry preserves
½ cup sliced almonds

Preheat oven to 350°.

Grease and flour a 10" springform pan.

In a large bowl, combine flour and ¾ cup of sugar. Cut in the butter with a fork, or use a food processor. Set aside 1 cup of this mixture. Add baking powder, baking soda, salt, sour cream, 1 egg and almond extract and blend well. Spread this batter over the bottom of the springform pan.

In a small bowl, combine cream cheese, ¼ cup sugar and remaining egg and blend well. Pour over batter in pan. Carefully spoon the preserves over the cheese filling. Mix the reserved cup of crumb mixture with almonds and sprinkle on top. Bake for 45–55 minutes.

Lynn B. Popovich

227

Blueberry Coffee Cake
"Pour a cup of coffee and relax"

Easy
Serves: 8
Preparation: 15 min.
Cooking: 40–45 min.
Can be frozen

Cake:
¼ cup (½ stick) margarine, softened

¾ cup sugar

1 egg

2 cups flour

2 tsp. baking powder

½ cup milk

2 cups blueberries (fresh or frozen)

Topping:
¼ cup (½ stick) cold margarine, cut into pieces

½ cup sugar

⅓ cup flour

1 tsp. cinnamon

Preheat oven to 375°.

Grease a 13"x9" pan.

Cake:
In a large bowl using an electric mixer, cream margarine and sugar; add egg. Mix flour and baking powder. Incorporate half the flour into the margarine mixture followed by half the milk; repeat with the remaining flour and milk. Fold in blueberries. The mixture will be thick. Spread into greased pan.

Topping:
Using an electric mixer, mix cold margarine, sugar, flour and cinnamon just until blended. Sprinkle topping mixture over coffee cake batter. Bake for 40–45 minutes. Cool before serving.

Ginny Z. Monroe

Judy's Carrot Cake
"A processor makes this cake a snap"

Easy
Serves: 12
Preparation: 25 min.
Cooking: 30–40 min.

Cake:
2   cups flour
2   tsp. cinnamon
1   tsp. salt
2   tsp. baking soda
2   cups sugar
1¼ cups oil
4   eggs
2   tsp. vanilla
1   cup chopped walnuts
3   cups grated carrots
Frosting:
1   16-oz. pkg. powdered
    sugar

½   cup (1 stick) butter,
    softened
8   oz. cream cheese
1   tsp. milk , or more as
    needed

Preheat oven to 350°.

Grease a 13"x9" pan.

Cake:
Sift all dry ingredients together. In a large bowl using an electric mixer, mix oil and eggs; beat well. Add flour mixture, vanilla, nuts and carrots; stir well. Pour into prepared pan. Bake for 30–40 minutes.

Frosting:
Using an electric mixer, beat sugar, butter and cream cheese. Add milk until frosting is desired consistency. Spread onto cooled cake.

Judy Ryave

Apple Cup Cakes

Easy
Serves: 18
Preparation: 20 min.
Cooking: 20 min.

¼   cup sugar
1   tsp. cinnamon
1   pkg. yellow cake mix
1⅔ cup smooth applesauce
2   eggs
2   egg whites

Preheat oven to 350°.

Line muffin pans with muffin cups.

Mix sugar and cinnamon in a small bowl and set aside.

Using an electric mixer, mix the cake mix, applesauce, eggs and egg whites until smooth. Drop a tablespoon of batter into each cup and sprinkle with cinnamon mixture. Top with another tablespoon of batter. Finish with the cinnamon mixture. Bake for 20 minutes.

Jean Clem

Cannoli Cake
"Dazzling and delicious"

Moderately difficult
Serves: 10
Preparation: 45 min.
Cooking: 30 min.
Must be made ahead

6   **eggs, separated**
1   **cup sugar, divided**
¾   **cup flour**
1   **Tbsp. baking powder**
½   **tsp. salt**
2   **tsp. vanilla, divided**
2   **Tbsp. water**
32   **oz. ricotta cheese**
8   **oz. cream cheese**
1   **cup powdered sugar**
¼   **cup semi-sweet chocolate chips**
½   **cup freshly squeezed orange juice**

Frosting:
3   **Tbsp. butter**
3   **Tbsp. milk**
1¾ **cups powdered sugar**
¾   **tsp. vanilla**
2   **cups whipping cream**
⅓   **cup semi-sweet chocolate chips**

Preheat oven to 375°.

In a small bowl, with mixer on high speed, beat the egg whites until soft peaks form. Gradually add ½ cup of sugar, beating until sugar is completely dissolved and stiff peaks form. Set aside.

In a large bowl, with mixer on low speed, beat the egg yolks, flour, baking powder, salt, ½ cup of sugar, 1 teaspoon of vanilla and the water until blended. With a spatula gently fold the egg whites into the yolk mixture ⅓ at a time. Spoon the batter into 2 ungreased 8" cake pans and bake for 30 minutes, or until the cake is golden on top and springs back when lightly touched. Invert the cakes on a wire rack and cool completely in their pans.

In a large bowl, with the mixer on low speed, beat ricotta, cream cheese, powdered sugar and remaining vanilla until smooth. Stir in ¼ cup chocolate chips.

Remove the cakes from their pans. With a serrated knife, cut each layer in half horizontally. Brush each layer with orange juice. Place the bottom layer, cut side up, on a plate. Spread ⅓ of the cheese filling on this layer. Repeat with two more layers, finishing with the last layer on top. Smooth any excess filling from around the cake.

Frosting:
In a small bowl, with mixer on medium speed, beat softened butter, milk, powdered sugar and vanilla until smooth. In another bowl, whip the cream to stiff peaks. Gently fold the frosting mixture into whipped cream. Spread frosting over cake. Melt chocolate chips over low heat. Pour into a decorating bag with a small tip. Draw concentric circles to the edge of the cake. Using a toothpick, draw lines through the circles from the center to the edge of the cake. Refrigerate at least 3 hours before serving.

Kit Muire

Chocolate Truffle Cake
"Wow"

Moderately difficult
Serves: 8
Preparation: 20 min.
Cooking: 15 min.
Must be made ahead

12 oz. semi-sweet
    chocolate
½ cup (1 stick) unsalted
    butter
1½ tsp. flour
1½ tsp. sugar
1 tsp. hot water
4 eggs, separated
1 cup whipping cream
1 Tbsp. sugar

Preheat oven to 425°.

Butter bottom of 8" springform pan.

Melt chocolate and butter in top of a double boiler. Add flour, sugar and water; blend well. Add egg yolks, one at a time, beating after each addition. Beat egg whites until stiff but not dry. Fold into chocolate mixture. Turn into pan and bake for 15 minutes. Cake will look uncooked in center and will sink in middle. Chill until set.

Whip cream and sugar until soft peaks form. Spread in thick layer over top of cake. Serve. Will keep in refrigerator up to 2 weeks.

Una Melikian

Decadence
"The rich flavor is truly terrific"

Easy
Serves: 12–16
Preparation: 30 min.
Cooking: 50–55 min.
Must be made ahead

1½ cups (3 sticks) butter
¾ lb. semi-sweet chocolate
¼ lb. unsweetened
    chocolate
1¼ cups sugar
¼ cup dark rum
1 tsp. vanilla
8 eggs
raspberry jam
whipped cream

Preheat oven to 325°.

Butter a 10" springform pan. Wrap outside with foil.

Melt butter, chocolates and sugar in a double boiler, stirring over low heat. Remove from heat and stir in rum and vanilla. Whisk in eggs one at a time. Pour into prepared pan. Set in larger pan. Fill larger pan halfway with water. Bake until a toothpick stuck in the center comes out clean, about 50–55 minutes. Remove from oven and let cake stand in water bath 15 minutes. Remove cake from water bath and let cool.

Remove pan sides. Spread jam on top of cake and refrigerate. Using a sharp knife that has been dipped in hot water; slice cake. Clean knife and reheat between each cutting. Serve with whipped cream.

Mary Lou Scarfone

231

Sugar On Top Cookies
"Sweet chunky treats"

Easy
Yields: 6 doz.
Preparation: 20 min.
Cooking: 15 min.

1 cup brown sugar
1 cup white sugar
1 cup (2 sticks) margarine
2 eggs
2½ cups flour
2 tsp. baking powder
1 tsp. baking soda
⅛ tsp. salt
1 cup coconut
1½ cups oatmeal
1½ cup white chocolate chips
1 cup raisins
¾ cup chopped walnuts
white sugar for dipping

Preheat oven to 350°.

Lightly grease baking sheets.

In the bowl of an electric mixer, cream together sugars and margarine. Add eggs and mix well. Add flour, baking powder, baking soda and salt and mix with a spatula. Add the coconut, oatmeal, white chocolate chips, raisins and nuts. Combine and form into walnut-sized balls. Dip the tops in the white sugar and place on the cookie sheets. Bake for about 15 minutes, or until browned.

Lucille B. Cardone

Grandma Graham's Sugar Cookies
"A favorite for five generations"

Easy
Yields: 3 doz.
Preparation: 30 min.
Cooking: 10 min.

½ cup shortening
½ tsp. salt
½ tsp. grated lemon rind
½ tsp. nutmeg
1 cup sugar
2 eggs, beaten
2 Tbsp. milk
2 cups flour, sifted
½ tsp. baking soda
1 tsp. baking powder

Preheat oven to 375°.

In the bowl of an electric mixer, blend shortening, salt, lemon rind and nutmeg. Add sugar and mix.

In a separate bowl, whisk the eggs and milk and gradually add to sugar mixture. Combine well. Sift together the flour, baking soda and baking powder. Add to the creamed mixture. Mix well.

Drop by teaspoons onto a baking sheet and flatten with the back of a wet spoon. Bake for 10 minutes, cool and serve.

Annie Hague

Duquesne Club Macaroons

"There are no better macaroons"

Moderately difficult
Yields: 4 doz.
Preparation: 30 min.
Cooking: 20 min.

parchment paper
1½ cups finely ground
    almond paste, tightly
    packed
1   cup sugar
1¾ cups powdered sugar
4   lg. egg whites, divided

Preheat oven to 325°.

Line two half-sheet pans with parchment paper.

To achieve the appearance of well cracked cookies, select finely ground almond paste. Put almond paste and both sugars in a 5 qt. bowl of an electric mixer fitted with the paddle attachment.

With the machine on low speed, break up the almond paste with both sugars, until the mixture is crumbly. Add one of the egg whites to the mixture and mix until the wet and dry ingredients begin to bind. Add the remaining egg whites in a slow, steady stream. The mixture should now form a soft mass that is shiny, not too wet and slightly sticky.

Place the mixture into a pastry bag fitted with a size 7 round tip. Pipe out 1¼" round balls onto the prepared sheets. Space balls 1½" apart. Each pan should accommodate 24 balls. Use a clean, lightly moistened towel to tap down the points.

Set one pan at a time into the oven and bake for 18 to 20 minutes, or until the cookies are light tan in color and well cracked. Remove from the oven and let cool completely before removing from the parchment paper. Trying to remove them before they are cooled will cause the centers to stick to the paper. Store the cookies in an airtight container to prevent drying, or freeze for up to one month.

Keith A. Coughenour
Duquesne Club

233

Chocolate Chip Peanut Butter Cookies
"Always a great combination"

Easy
Yields: 4 doz.
Preparation: 10 min.
Cooking: 11 min.

1   cup flour
1   tsp. baking soda
1   cup (2 sticks) margarine
1   cup peanut butter
1   cup brown sugar
1   cup white sugar
1   tsp. vanilla
3   eggs
1   12-oz. pkg. semi-sweet chocolate chips

Preheat oven to 350°.

Sift together flour and baking soda. In a separate bowl, using an electric mixer, mix margarine, peanut butter, brown and white sugars, vanilla and eggs. Gradually beat in the flour mixture. Stir in the chocolate chips. Place dough by tablespoons on an ungreased baking sheet and bake for 11 minutes.

Debra Gibbs

Swedish Oatmeal Cookies
"Crispy and delicate"

Moderately difficult
Yields: 3 doz.
Preparation: 45 min.
Cooking: 8–10 min.

1   cup flour
½   tsp. salt
½   tsp. baking soda
¾   cup shortening
½   cup brown sugar
½   cup white sugar
¼   cup boiling water
1   tsp. vanilla
3   cups oatmeal

Preheat oven to 350°.

Grease baking sheets.

Sift the flour, salt and baking soda. Set aside.

Using an electric mixer, cream the shortening and sugars. Add the boiling water and vanilla to the creamed sugars, mixing thoroughly. Add the flour mixture, then the oatmeal, again mixing thoroughly. Form 1½" diameter sized balls and place on the baking sheets. Flatten each ball with the bottom of a wet spoon until very thin, about ⅛" or less. Make sure to wipe off the spoon each time and moisten again.

Bake until golden brown, 8–10 minutes.

Mary Murphy

Mother's Apricot Mumble
"Effortless"

Easy
Yields: 18 bars
Preparation: 15 min.
Cooking: 20–25 min.

¾ cup (1½ sticks) unsalted butter, softened
1 cup brown sugar, packed
1½ cups flour, sifted
½ tsp. baking soda
1½ cups rolled oats
1 10-oz. jar apricot filling

Preheat oven to 400°.

Grease a 13"x9" pan.

Using an electric mixer, cream butter and brown sugar in a large bowl. In a separate bowl, mix the flour and soda. Add to the butter mixture. Stir in the oats.

Put half the dough mixture into the prepared pan. Spread apricot filling on top. Crumble remaining dough over the apricot layer and bake for 20–25 minutes. Cool. Cut into bars.

Judy B. Scioscia

European Raspberry Bars

Easy
Yields: 16 bars
Preparation: 20 min.
Cooking: 40–50 min.

2¼ cups flour
1 cup sugar
1 cup pecans, chopped
1 cup (2 sticks) butter, softened
1 egg
1 10-oz. jar raspberry preserves

Preheat oven to 350°.

Grease an 8"x8" baking pan.

In a large mixing bowl, combine flour, sugar, pecans, butter and egg. Beat slowly with an electric mixer until mixture is crumbly, 2–3 minutes. Reserve 1½ cups of crumb mixture. Press the remaining mixture onto the bottom of the baking pan. Spread preserves to within ½" of the edge of the pan. Crumble remaining crumb mixture on top of the preserves. Bake for 40–50 minutes, or until lightly browned. Cool. Cut into bars.

Lynn B. Popovich

235

Berry Cheese Bars

"You'll give thanks for these cranberry bars"

Easy
Yields: 18 bars
Preparation: 30 min.
Cooking: 45 min.

2   cups unsifted flour

1½ cups quick cooking
    rolled oats

¾   cup plus 1 Tbsp. firmly
    packed brown sugar,
    divided

1   cup (2 sticks) butter

1   8-oz. pkg. cream
    cheese, softened

1   14-oz. can sweetened
    condensed milk

¼   cup fresh lemon juice

1   16-oz. can whole
    cranberry sauce

2   Tbsp. cornstarch

Preheat oven to 350°.

Grease a 13"x9" baking pan.

Rub together the flour, oats, ¾ cup of the brown sugar and the butter until crumbly. Set aside half of the mixture. Press remaining mixture into the prepared pan. Bake for 15 minutes. Allow to cool.

Meanwhile, using an electric mixer, beat cream cheese until fluffy. Gradually beat in the milk until smooth. Stir in the lemon juice. Spread over the cooled crust.

Combine the cranberry sauce, cornstarch and the remaining 1 tablespoon of brown sugar. Spoon over the cheese layer. Top with the reserved crumb mixture. Bake 45 minutes, or until golden brown. Cool and cut into bars. Refrigerate leftovers.

Betty

Apple Raisin Bars

Easy
Yields: 30 bars
Preparation: 30 min.
Cooking: 25 min.

1½ cups uncooked rolled oats, old fashioned or quick
¾ cup flour
½ cup brown sugar, packed
¼ cup sugar
¾ cup (1½ sticks) margarine
2 8-oz. pkg. cream cheese
2 eggs
1 cup chopped apple
⅓ cup raisins
1 Tbsp. sugar
1 tsp. cinnamon

Preheat oven to 350°.

Grease a 13"x9" pan.

Combine oats, flour and sugars in a medium bowl. Cut in margarine until the mixture resembles coarse crumbs. Set aside 1 cup of the oat mixture. Press remaining mixture into the prepared pan. Bake for 15 minutes.

Combine cream cheese and eggs, mixing well. Pour over the partially baked crust. Top with remaining ingredients and sprinkle with the reserved oat mixture. Bake for 25 minutes. Cool and cut into bars.

Lynn B. Popovich

Pecan Squares
"A pecan lovers paradise"

Easy
Yields: 16
Preparation: 50 min.
Cooking: 30 min.

Crust:
1½ cups flour
½ cup (1 stick) butter, room temperature
¾ cup brown sugar
½ tsp. vanilla
Filling:
½ cup (1 stick) butter
½ cup brown sugar
½ cup honey
3 Tbsp. heavy cream
1 tsp. vanilla
2 cups pecan halves

Preheat oven to 350°.

Lightly butter an 8"x8" baking pan.

Mix crust ingredients. Pat evenly onto the bottom of the prepared pan. Bake until golden brown, about 16 to 20 minutes. Let cool at least 10 minutes.

Put butter, sugar and honey into a medium saucepan. Bring the mixture to a boil, stirring constantly. Add the cream and return to just boiling; remove from heat. Add vanilla and pecans, then pour over the crust. Return to oven and cook mixture until bubbly and firm, about 30 minutes. Cool completely on a wire rack. Cut into squares to serve.

Karen C. Roman

237

Moca Java Bars
"A yummy blend of flavors"

Easy
Yields: 3 doz.
Preparation: 45 min.
Cooking: 20–25 min.

Bottom Layer:
1¼ cups flour

1   tsp. sugar

1   tsp. baking powder

dash of salt

⅔   cup (1¼ sticks) butter

2   Tbsp. strong coffee, cold

1   egg yolk

1   12-oz. pkg. chocolate chips

Top Layer:
½   cup (1 stick) butter

1   cup sugar

1   Tbsp. vanilla

2   eggs plus 1 egg white

2   Tbsp. strong coffee

1   cup nuts, chopped

powdered sugar

Preheat oven to 350°.

Lightly grease a 15"x10" jelly-roll pan.

Bottom Layer:
Combine flour, sugar, baking powder and salt in a large bowl. Cut in butter until the mixture resembles coarse crumbs.

In a small bowl, mix 2 tablespoons of coffee and egg yolk, blending well. Stir into the flour mixture and moisten to form the dough. Press onto the bottom of the pan. Bake for 10 minutes. Remove and sprinkle chocolate chips over the top and return to oven for 2 minutes. Remove and evenly spread the chocolate with a spatula. Allow to stand for several minutes.

Top Layer:
Cream butter, sugar and vanilla. Beat in eggs and egg white, one at a time. Add 2 tablespoons of coffee (mixture will appear slightly curdled). Stir in nuts and spread over the bottom layer. Return to the oven and bake for 20–25 minutes, or until the top is brown.

Remove and dust with powdered sugar. Cool in the pan and cut into bars.

Lynn B. Popovich

Almost Killer Brownies

"Drop-dead delicious"

Easy
Yields: 1 dozen
Preparation: 25 min.
Cooking: 25 min.

1   14-oz. pkg. caramels
⅔   cup evaporated milk, divided
1   pkg. German chocolate cake mix
¾   cup (1½ sticks) butter, melted
½   tsp. vanilla
1   cup nuts, chopped
1   12-oz. pkg. semi-sweet chocolate chips

Preheat oven to 350°.

Lightly grease a 13"x9" pan.

In a saucepan, melt the caramels and ⅓ cup of the evaporated milk. In a large bowl, mix the cake mix, remaining ⅓ cup of evaporated milk, melted butter, vanilla and nuts. Pour half of the cake mixture into the pan. Bake for 6 minutes. Remove cake from the oven. Sprinkle with the chocolate chips and pour caramel over the top. Cover with remaining cake mixture. Bake 25 minutes. Cool completely before cutting.

Kelly Postma

Surprise Cookies

Easy
Yields: 24 cookies
Preparation: 20 min.
Cooking: 12 min.

1   cup (2 sticks) unsalted butter, room temperature
½   cup sugar
1   tsp. vanilla extract
2   cups flour, sifted
1   cup finely chopped walnuts
1   5¾-oz. pkg. chocolate kisses

powdered sugar

Preheat oven to 375°.

Grease cookie sheets.

In a large bowl, cream the butter at medium speed. Gradually add the sugar and vanilla and continue mixing until fluffy. At low speed, stir in the flour and nuts and continue beating until well blended.

Take approximately two tablespoons of dough, put one kiss in the middle and roll into a ball. Repeat until dough is gone.

Place balls on prepared cookie sheets. Bake 12 minutes, or until bottom is slightly brown. Place on a rack. While still warm, roll in powdered sugar. Roll again when cool.

Laurie R. Bly

239

Sesame Cracker Cookies
"1,2,3 - dessert"

Easy
Yields: 2 doz.
Preparation: 5 min.
Cooking: 10 min.

½   cup brown sugar

½   cup (1 stick) butter,
     softened

1   box club crackers

sesame seeds

Preheat oven to 325°.

Cream brown sugar and butter. Spread on the crackers. Sprinkle heavily with sesame seeds.

Transfer crackers to a cookie sheet and bake for 10 minutes. When cool, cut into desired size. Store in an airtight container.

Nan V. O'Connor

Margie's Cracker Cookies
"Deliciously different. Everyone wants the recipe"

Easy
Yields: 2 doz.
Preparation: 30 min.
Must be made ahead

1½ cups brown sugar

1   cup sugar

⅔   cup milk

1   cup (2 sticks) butter

2   cups graham cracker
     crumbs

1   box club crackers

1½ cups peanut butter,
     creamy or crunchy

12   oz. chocolate chips,
     semi-sweet or milk,
     melted

In a saucepan, heat brown and white sugars, milk and butter until melted. Add graham cracker crumbs and boil until thick, 6–7 minutes. Lay one package of the club crackers out onto jelly-roll pan.

Pour half the crumb mixture over the crackers. Add another layer of crackers and pour the remaining mixture on top. Add a third layer of club crackers and refrigerate at least one hour.

Melt together the peanut butter and chocolate chips. Pour over the top and refrigerate again. Cut into small squares.

Helen Brancazio

Caramel Candy Bar Cookies

Easy
Yields: 4 doz.
Preparation: 25 min.
Cooking: 20–25 min.

1 14-oz. pkg. caramel candies
⅓ cup milk
2 cups flour
2 cups quick cooking rolled oats
1½ cups packed brown sugar
1 tsp. baking soda
½ tsp. salt
1 egg
1 cup (2 sticks) butter
1 6-oz. pkg. semi-sweet chocolate chips
1 cup chopped walnuts

Preheat oven to 350°.

Grease a 13"x9" pan.

Heat candies and milk in a 2 qt. saucepan over low heat, stirring frequently, until smooth. Remove from heat.

Mix flour, oats, brown sugar, baking soda, salt and egg in a large bowl. Stir in the butter with a fork and mix until crumbly. Press half of the mixture into the pan. Bake 10 minutes. Remove from oven and sprinkle with chocolate chips and walnuts. Drizzle with caramel mixture and sprinkle remaining crumbly oat mixture over the top. Return to the oven and bake 20 to 25 minutes, or until golden brown. Cool 30 minutes. Run a knife around sides of pan and continue to cool. When completely cool, cut into bars.

Dee Sacco

Chocolate Crunch Delight
"Couldn't be easier"

Easy
Yields: 3 doz.
Preparation: 15–20 min.

1 lb. milk chocolate
2 1-oz. squares unsweetened chocolate
5 cups cornflakes
½ cup slivered almonds
dash of salt

Melt the chocolate in a bowl, over gently simmering water, or in the microwave. Stir in the remaining ingredients, mixing well. Drop by heaping tablespoons onto waxed paper and refrigerate until firm.

Melissa A. Doyle

Pizza Cookies
"Hold the pepperoni"

Easy
Yields: 8–12
Preparation: 20 min.
Cooking: 13–15 min.

½ cup (1 stick) butter
¾ cup brown sugar
1 egg
1 tsp. vanilla
¾ cup flour
dash of salt
½ tsp. baking powder
½ tsp. baking soda
1 cup rolled oats
½ cup shredded coconut, optional
1 cup chocolate chips
½ cup chopped pecans
1 cup mini M&M's

Preheat oven to 350°.

Grease a 12" pizza pan to within ½" of the edge.

Using an electric mixer, cream together the butter and brown sugar. Add egg and vanilla and beat until smooth. Add flour, salt, baking powder and soda. Mix well. Add the oats, coconut, chocolate chips and pecans. Stir until well blended. Spread cookie dough onto the prepared pizza pan. It may help to wet your hands a bit when doing this. Sprinkle the M & M's evenly over the top. Bake 13 to 15 minutes, or until golden brown. Cut into wedges and cool.

Annie Waterfall

Tutu Candies

Easy
Yields: 4½ doz.
Preparation: 15 min.

1 cup sugar
1 cup light corn syrup
1½ cups chunky peanut butter
6 cups Special K cereal
1⅓ cups semi-sweet chocolate chips
1½ cups butterscotch chips

Grease a 13"x9" glass baking dish.

In a large saucepan, mix the sugar and syrup. Bring to a boil, stirring constantly. Add the peanut butter and cereal, stir and remove from heat. Press mixture into the prepared dish.

In a double boiler, combine and melt the chocolate and butterscotch morsels. Spread on top of the cereal mixture and cool. Cut into squares and store until ready to serve.

Nancy Thompson Godfrey

Index

243

Index

Index

Index

Index

247

Index

Index

Index

Index

Index

Index

Measurements and Equivalents

MEASUREMENTS				METRIC CONVERSION		

MEASUREMENTS

dash	=	less than 1/8 tsp.
1 TBSP	=	3 tsp
2 TBSP	=	1 oz.
4 TBSP	=	¼ cup
5 ⅓ TBSP	=	⅓ cup
8 TBSP	=	½ cup
16 TBSP	=	1 cup
8 oz.	=	1 cup
16 oz.	=	1 lb.
2 cups	=	1 lb./1 pint
2 pints	=	1 qt./4 cups
4 quarts	=	1 gallon
8 quarts	=	1 peck
4 pecks	=	1 bushel

METRIC CONVERSION

Volume

1 tsp	=	5 ml
1 TBSP	=	15 ml
2 TBSP	=	30 ml
1 cup	=	240 ml
1 pint	=	480 ml
1 quart	=	960 ml

Weight

1 oz.	=	28 gm
1 lb.	=	454 gm
2.2 lbs.	=	(1Kg) 1,000 gm

Length

1 in	=	2.54 cm
39.37 in	=	1 meter

EQUIVALENTS

Apples	4 oz.	= 1 cup sliced
Bread	1 slice	= ⅓ cup dry crumbs
Butter	1 oz.	= 2 TBSP
	¼ lb. = ½ cup	= 1 stick
Cheese, dry	1 lb.	= 4 cups
grated	1 lb.	= 4-5 cups
cottage	½ lb.	= 1 cup
cream	3 oz.	= 6 TBSP
Chicken	3 ½ lbs. drawn	= 2 cups cooked, diced
Coconut, flaked	3 ½ oz.	= 1 ⅓ cups
Cream, heavy	1 cup	= 2 cups whipped
Eggs whole	5	= 1 cup
whites	8-10	= 1 cup
yolks	10-12	= 1 cup
Flour,	1 lb.	= 4 cups
for thickening	5 tsp	= 2 tsp arrowroot
	2 TBSP	= 1 TBSP cornstarch
	1 TBSP	= 2 tsp quick-cooking tapioca
Gelatin	¼ oz. env	= 1 TBSP (gels 2 cups)
Herbs	⅓-½ tsp. dried	= 1 TBSP Fresh
Lemon	1	= 2-3 TBSP juice
		= 1-2 tsp rind
Meat, cooked	1lb.	= 3 cups minced
Mushrooms	1 lb. fresh = 5 cups sliced	= 6 oz. canned
Nuts	1 lb. in shell = ½ lb. kernels	= 3-4 cups
Orange	1 med.	= 6-8 TBSP juice
		= 2 tsp rind
Potatoes	1 lb. raw	= 2 cups mashed
Raisins, seedless	1 lb.	= 2 cups
Rice	2-2 ½ cups (1 lb.)	= 8 cups cooked
Sugars, brown	1 lb.	= 2 ¼ cups packed
confectioners'	1 lb.	= 4 cups
white	1 lb.	= 2 cups

Contributors:

We wish to thank the following for their financial contributions toward the production expenses of Three Rivers Renaissance Cookbook IV.

Renaissance Benefactor
Drs. Gustav and Susan Eles
Trish and Sam Kinney
Ed and Anne Lewis
Dr. and Mrs. Thomas A. MacMurray
Smithkline Beecham Consumer Healthcare
Mr. and Mrs. George Szakach
Mr. and Mrs. Mark Zappala

Renaissance Supporter
Mr. Bill Behan, Papier
Dr. Joseph Bikowski
Mr. and Mrs. James C. Bly
Dr. and Mrs. Thomas Doyle
Mr. and Mrs. Wayne Hyjek
Interstate Hotels Corporation
Mr. and Mrs. Thomas Johnson
Mr. and Mrs. Philip Jones
Mr. and Mrs. Gary Kovac
Dr. and Mrs. Robert Mantica
Merrill Lynch, Sewickley, PA
Anne B. Metcalf
Mr. and Mrs. Thomas C. Moorhead
Mr. and Mrs. Wayne Murphy
Mr. and Mrs. Hugh W. Nevin, Jr.
Dr. and Mrs. Robert Nitzberg
Mrs. Daniel B. Oliver
Dr. and Mrs. Thomas Pangburn
Mr. and Mrs. William Alfred Rabe III
Mr. and Mrs. Ken Rom
Mr. and Mrs. Rick Ruperto
Mr. and Mrs. Richard J. Tito
Mr. and Mrs. Donald Traviss
Sara White and Dwight Howes

Renaissance Friend
Jean Bottcher
Dr. and Mrs. Timothy Brown
Patricia D. Carton
Mr. and Mrs. Donald Y. Clem
Mr. and Mrs. Charles Gross
Mr. and Mrs. Reg Henry
Mr. and Mrs. Niles Kenyon
Mr. and Mrs. John Lednak
Hope Linge
Mr. and Mrs. Lawrence Megan
Mr. and Mrs. David C. Monroe
Mr. and Mrs. David Murdoch
Mr. and Mrs. Richard Roberts
Dr. and Mrs. Anthony Scalercio
Mr. and Mrs. Mark Scioscia
Suzonne Smith
Anne B. Tomson
Mr. and Mrs. Roger Wright
Missy Zimmerman

Bio's

Credit for the book's design belongs to Donna Albert, an award-winning art director and designer based in Pittsburgh. After ten years in the advertising business, Albert took her talents free-lance and now owns and operates Midnight Oil, working with many of Pittsburgh's best known corporations and not-for-profits.

Kristine Ream, an experienced illustrator and portrait artist, created the illustrations for the cookbook. Now living in the South Hills, this Carnegie Mellon graduate has developed a diverse portfolio as a free-lance illustrator. Her work includes children's books, magazines, advertisements, and portraits.

The photographs in this book are the work of Frank Walsh, a Pittsburgh-based photographer who specializes in commercial and fine arts photography. Over the past 13 years, he has worked with advertising agencies, corporations, and publishers, developing a style that is innovative, provocative, and memorable. The special quality of the photographs in this book is achieved through his creative use of desktop publishing to evoke the look and feel of earlier photographic processes.